Language in Prehist‹

MW00335913

For ninety per cent of our history, humans have lived as 'hunters and gatherers', and for most of this time as talking individuals. No direct evidence for the origin and evolution of language exists; we do not even know if early humans had language, either spoken or signed. Taking an anthropological perspective, Alan Barnard acknowledges this difficulty and argues that we can nevertheless infer a great deal about our linguistic past from what is around us in the present. Hunter-gatherers still inhabit much of the world, and in sufficient number to enable us to study the ways in which they speak, the many languages they use and what they use them for. Far from 'primitive', they are linguistically very sophisticated, possessing extraordinarily large vocabularies and highly evolved languages of great grammatical complexity.

Barnard investigates the lives of hunter-gatherers by understanding them in their own terms. How do they, as non-literate people, perceive language? What do they use it for? Do they have no knowledge of grammar, or have they got so much grammatical sense that they delight in playing games with it? Exploring these and other fascinating questions, the book will be welcomed by all those interested in the evolution of language.

ALAN BARNARD is Professor of the Anthropology of Southern Africa in the University of Edinburgh, where he has taught since 1978. He has undertaken ethnographic research with hunter-gatherers in Botswana, Namibia and South Africa. He participated in the British Academy Centenary Research Project 'From Lucy to Language: The Archaeology of the Social Brain'. In 2010 he was elected a fellow of the British Academy, and he serves as an Honorary Consul of the Republic of Namibia. His numerous publications include *Social Anthropology and Human Origins* (2011) and *Genesis of Symbolic Thought* (2012), and this volume completes his series on human origins.

Approaches to the Evolution of Language

The evolution of human language is a rapidly growing area of study and research, undertaken from a wide range of perspectives. This new series provides a forum for the very best contributions to this fascinating subject. Taking an interdisciplinary approach, the series as a whole encourages a productive dialogue between those working in linguistics, biology, psychology, anthropology and cognitive science.

Published titles

Language Evolution and Syntactic Theory Anna R. Kinsella

The Evolution of Human Language: Biolinguistic Perspectives Richard K. Larson, Viviane Depréz and Hiroko Yamakido

The Evolution of Language W. Tecumseh Fitch

How Language Began: Gesture and Speech in Human Evolution David McNeill

Further titles planned for the series

Language Evolution: The Windows Approach Rudolf Botha

Language in Prehistory

Alan Barnard

Professor of the Anthropology of Southern Africa
University of Edinburgh

CAMBRIDGE
UNIVERSITY PRESS

University Printing House, Cambridge CB2 8BS, United Kingdom

Cambridge University Press is part of the University of Cambridge.

It furthers the University's mission by disseminating knowledge in the pursuit of education, learning and research at the highest international levels of excellence.

www.cambridge.org
Information on this title: www.cambridge.org/9781107692596

© Alan Barnard 2016

First published 2016

Printed in the United Kingdom by Clays, St Ives plc

A catalogue record for this publication is available from the British Library

Library of Congress Cataloguing in Publication data
Barnard, Alan (Alan J.)
Language in prehistory / Alan Barnard.
    pages   cm. – (Approaches to the evolution of language)
Includes bibliographical references and index.
ISBN 978-1-107-04112-7 (hardback) – ISBN 978-1-107-69259-6 (pbk)
1. Language and languages–Origin–History.   2. Sign language.   3. Human evolution. I. Title.
P116.B34 2015
417′.7–dc23   2015022578

ISBN 978-1-107-04112-7 Hardback
ISBN 978-1-107-69259-6 Paperback

For the Naro and their language

Contents

Figures

Tables

Preface

This is the third volume in a series of three. When I began writing the series, I never imagined that more than one volume would be required. In fact, though, each volume seems naturally to have succeeded the next. They were all written as complete in themselves, and each can be read quite independently of the others.

The first volume is called *Social anthropology and human origins* (Cambridge University Press, 2011). The idea was to look at issues in human origins with the eyes of a social anthropologist. The book brings together ideas from primate studies, archaeology, linguistics and human genetics. The focus is on both raw data and notions on which social anthropology has important things to say: technology, subsistence, exchange, family and kinship, for example.

The second volume is *Genesis of symbolic thought* (Cambridge University Press, 2012). Whereas *Social anthropology and human origins* covers material on primates, australopithecines and *Homo* alike, *Genesis of symbolic thought* is specifically concerned with *Homo sapiens*. It traces the earliest examples of symbolism, especially from recently discovered archaeological sites, and it reflects on them through debates within social anthropology, from Durkheim and Frazer to much more recent thinkers. The phrase 'genesis of symbolic thought' comes from Lévi-Strauss, who in 1945 stated that we can never know how and why symbolic thought came into being. My argument is that with developments since then in archaeological dating methods, in the science of genetics and with advances in linguistics, volcanology, climatology, neuroscience and many other fields, it should now be possible to look at the topic afresh, which is what I did in the book. My view is that full modernity began in southern or eastern Africa, possibly 130,000 years ago, possibly earlier, and certainly by 60,000 or 70,000 years ago.

The present volume, *Language in prehistory*, has a narrower focus, albeit still a 'big' one. It is specifically about the origins and evolution of language. *Language in prehistory* is essentially a book-length expansion of 'The flowering of language', a chapter within *Genesis of symbolic thought*. I look at this problem through the eyes of a social anthropologist, because that is what I am. This is what differentiates the present book from the literally hundreds of thousands that I have located through web searches on things like 'origin of language', 'origins of language', 'language origins' and so on. Language began among prehistoric peoples, specifically among African hunter-gatherers. It evolved to its current state among those and other hunting-and-gathering peoples too. Many such peoples have very complex languages: famously, the Inuit and Athapaskan peoples of North America. My own fieldwork language, Naro (also known as Nharo or Naron), which is spoken in Botswana and Namibia, has 86 person-gender-number (PGN) markers or pronouns and grammatical suffixes. For example, they have masculine, feminine and common genders, and nouns have singular, dual and plural suffixes. Other San or Bushman languages are equally intricate. /Xam, once spoken in South Africa, has at least 24 verbal prefixes and 6 verbal suffixes, and it has at least 14 ways to make a plural.

Why should a band of 20 or 30 non-literate hunter-gatherers need such grammatical complexity? For me the answer is pretty obvious. They need it to tell stories, to devise mythological systems and the sets of beliefs that surround these. Such stories and myths, and the very ability to narrate at all, enabled their ancestors (and ours) to populate the globe. Of course, *Homo erectus* populated most of the globe too, and probably without myth or narrative and without language.

Modern hunter-gatherers all over the world do have language and do have stories. Their ancestors developed the ability to tell stories many thousands of years ago. Language does not exist for simple communication alone, but for the ability to put sentences within sentences within sentences, etc., as within mythology. Simple communication became complex for purposes such as this, and we can study examples of this phenomenon on every continent. Whether language is recent in origin (50,000 years ago is a date often suggested) or developed gradually, perhaps from Neanderthal speech or from the earliest sign languages, maybe hundreds of thousands of years ago, linguistic complexity is universal among modern humans. So too is the ability to speak more than one language. This book examines theories of the origin and evolution of language and all that goes with them: cognition, communication, teaching and learning, the development of material culture and of culture in general, the ability to recognize past and present, the ability to relate events in these in narrative and the creation of mythologies and to tell the truth and to deceive through the telling of untruth, and indeed the ability to express such thoughts and ideas across linguistic boundaries.

Unfortunately, we cannot study prehistoric languages. They are gone, and there is no guarantee that the languages of the small populations of hunter-gatherers that live in the world today resemble those of the past any more than do the languages of pastoralists or agrarian peoples. My problem here then is to work out what I can of the prehistory of language, how it evolved, why it evolved and how it came to acquire the complexity that it did. I do this mainly through the tools I have acquired as a social anthropologist. Although in this book I touch also on ideas from linguistics, cognitive science and many other fields too, no knowledge of linguistic theory or terminology is necessary in order to understand it. Nor, for that matter, is a knowledge of anthropological theory. The previous books in this series had extensive glossaries, but the one in this book is perhaps more extensive. It is intended for practical use, but can indeed be employed for browsing as well, and in this sense it serves one purpose for which language itself is, it seems, designed: to enable and to facilitate creative thought.

Let me acknowledge the help of Naro people with whom I did field research, mainly in the 1970s. In that decade, and to some extent since then too, they taught me a little of their language and helped me to think, at least a little bit, in the way that they think. This book is dedicated to them as well as to their rich and wondrous language, which I once spoke but now speak only seldom and very badly. I also acknowledge the support of the many people whose ideas have helped shape this book, including Joy Barnard, Gertrud Boden, Robin Dunbar, Morna Finnegan, Tecumseh Fitch, Tom Güldemann, Willi Haacke, Chris Henshilwood, Jim Hurford, Wendy James, Chris Knight, Bob Layton, Claire Lefebvre, Jerome Lewis, David Lewis-Williams, Camilla Power, Dan Sperber and Ian Watts. Grateful thanks too for the help of Richard Fisher and Andrew Winnard of Cambridge University Press and to Linda Randall, who very skilfully copy-edited the first two books in this series, and Sue Browning, who edited this volume.

1   Introduction

Modern humans have spent little over 10,000 years as non-hunter-gatherers, but nearly 190,000 years before that as hunter-gatherers. Even if we were to date the origin of language to 50,000 years ago, that still gives us 80 per cent of our time on earth as pure hunters, gatherers and fishers, and most of this time as imaginative, talking and communicating people. I believe it was rather longer ago than this. Human beings are linguistic, evolutionarily adaptive hunter-gatherers, usually not literate, but with the same minds as those possessed by, as the famous anthropologist Claude Lévi-Strauss (1968: 351) once put it, a Plato or an Einstein.

This book is about the origins of language and its evolution. The key difference between it and most other books on the subject is that it is written by an anthropologist rather than by a linguist. It therefore looks at the problem a little differently. The problem, however, is that there exists no direct evidence for the origin and evolution of language, so we have to infer it from the wealth of material we do have from archaeology, from studies of language acquisition by children, from comparative studies of language diversity and so on. My specialization happens to be hunter-gatherer studies, so I have tried also to bring some of my knowledge of such people to bear on language evolution. In my own fieldwork, as well as in my reading, I have tried to understand hunter-gatherers in their own terms. How do they, as non-literate people, see language? What do they use it for? Are they ignorant of grammar, or have they got so much grammatical sense that they delight in playing games with it? Indeed, are they more grammatically sophisticated than those in the West? Like a Plato or an Einstein, do they spend their time exploring the intricacies of philosophical or scientific problems? Or indeed grammatical ones? The answer to that, it may surprise some, is a qualified 'yes'.

In this book I make a number of assumptions. First, I know that hunter-gatherers are just as intellectually sophisticated as I am. I know that they are interested in grammar, and that the grammar of their languages is as complex as those of non-hunter-gatherers. Furthermore, possessing just one language is very unusual for them. Typically, individual hunter-gatherers can speak many languages. Mythology and other forms of narrative are of fundamental importance. Important too, on a global scale, is migration. However, hunter-gatherers are not (as is sometimes said) 'nomadic'. They migrated across and through several parts of the globe long ago as *Homo georgicus* and *H. erectus* (1,800,000 BP), as *H. antecessor* (800,000 BP), as *H. heidelbergensis* (600,000 BP), as *H. neanderthalensis* (perhaps 250,000 BP) and as *H. sapiens* in the Middle East (125,000 BP), to India (perhaps by 70,000 BP) and to Australia (around 60,000 or 48,000 BP). Most hunter-gatherers, though, are not nomadic, *except* within territories they know. Specialists in the study of southern African hunter-gatherer populations tend to assume a great antiquity on the subcontinent: several tens of thousands of years at the very least. There is also some question about when we can reasonably talk of 'hunter-gatherers', as opposed to the vegetarian species that preceded them. Jennie Robinson (2014), for example, takes quite a strict view. She distinguishes *Homo sapiens* from early *Homo*, but notes that early *Homo* did have a shorter gut than australopithecines (allowing food that is more digestible) and an ever-expanding brain. She also points out that hunting-and-gathering behaviour is said to be unique to humans, though not hunting-and-gathering activities. One could distinguish here the arboreal activities of chimpanzees from the quite different savannah-based activities of early hominins. However, even here there remain problems of definition: chimps as well as humans have been recorded to swap sex for meat (see e.g., Gomes and Boesch 2009). Evidently, they do this without the necessity of words for the actions.

The beginnings of language

My own view is a bit more radical than some. In line with other recent writers, I am happy to grant, or at the very least to consider granting, some form of language to early humans: Neanderthals, Denisovans and *Homo heidelbergensis*. The Denisovans were the Palaeolithic inhabitants of Denisova Cave in southern Siberia, from about 175,000 years ago. We do not know whether they had either language or some sort of proto-language, or whether their language was spoken or signed. Yet such a scenario would allow several more tens of thousands of years for linguistic humanity than is generally assumed. Theories of the earliest stages of proto-language abound. For example, Tecumseh Fitch, Michael Arbib and Merlin Donald (2010: 141–2) cite four models for proto-language: Derek Bickerton's lexical model, Charles Darwin's musical hypothesis, Merlin Donald's mimetic model and Michael Arbib's gestural model. Each model posits one core feature that was supposed to have evolved first, and from which other features followed.

We cannot at this stage make much of a guess as to what these early branches of humanity may have signed or said, but whatever it was they were at least *thinking* along the same lines as much of modern humanity. They were in modern terms 'primitive' hunter-gatherers. Yet they were not really primitive at all if we understand the nature of humanity itself as being linguistic and possessing some sort of grammar. Although we will never know the complete details of the evolution of language, we can infer a great deal from what is around us. Hunter-gatherers still inhabit much of the world, not in large numbers but in numbers that enable us to study the ways that they speak, the many languages they use and what they use their languages for. What is most important is to recognize that hunter-gatherers today are every bit as linguistically sophisticated as anyone else. Edward Sapir (1933: 155) put it wonderfully: 'Of all aspects of culture, it is a fair guess that language was the first to receive a highly developed form and that its essential perfection is a prerequisite to the development of culture as a whole.' As a specialist in North American languages, including several spoken by hunter-gatherers, he knew that these languages exhibited great grammatical complexity as well as rich and quite unusual ways to express even simple concepts.

Of course, I myself am not a hunter-gatherer. But as an anthropologist specializing in hunter-gatherers I have spent many years with people who are. This has been mainly in southern Africa, though I have visited hunter-gatherers elsewhere and have a lifetime's experience in academic studies of these peoples. I mention this because I have received correspondence from linguists who assume that hunter-gatherer peoples do speak more primitive languages than non-hunting peoples. I have never had such correspondence from any that assume the reverse, though it would not surprise me if some among my fellow anthropologists might indeed make this assumption. Hunter-gatherers have, both collectively and individually, extraordinarily large vocabularies, and they speak highly evolved languages of great grammatical complexity. They do not have just a few words for trees and bushes, but vocabularies with hundreds of words for botanical categories. This might hint at one origin for early language: to gesture, sign or talk about the natural environment. Richard Lee (1979: 464–73) lists 220 species known to the Ju/'hoansi (formerly known as the !Kung), of which they can name 11 that are unknown to botanical science. Likewise, though not quite so many, are their zoological categories, including 58 species of mammal (1979: 474–8). This book, in part, explores why hunter-gatherers should speak such rich languages.

Hunter-gatherers need complex language every bit as much as do computer programmers, nuclear physicists and philosophers. Perhaps Neanderthals and Denisovans did not need quite as much language, but our *Homo sapiens* linguistic abilities are not *that* far off. As the amateur American linguist Benjamin Lee Whorf implied, supposedly 'primitive' languages (that is, the languages of 'primitive peoples') are not primitive at all. They display cognitive functions that are at least as sophisticated as those of Western, university-educated scientists. Whether they are truly *more* sophisticated (as Whorf seemed to believe, see Carroll 1956) has long been a subject of debate. Whorf made this pronouncement in the 1930s, and debate on the matter still continues to this day. Nearly all professional linguists now hold to the view that the languages of hunter-gatherers are at least as complex as those of anyone else. Whatever the advantages of food production, that means of subsistence does not bring either greater understanding of the environment (which was already there in late hunter-gatherer times) or greater grammatical complexity. Late hunter-gatherers already had those abilities. Before that, it becomes more difficult to know or even to speculate about. Language, or rather proto-language, was evolving, and the process was slower than some linguists think, but it did take some time before humans became fully human in a linguistic sense. Why should a hunter-gatherer people need 24 verbal prefixes and at least 14 ways to make a plural? The answer is simple: they are not really a primitive people at all. They are 'us'.

We do not know exactly when language began. However, the figure of 50,000 BP (see Klein 2009: 650–3) seems far too recent to me, especially given the possible settlement of Australia as early as 65,000 BP (Oppenheimer 2004: 82). A date of 60,000 is more commonly cited, but Australia was, of course, settled by technologically competent, language-using humans. They migrated to the continent by sea before being (mainly) cut off from the rest of humanity until the eighteenth century. Australian Aborigines were using complicated languages before Europeans, although not before Africans. The original ocean voyage of the first Australians was probably accidental. Yet their ability to master their environments, to develop ways of describing them and, importantly, to create mythological and spiritual explanations of everything they encountered suggests great cultural as well as linguistic sophistication. This is not to diminish Richard Klein's argument for a world epicentre of cultural revolution and a point of migration from eastern Africa around 50,000 years ago. However, it does tell us that *something else* is needed in order to explain the existence of Aboriginal society and cultural complexity.

We do not really know exactly what constitutes 'language'. Virtually all the 5,000 or 7,000 (the figures are in dispute) languages found in the world today are in some way complex and, certainly, constantly changing. It is entirely possible that some elements of language evolved before others, but the proposed date of 50,000 BP probably reflects material cultural development more than it does the development of language. Language was in place before humankind got to Australia, and languages continued to evolve. However much language may have changed, it did not do so differently or separately in Australia and the rest of the world.

Some scholars like to speak in terms of a Proto-World language, or at least to argue a common origin for all languages as well as for 'language' in the abstract. American linguist Merritt Ruhlen (1994a, 1994b) is a prominent advocate of this view. My own view is rather different, for I tend to think in terms of a multiplicity of languages, at least from very early in human evolution. Linguist James Hurford puts it like this:

Current estimates put the number of living distinct languages at over 7,000. It is likely that in prehistory, even though the human population was much smaller, the number of languages was greater. The number of different languages that have ever existed is far greater than the number we can count now. To grasp this, we have to abandon the notion of global languages like English, Chinese, and Arabic, spoken by millions. (Hurford 2014: 16)

As a social anthropologist I have both a different background and a different way of viewing the problem from most linguists. I have seen and heard the multiplicity of languages in action among today's hunter-gatherers, especially in southern Africa where I do fieldwork. And although most social anthropologists today are not much interested in such evolutionary problems, I have to ask myself whether something quite similar may have been happening deep in prehistory. As population geneticist Louis Cavalli-Sforza (2001: viii) has suggested, history is not a science. However, he tells us, we can reach the truth, if not by experimental replication, then by coming at the problem through the understandings of a diversity of academic disciplines. For language, this can include either internal evidence, in other words, that from within linguistics, or external evidence, from social anthropology or any number of other disciplines (see Aitchison 1996: 11–12). In short, there are two main theories of language origins: a *common origin* for all groups of the earth's peoples, or *separate origins* for each. My own view, though, is rather different.

I believe that, almost from the beginning, a plurality of languages was present. As among hunter-gatherers today, in earlier times, hunter-gatherers in one location could speak several languages and could understand many more. As Hurford's comment implies, in the past, both language diversity and multilingualism were the norm, and languages have been lost at a phenomenal rate ever since people started to use language. According to Hurford's estimate, this was perhaps 100,000 years ago. And according to mine, which would include some kind of proto-language in use among Neanderthals, Denisovans and so on, even before this. McMahon and McMahon (2013: 232) also suppose proto-language developing through stages over a long period and possibly resembling what they refer to as 'living linguistic fossils', 'like pidgins, the language of young children, or the signs of language-trained apes'. Whether Neanderthals also used many languages, I hesitate to speculate. But why not?

Back in prehistory

If we do not know exactly when language began, or even how many languages there were in the beginning, at least we know what constitutes 'prehistory'. This was the time before writing was invented, when people lived as hunter-gatherers, as pastoralists or as subsistence farmers. It is, in a real sense, humankind's *natural* existence, as measured by the length of time humans have lived that way or in those ways.

We owe the concepts 'prehistory' and 'prehistoric' to several people. Among these were the Danish antiquarian Christian Jürgensen Thomsen (from around 1816, when he was appointed head of antiquarian collections at what became the National Museum of Denmark) and several of his Scandinavian students and colleagues. The latter include J. J. A. Worsaae, Bror Emil Hildebrand, Oscar Montelius and Sven Nilsson. Also important were the French archaeologist Paul Tournal (probably the first to use the word *anté-historique*, in the 1830s), the Scottish-Canadian archaeologist Sir Daniel Wilson and, perhaps above all, the English banker and amateur archaeologist Sir John Lubbock, in later life known as Lord Avebury (see e.g., Rowley-Conwy 2006; Renfrew 2008: 3–13). Wilson (1851) used the adjective 'prehistoric' in *The archaeology and prehistoric annals of Scotland*, as did Lubbock (1865), in his seminal work, *Pre-historic times*. Eventually, the nominal form, 'prehistory', came into use within archaeology and ultimately also into general use in the English language.

But what exactly do we mean by 'language'? Writing in a supplement to the *American Journal of Physical Anthropology*, L. A. Schepartz tackles the question of whether or not (complex) 'language' is related to the emergence of *Homo sapiens* by around 200,000 years ago or instead to later events such as the appearance of this species in Western Europe. His definition specifies that language is 'a system with external aspects relating to speech production and internal aspects involving cognition and symbolism' (Schepartz 1993: 91). His findings are that there is no relation between palaeontological and archaeological evidence and the emergence of language in those times, but rather that the *capability* for language existed much earlier. Since 1993, when Schepartz published his paper, this has also been suggested more recently by the discovery of the FOXP2 mutation, that is, the so-called 'gene for language', among Neanderthals as well as among *H. sapiens* (Krause *et al.* 2007; see also Wade 2006: 47–50; Wells 2010: 98–106). FOXP2 is a gene found in other mammals too, but, for example, in rats and mice it simply regulates breathing. In these creatures, it of course has nothing to do with language or speech. Yet in humans, it does precisely this: it enables the use of grammar. The mutation was apparently highly advantageous, and it spread rapidly throughout humanity at some point in prehistory. We know this because of a British family who have now been intensively studied and some of whose members, in fact, lack this mutation, or they have undergone another one, to reverse it, and therefore they seem to have difficulties both in grammatical construction and in speech.

More recently, Dan Dediu and Stephen Levinson (2013) have argued, quite against the prevailing understanding, that Neanderthals possessed a capacity for language too, and this capacity was not that different from our own. They look to an origin of language fully half a million years ago, before the divergence between *Homo sapiens sapiens* and *H. neanderthalensis*. Their view is that genetic and linguistic features of humanity co-evolved, and even that pre-*Homo sapiens sapiens* individuals may be responsible for the origins of linguistic features found in some languages today. This is not implausible, given that there is evidence of contact and cultural borrowing between Neanderthal and *H. sapiens sapiens* groups. It is also borne out biologically by the findings of D'Anastasio *et al.* (2013), who report on the analysis of a Neanderthal hyoid bone found in 1983 and first described a few years later, in 1989. The hyoid is a horseshoe-shaped bone under the chin and is important for speech. The implications of the analysis by D'Anastasio and his colleagues are that Neanderthals, or at least *this* Neanderthal dated at 60,000 BP, had the capability of speech. On the other hand, the position of the larynx has been the subject of debate on exactly how Neanderthals (with a presumably lower position of the larynx) might have produced the same sounds as modern humans. Early dates for language are possibly implied in archaeological evidence of symbolism, and therefore religion, dated to at least 75,000 BP and possibly earlier (e.g., Henshilwood 2009: 45). However, this suggestion remains controversial. Symbolism still requires some sort of linguistic expression, so presumably a kind of language preceded symbolic thought. Jean-Louis Dessalles (2007 [2000]: 76) suggests 100,000 BP for language itself, and this seems, if anything, a conservative estimate. Certainly, as I have argued (Barnard 2012: 138–40), there are indications of symbolic thinking much earlier than this.

Archaeology, anatomy and genetics, it seems, are conspiring against conservative forces in linguistics to push back the date of the earliest language, and even of the species that first possessed it. And these other disciplines have in their ranks people with reservations too. In an attack on Dediu and Levinson, the team of Berwick, Hauser and Tattersall conclude: 'At the archaeological level, our core linguistic competence does not fossilize. As for molecular evidence, we are nowhere near identifying the relevant "language genotype" and they provide no "language phenotype" to guide us. For the present, abstinence from speculation may be the best remedy' (Berwick *et al.* 2013).

Apart from what language may be, there is also the important question of language diversity. If Neanderthals could speak, could they converse with *H. sapiens sapiens*? This seems unlikely if their vocal apparatus differed substantially from ours and also since their mobility was, in our terms, so restricted (Féblot-Augustins 1993). As Ian Tattersall (1998: 166–73) noted in earlier work, language is a product of the brain, whereas speech is located in the vocal tract. None of this is preserved in the fossil record, although the roof of the vocal tract, in the base of the skull, is preserved. Nevertheless, he argues that it is unlikely that Neanderthals possessed either a form of speech that could be used for communication with *H. sapiens sapiens* or language. Neanderthals, he adds, presumably lacked the 'sheer cleverness' that we possess, along with the related cognitive skills such as the use of art and symbols. In a later book (2008: 76), he goes further, suggesting that *Homo heidelbergensis* (the common ancestor of both modern humans and Neanderthals) also had the mental capacity and the linguistic abilities of modern humanity. About 300,000 years ago, that species had acquired the ability to make stone tool cores and thereby to instigate a revolutionary advance in technology that required at least showing and teaching the young to do the same. Whether they truly thought in symbolic terms or invented forms of description for what they were doing and teaching we do not know.

Considering just *H. sapiens sapiens*, was language invented just once among us, or many times? The great comparative linguist Morris Swadesh died in 1967. Through much of his life he argued the one-origin view. In the book he was working on at the time of his untimely death, he put the date of the divergence of languages variously at 'half a million or so years ago' (Swadesh 2006: 215) or 'somewhere above twenty thousand years'. He added that there is 'little reason to suppose that the time depth of diversification for all known languages should be as much as 100,000 years' (2006: 226). In brief, working out the time depth seemed to be an almost insurmountable problem, even for him, the inventor of glottochronology. However, even he seems to have conceded that an origin of language deep in humankind's past, and in continuity with its present, is plausible.

The hardest problem in science?

The question of language origins has been around a few hundred years. It was of major concern among intellectuals, especially in France and in Scotland, in the eighteenth century. Charles de Brosses, president of the parliament of Dijon, was instrumental in establishing the topic as worthy of scientific discussion (Nicolaï 2006). He also promoted it in archaeological work, in theoretical work on the origins of religion and in predicting the existence of an Australian continent. Rousseau, Herder, Adam Smith and many others devised theories of the origin and evolution of language. The Scottish judge Lord Monboddo wrote many volumes on the subject; several were attacks on his chief opponent, Lord Kames, who regarded even Native North Americans as a different 'species' from himself (see Barnard 1995). It must be said, though, that the Linnaean idea of a species was not at that time fully recognized. Monboddo thought the Orang Outang (again, a disputed concept) was 'a Man'. But for a start, the idea of Orang Outang undoubtedly included chimpanzees, who, along with the orang-utans of Southeast Asia, were regarded as tool-using and hut-dwelling but not quite linguistic human beings. My readings of both Linnaeus and Rousseau suggest that neither were that distant in their views. These apparent 'apes' were virtually human, but they did not (yet) have language. Therefore, like Peter the Wild Boy of Hanover and Memmie Le Blanc, Wild Girl of Champagne, they were considered fully human but pre-linguistic. The relation between language and humanity was, in other words, then a matter of debate and not something intellectuals all agreed upon.

In the nineteenth century, the tide eventually turned against the topic even as one worthy of discussion. The Société de Linguistique de Paris was founded in 1864, but two years later, so heated had become the discussion of language origins that all debate on it was banned! One cause, it seems, had been the publication of Darwin's (1859) *Origin of species*. Yet there remained no way of tackling what was at that point simply argument over theory. There was never any real evidence for language origins as we would understand the nature of evidence. A few years after the ban in Paris, the Philological Society of London, founded in 1842, issued a similar edict. So no one in Paris or London, it seems, could argue on the matter. Language evolution is quite possibly, in the words of Christiansen and Kirby (2003b: 1) 'the hardest problem in science', and it would take a long time before it was to become acceptable again as something that linguists, or indeed other scientists of any sort, would be happy to argue about. Through these times, it must be remembered, there were as yet no 'Neanderthals' as we understand the species. The fossil that became 'Neanderthal Man' was discovered in the Neander Valley of Germany in 1856, though we now know that similar if unnamed skulls had been unearthed in Belgium in 1829 and in Gibraltar in 1848. The relations among these creatures were completely unknown prior to Darwin's *Origin* (1859) or, more to the point, his *Descent of man* (1871).

The origin of language, or *of languages* has, however, met with a remarkable resurgence overs the last 30 years or so. Long before the ban by the Société de Linguistique de Paris, protagonists had disagreed with one another, but as often as not their theories really focused on different aspects of language. Rousseau's (1986 [1781]) posthumous paper, for example, emphasized the place of music in the origins of language and argued that language began in the musical south of Europe before moving to northern Europe. Herder's (1986 [1772]) essay saw linguistic origins in nature itself, but his real concern was in rejecting the idea of language as divinely inspired. At various points through the centuries the topic returned in intellectual discussions, and debates often seem to have taken such forms as this. Adam Smith's much more secular (1767: 437–78) 'Dissertation on the origin of languages', or, to give it its full title, 'Considerations concerning the first formation of Languages, or the different genius of original and compounded Languages', was first published as an appendix to the third edition of *The theory of moral sentiments*. It concerns the evolution of parts of speech. Oddly, in light of Benjamin Lee Whorf's twentieth-century relativism and indeed (presumed) primitivism, Smith (1767: 478) finds favour in Latin over the 'prolixness, constraint, and monotony of modern Languages'. Whorf's ideal language seems to have been Hopi: 'English compared to Hopi is like a bludgeon compared to a rapier' (Whorf 1956a: 85); time and matter in Standard American English are 'linguistically conditioned', whereas the Hopi sense of space is 'pure' and free from such extraneous notions (1956b: 158–9). Foucault, Derrida and others resurrected the problem in late-twentieth-century post-structuralist and postmodernist circles, but ultimately it returned in earnest in the 1990s. In that decade, the increase in general interest within linguistics, combined with advances in genetics, neuroscience and many other fields, enabled serious debate once again.

Christiansen and Kirby (2003c: 305) have raised a number of issues with regard to the origin and evolution of language. These include: developing an evolutionary approach, the place of natural selection and the potential convergence of archaeological and genetic evidence. There are also speech versus gesture theories, the question of how unique human language really is and comparisons to non-human communication. Related fields of enquiry include studies of apes with regard to the evolution of language, explaining universal properties of language through computer simulation and the relation of culture to biology in the evolutionary sciences. I believe that all these are relevant. However, still they miss one key point, which for me is crucial: what language does that we cannot do without. In other words, what is the point of having and using a language? Why do we need them?

In recent decades, there have been great changes in attitudes about language origins. These include the reduced interest in the theory of universal grammar (or Universal Grammar), and a greater interest in the gradual development of language. Noam Chomsky, the world's leading linguist, and indeed some would say the world's leading public intellectual, has been reluctant until very recently to discuss language origins at all (e.g., Chomsky 2012). He has preferred instead to concentrate on specialist and often highly technical interests within theoretical linguistics. These have included, since the 1950s, the Standard Theory, the Extended Standard Theory (X-bar theory), the Revised Extended Standard Theory (Move α), Principles and Parameters Theory, Government and Binding Theory and the Minimalist Program, including the idea of Merge. These theories within transformational grammar have competed with a number of non-transformational theories and ideas, including Relational Grammar, Lexical-Functional Grammar, Generalized Phrase Structure Grammar, Head-Driven Phrase Structure Grammar, Categorical Grammar and Tree-Adjoining Grammar. Non-linguists (and perhaps linguists too) will be pleased to know that discussion of the minutiae of such notions will not feature in this book! As a sometime linguist in my youth I was once interested, but have long ago ceased to try to keep track of such things.

Today's problems

Today there has also been a growing interest in gesture as a precursor to speech, a recognition that Neanderthals probably had some form of linguistic communication and a realization that differences between Neanderthals and Cro-Magnon are more cultural than biological. We know too that Neanderthals certainly exhibited some kind of symbolic behaviour, and that this was on occasion the product of contact between *Homo sapiens, H. neanderthalensis* and other 'archaic' species over the last 160,000 years (J. M. Renfrew 2009; Taçon 2009: 70). Music has also gained in importance as something language specialists need to consider, and, above all, the relation between social organization and language has become recognized as important and still needs further study (see also Beaken 2011: xiii–xv).

However, perhaps the most interesting development of the last few decades has been the creation of Nicaraguan Sign Language, or NSL. In the early 1970s, deaf Nicaraguans generally lived an isolated existence. There was no deaf community in the country and therefore no sign language. All this changed around 1977, when a school for the deaf was built in the city of Managua. The initial group of 50 deaf children grew eventually to several hundred, and at the request of the Nicaraguan government, American linguist Judy Kegl began a study of the emerging language. The children themselves had turned the pidgin into a creole-like form, with verb agreement and other aspects of *real* language that turned out to be quite unintelligible to outsiders (Kegl 2002). Other researchers followed Kegl, and theories and debates appeared in the literature explaining the differences between the pidgin and the later form. Above all, the debates showed that: 'Language is an inherently social phenomenon, and must be studied as part of larger sociocultural systems' (Senghas *et al.* 2005: 288). Thus empirical research on the actual emergence of a language, in more or less natural conditions, proved possible. And for once, it put theoretical pronouncements in a context of observable phenomena. It did not matter at all, nor does it matter, that this is a sign rather than a spoken language. The principles are basically the same. Sign language, just like speech, is a form of language in its broadest sense.

Origins of grammar

All language, signed or spoken, has grammar. Grammar is essentially *syntax*: the bit of language that lies between *phonology* (the system of sounds that makes up speech) and *semantics* (the bit that carries meaning). The linguist Geoffrey Leech (1974: 13) once envisaged the relationship like this: the speaker encodes semantics, realized ultimately as a phonological representation, while the listener decodes what is said, which is realized as the semantic representation. Syntax mediates between the two (see Figure 1.1).

How language came to give us syntax, or grammar, is open to debate, although to me the arguments of Heine and Kuteva (2007) are quite convincing. They propose a six-layer scheme for the evolution of grammar: (1) nouns, (2) verbs, (3) adjectives and adverbs, (4) demonstratives, negation, etc., (5) pronouns, etc. (enabling early clause subordination) and finally (6) markers for agreement, passive voice and adverbial clause subordination (2007: 298–306). Their model suggests further that language evolved *gradually* and that the lexicon preceded syntax. In other words, in the beginning was the word.

Heine and Kuteva are more equivocal on the debate between Chomsky (e.g., 2002) and others (e.g., Pinker and Jackendoff 2005) on whether language exists primarily to express thought (Chomsky's view) or more for communication, although broadly they accept that language does exist for communication. This debate does interest me greatly, though in the end language really is both for communication (among a bunch of people) and for thought: *private* communication. The widespread use of pronouns like 'you' points to this. Why say 'you' if you are talking to yourself? Frederick Newmeyer (2003) has argued something similar. The debate 'language for communication' versus 'language for thought' is kind of a red herring. If sometimes I emphasize the latter it is only because the former seems to be dominant: we *do* think through language, and that aspect of it has to be understood.

Heine and Kuteva are also equivocal on the question of whether children create language or adults do. That question is not a trivial one. Indeed, a great deal has been written on it, especially in relation to the emergence of NSL. Nor is there agreement, however. For example, Elizabeth Traugott (2003: 626) points out that although understanding communication may be a task for children, grammatical innovation in a formal sense is still in the hands of adults. So *how* does grammar come into being? This related question is very much open to debate. Lévi-Strauss (1968: 351) commented that humankind is 'about one or two million years old', but that 'we are not ready to grant him a continuous thinking capacity during this enormous length of time'. He adds:

I see no reason why mankind should have waited until recent times to produce minds of the caliber of a Plato or an Einstein. Already over two or three hundred thousand years ago, there were probably men of a similar capacity, who were of course not applying

Listener decodes

↑   PHONOLOGY

       SYNTAX

       SEMANTICS   ↓

Speaker encodes

Figure 1.1 Semantics, syntax and phonology
Source: adapted from Leech 1974: 13

their intelligence to the solution of the same problems as these more recent thinkers; instead, they were probably more interested in kinship! (Lévi-Strauss 1968: 351)

No doubt they were. But as any social anthropologist will know, kinship has its own 'grammar'. It is learned, but it is also instinctive, or virtually instinctive. If I call a junior relative 'daughter', she will learn to call me 'father' and treat me appropriately. If I call her 'niece', the relationship and the behaviour may be different. One grows into a kinship system that is already there. Grammar is probably a bit like that too. And without either kinship or the problems of a Plato or an Einstein, our ancestors could easily have amused themselves with indicatives and subjunctives, or gerunds and gerundives. The next question we might ask is where to put them. In a language like Latin, with precise morphology for each word, rules depend on this and not where the word sits in a sentence. Word order is not so important because the word takes its meaning from its ending. In English, on the other hand, word order does matter. The usual English word order is SVO (subject – verb – object), whereas in Latin or Japanese, for example, it is SOV (subject – object – verb). If it does not matter much in Latin, it does matter in Japanese. That is why language is still difficult for the learner, as anyone trying to teach a language will know. Both children and adults get their grammar wrong at times. And of course language change is usage through the generations: it is not simply that the young imitate the old.

So which came first, English word order or Japanese word order? According to Derek Bickerton (2012: 465–6), claims based on what we know of language change in more recent times are irrelevant, because a pendulum process is the most likely explanation for the direction of change. In more recent times, shifts from SOV to SVO are more common, but this has not necessarily always been the case. The time depth of the existence of language is simply far too long for the problem to be that easy. Still, this discussion presupposes we are talking about a *single* origin for all languages. Many take such a view, but others, such as Joanna Nichols (1998, 2012), have argued against it. Her view is that 'language originated gradually over a diverse population of pre-languages and pre-language families' (Nichols 2012: 572). In other words, at first there was verbal communication that lacked the characteristics of modern languages. She dates this at 100,000 to 200,000 years ago. This is a view with which I have some sympathy. Everything is complicated, and that is why the problem is so fascinating.

This book will explore the idea of where grammar comes from, but it is not essentially a book about grammar or about any other specific attribute of language. My concern, rather, is mainly with the very idea of language: what it can do, how it relates to cognition and memory, how it relates to the ability to make tools, or to learning and teaching and, above all, when and how it began. Essentially, I am pretty agnostic about (1) the degree to which we can find precursors in primate communication, as Michael Tomasello and Josep Call (2007) suggest, or, alternatively (2) whether genetic mutation was the driving force, which is Chomsky's (2005) interpretation. One strength of the former view is that it is to some extent observable. The strength of the latter is that it seems to explain so much that is *not* observable. Evolutionary anthropologist Tomasello (e.g., 1999, 2008) has also turned his attention to the uniquely human notion of learning in childhood, with an emphasis on issues such as the development of cognition, the significance of symbolic representation, the idea of cooperation and the acquisition of the notion of deception. In all this, he is on the edge of that boundary which separates apes from humans, though I fear he sees the boundary rather differently either from Chomsky or from most social anthropologists today. In social anthropology, culture is generally regarded as a human trait, and the boundary between non-human primates and humans is seen as rigid and transcended (within hominins) only by human beings. Primatologists tend to define it more broadly to mean learned behaviour.

Just as there is a clear difference between language and communication, there is an equally clear difference between language and speech. A recent article in *Current Biology* points to similarities between human speech and the 'wobbles' of geladas (Bergman 2013). But so what if they sound like humans? At best, this approach yields suggestions in our search for analogies. It does not tell us much about the actual evolution of human speech. And the evolution of human speech does not necessarily even give us a clue about the evolution of language, whose distinguishing feature is, of course, grammar.

A few theories

If 1866 marks the ban on discussion of the origin of language in Paris, it is worth recalling that not long before then, theories were absolutely rife. That was, after all, the reason for the ban. F. Max Müller (1861: 329–78) reviewed a number of theories: (1) the *bow-wow* or *cuckoo* theory, which saw in words the imitation of the sounds of animals, (2) the *pooh-pooh* theory, in which the first words were derived from interjections, (3) the *ding-dong* theory, in which words stemmed from a kind of natural resonance and (4) the *yo-he-ho* theory, where the collective rhythm of muscular activity gave birth to language. The present book may not cover *all* theories of language origins, and certainly it does not cover these early ones. One researcher in the 1970s counted 23 theories of how language began (Aitchison 1996: 5), and some of us have added a few since then. All these theories concerned the very beginnings of language, though, and not the evolution of language and the development of grammar. It is as if there was an assumption that evolution was natural, and simply happened.

To some extent, we have retained this understanding. Robin Dunbar (1996) takes this as his starting point too: language evolved from manual grooming among primates. When grooming came to require too much time, grooming relationships became 'vocal grooming' or gossip. However, critics like Camilla Power (1998) point out that the very ease of vocal grooming renders that activity ineffective. Why should I engage in gossip just to save time on physical grooming, and indeed how does one get from the physical to the vocal? The transition is not at all easy to explain.

At the other end of the spectrum, one of the longest-running debates in all the social sciences is: which came first, the social contract or the family? Hobbes, John Locke, Jean-Jacques Rousseau and many others held that the social contract came first. Sir Robert Filmer and later Sir Henry Maine argued that it did not: the family is the basis of all human societies. Maine's (1913 [1861]) ideas became crucial for anthropology. In arguing against the very idea of a social contract, Maine asserted that the ancient family was the basis of society. He objected to legal fictions assumed in social contract theory and instead traced social organization from belief in divine authority (especially in the East) or later in aristocratic authority (especially in the West). Eventually, such authority formed the basis of case law, as in the English legal tradition. Ultimately, society itself came to mirror the family of early societies. The social order was patriarchal, and society was a group of families, not a collection of individuals – as it came to be perceived in later times.

From Maine is derived the fundamental theory which forms the backbone of social anthropology. Rightly or wrongly, we are all in a sense followers of Maine. The anthropological traditions of Morgan, McLennan, Radcliffe-Brown, Fortes, Evans-Pritchard and many others are all essentially Maine's, and even those of their opponents are often implicitly similar in their focus on kinship over society in general. In hunter-gatherer social organization, kinship is typically cognatic or bilateral. This means that children are reckoned to be equally and similarly related to their fathers and their mothers. Typically too, there is a lack of gender hierarchy, although males and females may have different roles in subsistence (men do most of the hunting, and women the gathering) and in ritual (particularly with initiation rituals). Of course, this was not necessarily the case among *Homo erectus*.

Finally here, let me say just a few words concerning reviews of the first two volumes in this series. Both volumes seem to evoke praise for effort: confronting the unknown of biology, biological anthropology and so on. Yet both also produce criticism for a lack of diagrams (presumably, compared to North American texts), and references, as well as an audience unidentified by me. Actually, I think there are quite enough references. My books are not, in themselves, bibliographies (cf. Barnard 2011: xii, 2012: 140), and my intended audience was anyone interested, whether academic, PhD student, undergraduate or lay person. Much the same goes for the present book. It is not written specifically for linguists, anthropologists or anyone else. It is about language, and my goal is to pull together all that might help to enlighten us on that subject. I hope too that it provides a unique perspective on this problem.

2   Population diversity and language diversity

Language is often rich in symbolism and varied in things like word order and grammatical complexity. Such variation is necessary for the ways in which language is actually used: for simile and metaphor, for deception, for making up riddles, for telling stories (whether true or fictional), for making jokes and for idle chit-chat, as well as for imparting knowledge. We know that language as it exists today among non-hunter-gatherers was actually developed within not only non-literate but also foraging communities, and certainly not in technologically advanced ones (see Barnard 2012: 90–1). It is wise therefore always to keep our origins as foragers or hunter-gatherers in mind.

It may also be appropriate to reflect too on the fact that hunter-gatherers can be nearly as diverse as languages. There are, of course, many similarities among hunter-gatherer peoples, for example, in their sharing practices, their lack of or reluctance to accumulate property, their extensive kinship networks, their tendency to occupy large areas and their relatively simple technologies. Yet the differences can be considerable too, as Robert Kelly (2013 [1995]), among others, has demonstrated. Many hunter-gatherers are 'immediate-return' in economic structure, but 'delayed-return' hunter-gatherers, that is, those who store things or otherwise plan for the future, are found as well (Woodburn 1980, 1982). There exist both *egalitarian* hunter-gatherers (which is most of them) and *non-egalitarian* groups: Northwest Coast peoples, Ainu and presumably prehistoric groups evolving social complexity. The last category includes, for example, the prehistoric peoples of Europe in their long evolution towards the Mesolithic and its social complexity. There are also diverse kinship structures, mainly cognatic but occasionally matrilineal, and in the case of Australia mainly patrilineal. These entail very different ways of thinking about people and about kin relationships. In short, although hunter-gatherers are one kind of society, there are different sorts of 'hunter-gatherers'. Also, in the distant past there were hominins who were vegetarians. Not all creatures who gathered food were hunter-gatherers, though since the earliest days of *Homo sapiens* they were. As archaeologist Mark Pluciennik (2014: 55) points out, the category hunter-gatherer was invented in relation to Western, economic concerns: 'nascent capitalism, property rights, colonial practices and attitudes,

and as part of the developing Enlightenment and scientific passion for classification'. Yet that, of course, does not make it a non-category, but rather a
necessary category of its time.

Throughout prehistory, most hunter-gatherers have, in James Woodburn's
(1980, 1982) terms, lived in immediate-return economic systems, and
their social structure was egalitarian. This means that they cooperated in
hunting-and-gathering activities: modern groups like the Ainu and Northwest
Coast peoples are the exception. Hunters no doubt told stories about the hunt,
and this remains the most common daytime point of discussion among living
hunter-gatherers. The night is given over to argument (see Wiessner 2014).
Woodburn remarks that immediate-return economics precludes a number of
things: ordered relationships of long-term dependence, making nets for hunting
(which takes time, as well as cooperation, among hunters), making boats (which
requires planning ahead), and so on. Presumably he has to exclude Australian
Aborigines since they will have had to make boats in the first place in order to
get to Australia, and they are excluded in any case on social grounds: they (in
Woodburn's words) must plan ahead through 'farming out' their women (but cf.
Layton 1986). At least in recent times, this is necessitated because of their complicated kinship structures. In contrast, immediate-return economics depends on
food being eaten the day it is acquired, without storing or processing. Sharing
is required, if for no other reason, because it is more economically sensible than
saving. So where is language in all this? Well, pretty much everywhere, since
socially complex hunter-gatherers, which these people are, possess the means to
express in language most anything that needs to be expressed.

Hunter-gatherer ethnography

Our knowledge about modern hunter-gatherers comes mainly from ethnography, although through archaeology we also know a good deal too about earlier
hunter-gatherers. Our theoretical knowledge began with French thinkers such
as Montesquieu (see 1989 [1748]: 290–2), and some of the Scots, particularly
Adam Smith, who overturned the emphasis on politics and gave prominence to
economics instead. Through some comparisons, I want to touch here on ways
in which hunter-gatherers are similar, as well as on some ways in which they are
not. Hunter-gatherer lifestyles are, of course, related to hunter-gatherer ways
of speaking and classifying the world. If anything, such peoples have greater
understanding of environmental relations and often a much larger vocabulary
to express ecological knowledge than do agro-pastoralists or city-dwellers.
The fundamentals of language are the same everywhere, but the specifics differ a great deal and are, of course, culturally conditioned.

In particular, speech is often different in different communities. For example,
the idea of 'You speak; then I speak' tends to be a *non*-hunter-gatherer one,

although as sociolinguists will know, it can occur elsewhere. Still, examples do seem to be more prevalent in Aboriginal Australia, the Canadian Arctic and Subarctic, and so on, rather than in urban settings (see Swann 2009 [2000]). To understand language otherwise, we need to think of other permutations. 'I speak, I speak, I speak ...; you do not have to say anything', can be a more hunter-gatherer way of verbal interaction, as indeed are play and mimicry in speech. Jerome Lewis (2009) gives vivid examples from his field research with the Mbendjele Pygmies of central Africa.

Also, the definition of a 'word' is to some extent dependent on the ability to write. In general, hunter-gatherers cannot write, but they can put words together in sentences, with recursion, dependent clauses and all the other aspects of grammar that are known in languages of the literate. When we think of language, we would do well then to forget altogether the fact that we, who can read this book, are literate. Words take on their meanings according to how hearers and speakers recognize them. The bound morpheme z in English 'means' plural, but only as part of a word, say, 'dogs' as opposed to 'dog'. In the word 'dogs' the phonemic /z/ ending is instantly recognizable as a plural marker, whereas a z by itself is not. Hearers can recognize words out of context, but they cannot usually recognize smaller units of meaning such as these, except within speech. Generally speaking, that is how 'words' are defined outside of literary usage.

It is also possible that the emphasis on words is misguided. Language, of course, also entails grammar, and in many languages (like Inuit or Athapaskan languages), words as we think of them in English are not really the key forms. In English, words are made up of one or two morphemes, sometimes a few more. They have a stem and perhaps a prefix and/or a suffix. 'Dog' or 'dogs', 'pony' or 'ponies', 'audible' or 'inaudible', for example. Alison Wray (1998, 2000) has argued that it is possible that, in fact, words such as these, and longer units more generally, evolved earlier than shorter units. These longer units, in proto-language, were in her terms 'holistic'. In short, they expressed ideas more like phrases or sentences, as indeed is the case in Inuktitut today. Inuktitut dialects typically have around 450 affixes. According to Wray's thinking, Inuktitut sentences might easily have come into being later than the phrases that are characteristic of Inuktitut. As for the well-known assertion that Inuktitut has 4, 7 or even 400 words for 'snow', this notion has been summarily debunked (Pullum 1991: 159–71). In part, it all depends on what one means by a 'word'. I once spent a couple of weeks in China, where people definitively understand a 'word' as a lexical unit. So literate are Chinese people that they seem to prefer pictographs to speech, although of course they communicate through speech. In a sense, dialect diversity does not matter that much, since one can speak almost any variety of (simplified characters) Chinese with the 'words' remaining the same. In Chinese understanding, 'words' are about pictorial symbols rather than phonology (see Figure 2.1).

男人   man

女人   woman

儿童   child

Figure 2.1 An example of Chinese simplified characters

However, it may not be as simple as all that, even for Inuktitut: the most lexically complex language or languages on earth. In Inuktitut languages, not only does a single morpheme not have any meaning out of context, but quite long strings of morphemes may not have any either. Another linguist, Derek Bickerton (2009: 61–70), argues against both Wray's emphasis on the early existence of holistic units and the 'singing Neanderthals' idea of Steven Mithen (2005). Both these depend on an evolutionary trend towards language: that language is derived ultimately from animal communication systems (ACSs). However, Bickerton argues, this is not the way it is. Animal communication is one thing, and human communication is quite another. As we shall see, language, whether spoken or signed, involves complex grammar as well as communication. Seeing language simply as an ACS misses the point about what it truly is. Language *is* for communication, of course, as, for example, Lupyan and Dale (2010) note, with reference to the relation between social structure and language structure: the former influences the latter. The ways in which languages are learned and used does affect usage in matters of grammar. However, really things can be much more complicated, especially when I-language (Chomsky 1986: 21–4), or internal thought processes, are also taken into account. In both thinking and writing, we understand through the words we possess. This is as true of non-literate Inuit as it is for literate Inuit, and for Inuit in general as much as for English speakers. And even for those who use pictographs.

In the end, all humans are essentially hunter-gatherers. Given our genetic makeup, the human species, as well as those of our immediate predecessors such as Neanderthals, Denisovans and *Homo heidelbergensis*, are clearly hunter-gatherers in temperament. That is what is in our genes (Wells 2010).

Signing and talking

Language has two quite different forms or 'modes': signing and speaking. Sign language today is generally thought of in terms of the many languages used by deaf people. Contrary to what many hearing people think, sign languages are diverse and often linguistically complicated as well. In other words, they are *genuine* languages. They have grammar, often grammar quite different from that of neighbouring speaking-and-hearing communities, even though the languages of such communities may also share gestural features. The village sign languages of developing countries are, in fact, often used by hearing people too, and are not uncommon in communities in which there are a high number of deaf people. A 'high number' here can mean, say, 3.5 per cent – or 40 times the average elsewhere (Meir *et al.* 2010: 3). Some sign linguists distinguish *village sign languages*, which emerge spontaneously within such a community, from *deaf community sign languages*, which are formed in a diverse and often artificial community such as when deaf people are brought together at an educational institution (Meir *et al.* 2010: 4–8).

However, at one time (it is often assumed) gesture was the *only* form of language. This tends to be the prevailing view in neuroscience, where the origins of language are sometimes traced to primate gestural communication (see e.g., Arbib 2012; Corballis 2011). In a way, this should be obvious. Gesture and speech are produced similarly and in the same parts of the brain (see McNeill 2012). They evolve together within the human brain and, according to David McNeill, there is little point seeing one as either evolving first or being built on top of the other. If gestures exhibit grammatical properties, which in his view they do, the argument for seeing gesture as a form of language becomes ever so much more obvious.

My view is that too much effort has perhaps been given to this concern, in spite of its obvious truth at some level: at least one prehistoric origin of language is in gesture or, more accurately, in sign, even if most language is, among modern *Homo sapiens*, spoken rather than signed. The chief exception is for sign languages used for communication with or among the deaf. Yet that is a far cry from the assumption of an origin in gesture, such as imputed among chimpanzees. If *Homo* communicated in that way, it is likely to have been something like 2,000,000 years ago, and not in same time frame as argued for a bridge between ancestral forms of communication and human speech (see Kenneally 2007: 123–38). The fact that both speech and sign are forms of the same thing and possess grammar is of great theoretical interest, and this is why McNeill (2012: 58–164) bases much of his argument on 'Mead's Loop'. Mead's Loop (named after the sociologist G. H. Mead) is the adaptation to see one's own gestures as if some else's, and vice versa. In brief, this 'twisting' of mirror neurons enables gestural images to be available in Broca's area of the brain (the left ventral premotor cortex). That area, in turn, enables the capacity for comprehension that is necessary for understanding language. McNeill (2012: 113) suggests that, depending on one's point of view on the matter, if gesture did come before speech, then Mead's Loop may have first occurred either at 1,040,000 years ago (the presumed divergence of Denisovans from modern humans) or at 466,000 years ago (the presumed divergence of Neanderthals from modern humans). Either way, this facility for communication is available to modern humans.

In fact, gesture and speech go together as forms of communication among humans generally. In sign language for the deaf, there can be unconscious 'body language'. There is also a conscious use of gesture along with speech in other communities, and both can, of course, be culturally constructed. In the northern Kalahari, there are gestural sign 'languages' with vocabularies of more than 100 words, including nouns, verbs and adjectives, roots and quali- fiers, declaratives, imperatives and interrogatives. The degree to which these are part of 'true' language is, of course, an open question. Ts'ixa, a Khoe lan- guage spoken in Botswana, is a particularly good example of a mixture of speech and gesture, but similar usage is found across language boundaries and to some extent among agro-pastoralists in the area (Anne-Maria Fehn, personal communication). In comparison to other forms of signing, however, this figure is very slight: even Koko the gorilla's attested 'sign language' includes at least 375 signs (Corballis 2011: 47).

Human sign languages in southern Africa are mainly used when hunting in order that animals do not detect the presence of humans. It is sometimes said that there is a trade-off between speaking (which can be done in the dark) and gesturing (which can be done without the interference of noise). Bi-modal hunting communication (i.e., speech plus gesture) allows both, or rather, one or the other at any given time. My presumption is that hunting sign language was originally a hunter-gatherer form, and that in southern Africa at least, it was later extended to neighbouring agro-pastoralist peoples. A question that might come naturally from those unfamiliar with spoken Khoisan languages might be: are any Khoisan languages impoverished without supplementation by gesture? The answer, quite definitely, is *no*. As I noted in the preface to this book, Naro has 86 PGN markers. /Xam has at least 32 verbal prefixes and suffixes, and for nouns, at least 14 ways in which to form a plural (see Bleek 1928/9, 1929/30). And there are many other complex features in these and other Khoisan languages. However, these languages are very diverse, and not all Khoisan languages are indeed complex (see Honken 2013).

In this regard, Ernst Haeckel (1869: iv) was quite wrong when he wrote that the peoples of southern Africa 'have remained, down to the present day, at the lowest stage of human development'. Or, 'That this is true not only in respect of their entire physical and moral characteristics, but also in respect of their language.' For a start, 'Khoisan' is not a single language, or even a single language family, but several: if anything, it is a *Sprachbund* (that is, a group of previously unrelated languages that have come together) rather than a language family. That is, Khoisan is a geographically defined cluster of gen- etically unrelated languages (see Güldemann 1998). They have coalesced in the same geographical area rather than dispersed from a common source. And certainly, peoples with supposedly simple technologies do not necessarily, or even probably, possess simple languages. If anything, the opposite is likely to

be true, and far from being 'at the lowest stage of human development', southern African hunter-gatherers are the direct descendants of those who *created
symbolic thought* in the first place (see Barnard 2012: 15–39, 122–41).

Here the findings of Doran Behar and his colleagues (Behar *et al.* 2008) are
relevant. His team estimated that the mtDNA (DNA inherited in the female
line) of Khoisan populations diverged from the rest of the human gene pool
between 150,000 and 90,000 years ago. Furthermore, it remained separate
until about 40,000 years ago. According to Maggie Tallerman and Kathleen
Gibson (2012b: 31), respectively a linguist and a neuroscientist: 'Since the
Khoisan peoples have a normal human language faculty, this strongly suggests
that full language was already in place at the time of the split.' In other words,
we can date *full language* to before 90,000 BP. In fact, Tallerman and Gibson
summarize in their introduction to *The Oxford handbook of language evolution*, that recent findings in a variety of fields all point to at least 'some form
of language' 200,000 years ago or even significantly earlier. As they point out,
language accompanies other forms of symbolic thought, and the suggestion of
such an early date is very new, if not universally accepted by those linguists
with an interest in the problem. And of course, others would assume a yet earlier date, if we allow Neanderthals, Denisovans and *Homo heidelbergensis* into
the club. Studies of chimpanzee gestural 'language' have recently come to the
fore again, for example with a study showing 19 'apparently satisfactory out-
comes', in other words successful attempts at communication, out of 66 'gestural types' or gestures (Hobaiter and Byrne 2014). The significance of this
work lies in the fact that the research was conducted among wild chimpanzees
filmed for the purpose, and that it does hint at common features possibly in
existence before the divergence of chimps and humans. While very few would
admit chimps as linguistic beings, in terms of communicative abilities they
may be on the edge of inclusion. However, most certainly they lack symbolic
thought.

We in the social sciences must not forget that language is biologically
constrained. This is true in phonological patterns as well as in syntactic
ones (Berent 2013). Whatever the exact date for the beginnings of language,
or for the beginnings of spoken language or indeed some kind of mixed
gestural-and-spoken medium, language possesses universal patterns of many
kinds. These are phonetic, phonological, syntactic and presumably also semantic. In other words, the potential for using language as well as the biology for
doing so were there before language emerged. That is not to say that these
were not fine-tuned as human evolution progressed. Undoubtedly they were.
The boundary between language and symbolic thought is illusory, since modern human hunter-gatherers, like any other humans, are programmed to speak
both in phonologically complex ways and with symbolic purpose. Language,
of course, exists and probably has existed within the past several millennia for

many purposes (see Aitchison 1996: 16–25), and it is well not to lose sight of this. In *Genesis of symbolic thought* (Barnard 2012: 13–14), I hypothesized a date of around 130,00 years ago for the earliest symbolism, but it may be much earlier. It depends on when a form of language became possible and the degree to which language is necessary for symbolism and for the development of ritual. These may indeed have some sort of biological basis (see Ellis 2011; Wilson 2011).

Before language?

There were people before there were languages. It may be that language occurred pretty spontaneously (as Chomsky has always assumed), but it is also true that it had to begin somehow. Perhaps it was with the FOXP2 mutation or with some cluster of such mutations yet to be discovered? Using genomic evidence, Karl Diller and Rebecca Cann (2010: 113) dated human mutations in FOXP2 to 1,800,000 or 1,900,000 years ago. This means that humans were 'capable' of language, but not that they had developed it. 'Linguists who focus too much on design are likely to be disappointed in biological evolution, which is more like tinkering than like design. Single mutations often cause disease, disability, and dramatic disruption of systems. It usually takes many adjustments for a system to adapt positively' (2010: 113). However, they envisage *Homo erectus*, with twice the brain size as chimpanzees, as being well on the way to building a language capability, with the development of syntax as well as metaphor and grammaticalization. Fire could be controlled by 800,000 years ago, and the first fully modern humans, with, in their view, full language and not proto-language, were on the scene by 200,000 BP (2010: 113–14). This is rather earlier than often claimed, but on the basis of the full evolution of the brain and the existence of Mitochondrial Eve about that time, fully plausible. The date of Mitochondrial Eve, though, is rather difficult to measure: Ian Tattersall (2008: 90) suggests that 'Eve' lived in Africa some time between 290,000 and 140,000 BP.

In *The making of language*, Mike Beaken (2011: 115) suggests that in foraging societies there is generally an obligation for a brother to feed his sisters' children rather than his own. However, this is, in fact, not the case. What he refers to here is more typically what happens in a matrilineal society, and hunter-gatherers are only very, very rarely matrilineal. Rather, what we find among hunter-gatherers is an obligation of a man simply to watch out for the best interests of his sisters, who technically are 'avoidance' relatives. This does not literally mean that anyone physically avoids anyone but that their behaviour is governed by strict social obligations. These are related, in theory anyway, to the incest taboo and its social or metaphorical extension. A woman similarly looks after the best interests of her brothers. Yet as an ethnographer of the !Xóõ once put [...] from expressing estrangement, is perhaps [...] might be promoted by deep affection' (H[...] [...] example, when a man was injured it was h[...], not his wife, who was more distressed.

Pre-l[...] [...]ing to Aiello and Wheeler (1995), the add[...] [...] s (or before that, by some australopithec[...] [...]ng, which affected the ability of the gut to [...] ease in group size and to the greater intell[...] [...]ools and to teach tool-making skills to you..., [...] 114). An increase in the consumption of meat may also have [...] propensity for sharing meat, and possibly sharing mates. The exact stages in which these events first occurred are open to debate, and numerous hypotheses have been developed. For example, Robin Dunbar's (2003) 'social brain' hypothesis suggests an interplay between biological and social evolution: primate practices of grooming gave way to speech as a form of communication. He calculates that this must have taken place well before the predicted *Homo sapiens* 'natural' group size of about 150: what has become known as 'Dunbar's number'. According to Dunbar, a group size of 150 among any primates would imply that around 43 per cent of the time would be spent in grooming. He places the likely figure at which grooming gave way to language at more like 30 per cent (2003: 173–5). This implies that the transition in fact began among *H. ergaster* or *H. erectus*. By comparison, chimps spend about 20 per cent of their time grooming, and humans 20 per cent of our time in social interaction, and this mainly in conversation (Dunbar 2001: 190–1). If Dunbar is correct, then language began its evolution rather earlier that often assumed, and certainly before humanity left the African continent. Obviously, the population of the first migrants was small, with the figure of 150 being among those sometimes cited, although a larger figure for the breeding population may be more likely (see Stix 2008). Also, we do have to distinguish between the face-to-face unit and the dispersed community (see Layton and O'Hara 2010).

My suspicion is that all that can be implied is the earliest aspects of language: nouns and verbs, rather than fully formed, complex aspects of language such as those that imply the development of folklore, legends, fairy-tales and mythology. Adding to Heine and Kuteva's (2007) evolutionary trajectory, this gives us a scenario something like the one illustrated in Table 2.1.

Of course, what are defined here as 'skills' and 'categories' are only skills in a very loose sense. Also, the exact point at which categories appear in relation to skills is open to debate. My point is merely that there must be at least some association among these things, and an evolution from the earliest tool-making skills all the way to the creation of mythological systems can at least be imagined in a rough sequence, just as one can imagine evolutionary trajectories in

Table 2.1 *From pre-linguistic to linguistic humanity*

New skills	Categories
1. Tool-making	
2. Fire and cooking	
3. Family structures and notions of kinship	1. Nouns
4. The ability to migrate	2. Verbs
5. The ability to classify	3. Adjectives and adverbs
	4. Belief and symbolic thought
	5. Ritual, music and art
	6. Complex symbolic thought
	7. Mythology

the work of Dunbar (2003) or of Aiello and Wheeler (1995). Language must have begun somewhere and must have evolved and have brought with it complexity of thought, complexity of grammar and a use for these: the most obvious use being in the development of story-telling and myth.

After language, the spread of myth is equally obvious. Its precise evolution is difficult to ascertain, but the classic work of Mircea Eliade (e.g., 1963) and others set the scene. More recently, Michael Witzel (2012), a professor of Sanskrit at Harvard, has argued that the world's shared mythologies can be traced to a common origin some 100,000 years ago. These common myths, he argues, are still shared by most of the world's religions. South American, Eastern, Indic and European mythologies, then, have a common 'Laurasian' source, and the source accounts too for religious ideas and presumably linguistic features held in common. These mythologies, he says, differ from 'Gondwana' mythologies, those of most of Africa and of Australia and the Andaman Islands. All Witzel's land masses are named after primeval continent areas; they otherwise have no association with the continents we know today, though the names recall the metaphor.

Possibly since the Neanderthals, mythologies persist and form part of the religious desires and forms of religious expression that unite humankind. Unifying both these postulated mythological systems is a prior, 'Pan-Gaean', set of ideas dating from before the exodus from Africa which took place by 65,000 BP. (Some writers would say earlier.) Witzel (2012: 3) distinguishes his own approach from the two more standard approaches: either assuming universals in the human mind or seeking simple diffusion. He traces mythology backwards to African Eve, some 130,000 years ago, and uses methods that he claims are analogous to those of the natural sciences. Each myth has an origin, and the relation of one myth to another needs to be tested empirically.

Despite his obvious scholarship, I find Witzel's solution to the religious and mythological commonalities difficult to accept wholeheartedly. Nevertheless, his premise that this method works is worth some reflection: there are a number of common features among mythologies of the world, and these are historically deep.

Yuval Noah Harari, in his popular book *Sapiens*, puts it this way:

[H]umans evolved for millions of years in small bands of a few dozen individuals. The handful of millennia separating the Agricultural Revolution from the appearance of cities, kingdoms and empires was not enough time to allow an instinct for mass cooperation to evolve.

Despite the lack of such biological instincts, during the foraging era, hundreds of strangers were able to cooperate thanks to their shared myths. However, this cooperation was loose and limited. Every Sapiens band continued to run its life independently and to provide for most of its own needs. An archaic sociologist living 20,000 years ago, who had no knowledge of events following the Agricultural Revolution, might well have concluded that mythology had a fairly limited scope. (Harari 2014: 102)

Yet, as Harari (2014: 103) admits, this reasoning would be incorrect: 'myths *are* stronger than anyone could have imagined'. Harari is probably wrong about a number of things, but he is correct to see the importance of myth in enabling cooperation both in hunter-gatherer times and later. To share myth is more than to share language, because a shared mythology implies a shared belief system. The degree to which myth in general might have fostered empire building (one of Harari's concerns), though, is debatable. Of course, we do not know that languages were shared among many peoples, but the presumption in the writings of both Harari and Witzel must be that language at least exists in the times about which they write.

Dispersal from Africa

There is no question that the origins of modern humanity lie on the African continent and that *Homo sapiens* possessed language when the species spread across the globe. The traditional assumption, more specifically, is eastern Africa, although a southern African origin has also been argued (e.g., Henn *et al.* 2011). The phonetic similarities between Hadza, spoken in Tanzania, Sandawe, spoken in Kenya, and the click languages of southern Africa are sometimes cited as proof that there is a relation between these various populations. However, this is not as likely as it may seem: a population isolated from similar ones may experience a gene flow of perhaps 5 per cent per thousand years. This suggests, in fact, the replacement of 87 per cent of alleles or variants of a gene over 1,000 years and 98 per cent over 2,000 years (Cavalli-Sforza 2001: 153–4).

There is also a very real possibility of one very small group acquiring another language. This has undoubtedly happened many times among Pygmy groups (acquiring Bantu languages from their neighbours). Linguists and geneticists working together have indeed recently discovered the same in the case of my own fieldwork language Naro, which is a Khoe language. The earlier Naro population, it seems, spoke a Kx'a language (that is, one closely related to modern Ju/'hoan, 'Northern Bushman' or !Kung), before losing it in favour of the Khoe (or 'Central Bushman') language they use today (Pickrell *et al.* 2012). This does not mean a wholesale abandonment of one's native language, of course, but rather a linguistic shift with indeed several then existing languages giving way to one as the common language, perhaps for reasons of the number of speakers or the political dominance of one group (say, grandmothers) over others. I will have more to say about this later.

A review article by Amanuel Beyin (2011) cites 155 sources on Upper Pleistocene human dispersals, and most of them directly concern the question of African origins. Some are themselves reviews of earlier literature. Beyin's review covers both genetic and archaeological data and their implications for prehistory. Beyin (2011) looks especially at the two most prominent theories: (1) that a number of different populations entered the Levant, South Asia and Arabia both before and after the last interglacial period, or (2) that non-African modern humans are essentially derived from a single eastern African source. It is very difficult to pin down single dates for either of these proposed migrations except to say that the first is usually taken as the earlier possibility. That would be during the MIS-5 stage (roughly 130,000 to 85,000 BP), which has alternating warm and cold phases. The other (2) would be during the colder and later MIS-4 stage (85,000 to 74,000 or 71,000 BP). MIS (marine isotope stages) are calculated according to variations in oxygen isotope ratios, and MIS-4 is a stage when sea levels were lower than they are today. Thus travel across the present-day Red Sea would have been possible at that time.

Both the genetic and the archaeological details are complicated, but the implications of both theories are simple: in effect, there was either a single main migration or a series of migrations out of Africa to Asia, and ultimately to other parts of the world, before 71,000 years ago. This, and especially Beyin's second theory, fits well with Stanley Ambrose's (1998) notion of a 'volcanic winter' after the Toba explosion of 74,000 BP. Toba was a super-volcano that produced a cloud of ash that covered the earth, possibly for a duration of ten years or so. The results are known from studies on several continents. The meaning is clear: if there was such an overpowering explosion, the resulting ash cloud effectively reduced the total human population to as few as 2,000 individuals (Wells 2007: 140). Although that small number may seem unlikely, still some sort of population bottleneck is very likely. It has been suggested that the total number of migrants out of Africa was perhaps only 150 individuals, or in any case fewer than 1,000 (Stix 2008). This does not, however, rule out the possibility of different post-Toba population groups mixing in the Arabian peninsula or in India, before spreading to Southeast Asia and China and ultimately to Australia too.

The geneticist Stephen Oppenheimer (2009) suggests that the first inter-breeding among all these post-Toba groups occurred perhaps by around 85,000 BP, with the spread to China and Southeast Asia around 65,000 BP, to Australia as early as 65,000 BP (most say between 40,000 and 60,000 BP), and across the land bridge that stood across the present Bering Strait between 25,000 and 22,000 BP. Finding exact dates of migration, though, is rather difficult. It depends on integrating archaeological finds, known sea-level changes and speculations about probable route. Australia is an interesting case, especially since it is relatively isolated from the rest of the world. This is significant in that we must assume that language was in place from early times there, both because of this isolation in the thousands of years separating the spread of humans to the continent, and because of the assumption that language was needed in order to plan ahead. It was necessary, in other words, in order to migrate, and thus express plans on how to get there in the first place (see e.g., Oppenheimer 2004: 159–71).

Lake Mungo in New South Wales is the site of the earliest mtDNA (Bowler *et al.* 2003), variously estimated as being between 30,000 and 62,000 years old (plus or minus 6,000 years). It is certainly likely that Australia was settled before Europe, when Southeast Asia was one land mass (known by geologists as Sunda) and Australia was larger than it is today. It then comprised also Tasmania and New Guinea (a combined continent called Sahul). Between Sunda and Sahul was the Timor Sea, nearly 100 kilometres across even at the time of lowest sea level. Although perhaps concrete evidence is not abundant, assertion certainly is. For example, David W. Cameron and Colin P. Groves suggest that Australia boasts the earliest evidence of ocean-going craft, with an ability to travel at least 50 kilometres from land, also evidence of art, burial practice and cremation, of nets and fish traps and (incorrectly) of beadwork. Their conclusion is that these things

already existed in the common ancestor [of all humankind], before the colonization of Australia over 60,000 years ago. Language surely arose once, as did the control of fire and religion and music. These are cultural items for which there is no direct evidence, and yet the principle of parsimony suggests very strongly that they are very much earlier in their genesis [than is commonly supposed]. (Cameron and Groves 2004: 268–9)

In other words, those who arrived in Australia 60,000 years ago brought with them not only their ability to control fire but also their music, their religious ideas and the ability to talk with each other in *language* as we today would conceptualize it. Although the last few thousand years have seen contact between Australians and people of New Guinea, certainly before that the isolation of Sahul or Australia was long, and the population of the Australian continent was separated from the rest of humanity.

The number of languages spoken in Australia in 1770 is commonly estimated to be more than 200 (see Dixon 1980). Of course, the figure is open to interpretation, not least since languages can be defined as dialects, and some will be closely related to others. Nor were these 200 languages either primitive or recently evolved. As almost every linguistics student will know, dialects or not, a divergence of tens of thousands of years will create significant differences among languages. Apparently this was a surprise to the first settlers: the governor, Arthur Phillip, wrote to Sir Joseph Banks of his astonishment that the indigenous inhabitants of Botany Bay were using different words from those 40 miles (64 km) away (Dixon 1980: 9–10). If anything, what is surprising is that in his survey of Aboriginal languages, R. M. W. Dixon notes a number of grammatical and other similarities among Australia's diverse languages.

Among the most interesting evidence regarding the 'Out of Africa' hypothesis is a study of phonemic variation in 504 of the world's languages, sampled from the World Atlas of Language Structures (see Atkinson 2011: 247). Through a statistical sampling method, Atkinson plotted the number of phonemes in each of these languages against the distance from Africa where they are spoken, through migration along the obvious routes. He also plotted the mean phonemic diversity across language families: through a founder effect, languages lose phonemes if they are spoken by smaller populations. In both cases, evidence for a single, African origin of all the world's languages was unequivocal. The highest levels of phonemic diversity beyond Africa are found in language families autochthonous to Southeast Asia. They experienced the most rapid population growth, and therefore time to recover phonemic diversity. African languages have by far the largest number of phonemes, and South American languages the smallest. !Xũ (spoken in Namibia), for example, seems to have 141, and Pirahã (spoken in Brazil) has only 11. Other languages lie in the middle, for example, English with (depending on dialect) around 46. In general, Oceanic as well as South American languages have few phonemes, and European languages have more. Hawaiian has 13, Roro (spoken in Papua New Guinea) has 14 and Bandjalang (spoken in Australia) has 16.

If we plot the likelihood of two origins for complex language on such a basis, South America (which would be very unlikely) comes in as the second most probable source, according to Atkinson (2011: 248). Rather, the evidence does indicate a series of successive expansions and bottlenecks on a journey from Africa to all the other continents. Atkinson remarks on the consistency between his data and archaeological evidence for the origin and evolution of symbolic culture between 160,000 and 80,000 years ago. While later correspondents in *Science* would criticize details in his paper, the gist of Atkinson's work is safe enough.

Finally here, it is worth considering the possibility that, by analogy with the 'Movius Line', there is a difference between the relatively rapidly evolving languages of some parts of the world and those that might have developed more slowly. Just as in the 1940s the archaeologist Hallam Movius (1948) pointed out (rightly or wrongly) that Southeast Asia and the Far East retained 'backward' handaxe-making traditions, in contrast to those west of the 'Line', so too might the development of languages have been more or less advantaged by geographical circumstances. Thus, rapid linguistic evolution may not take place at the same rate across the globe.

Peopling of the Americas

A traditional date for the peopling of the Americas was around 11,000 BP, with the arrival across the Bering Strait of Clovis stone tool technology. Recently, there have been suggestions of rather earlier dates, as long ago as 45,000 BP (Alexiades 2009: 6; see also Jablonski 2002). Domestication of plants (manioc and maize) and the modification of landscapes may have occurred in Mesoamerica and then South America as early as 10,000 BP, with pottery developing later. There were also extensive trade networks in the pre-colonial Americas, including South America, as well as the evolution of complex political structures, including states (Alexiades 2009: 6–15). In spite of ethno-botanical evidence of Polynesian contact in the Andes, there is no accepted evidence of genetic influence from migrant populations from other continents (Schurr 2004).

Therefore, the details of the peopling of the Americas are in dispute. From a social anthropological point of view, what is perhaps more important than the exact date is the fact that American peoples, when they arrived in the Americas, were completely developed biologically, culturally and linguistically. The linguistic diversity of the Americas is, though, still open to debate (as is the linguistic diversity of Australia). Figures of 1,500 languages, or more, in South America alone have been suggested. We do not know. Nor do we know whether the first inhabitants of North America arrived from Asia in one migration, speaking one language, or in multiple and linguistically diverse migrations (see e.g., Campbell 1997). We only know that they arrived, spread and diversified. We also know that there are close similarities in genetic material among those who travelled farthest, those of Baja California, and the southern tip of South America. Indeed, the peopling of the Americas is enormously complex, in view of the probable multiplicity of founder lineages in these two continents (see Oppenheimer 2004: 279–342). Indeed, there are different male lines as well as distinct waves of migration through North America and down to Tierra del Fuego. The world's most extreme locations, in terms of distance from the great land masses of Africa and Asia, offer tests for the degree to which humans can adapt, and linguistic adaptation would seem to be a form like any other. If the most complex languages in the world are to be found in the Canadian Arctic (as they are), perhaps the second most complex of any are those found in the Canadian Subarctic.

To put it all together, then, humanity had already evolved speech after an earlier use of gesture for communication. Grammar and vocabulary became complex in Africa, before a small group of humans crossed to Asia and ultimately to Australia. Later, others crossed the Bering Strait to Alaska, across a land bridge then connecting Asia and North America, and migrated southwards and finally all the way to Tierra del Fuego. Both the first Australians and the first Americans possessed full language, and they possessed and transmitted mythology as well as practical knowledge and skills. Exactly how old their mythologies are, we do not know. Nor do we know for certain whether they are connected or not, but they may well be.

3   What did prehistoric people do?

This may seem pretty obvious. Hunters hunt, and gatherers gather. The reality is, of course, slightly more complicated. The ecology of hunter-gatherer societies is related to social phenomena, such as land use, land ownership, perceptions of nature (through language) and so on. Knowing this provides necessary background for understanding how hunter-gatherers perceive the world. This will be the subject of the following chapter.

Hunter-gatherer society: an eighteenth-century invention?

A few years ago I argued that hunter-gatherer society was an eighteenth-century Scottish invention (Barnard 2004a). The concept of 'hunter-gatherer society' simply did not exist before that. This is not to say that seventeenth-century Europeans did not understand what it meant to be an individual hunter-gatherer, but it *is* to say that they could not conceive of hunter-gatherers as living *in a society*. In the seventeenth century, the idea of *society* was not generally expressed as a count noun, as we do today: one society, two societies, etc. It was expressed in the abstract, with no indefinite article: *in society*. What is more, hunter-gatherers were understood to be people who lived beyond society, and not within it. The hunter-gatherer, therefore, was a society-less person:

In such condition, there is no place for Industry, because the fruit thereof is uncertain: and consequently no Culture of the Earth; no Navigation, nor use of the commodities that may be imported by Sea; no commodious Building; no Instruments of moving, and removing such things as require much force; no Knowledge of the face of the Earth; no account of Time; no Arts; no Letters; no Society; and which is worst of all, continuall feare, and danger of violent death; And the life of man, solitary, poore, nasty, brutish, and short (Hobbes 1991 [1651]: 89).

In the eighteenth century some writers, notably Rousseau (1973 [1750–62]), preferred to idealize the individual hunter-gatherer. This, however, had less to do with the acceptance of a hunter-gatherer lifestyle as *sociable*: Rousseau held that humans were naturally *not* sociable. It had more to do with perceiving the *economic* basis of society. Rousseau was, if you like, the first 'Marxist'. Later writers, notably Adam Smith, went further. Smith was indeed among the very first to see hunter-gatherers not only as sociable but also as possessing *society*. We might even credit Smith with anticipating (if only by accident) Robin Dunbar's (1993) notion of a 'natural' human group size in such a society, or indeed in any human society, of just under 150 individuals. (Dunbar's actual ideal human group size, predicted from the number of primates in a group with the same size of neocortex, is 143 rather than 150.) However, this does not allow for one mitigating factor: the possession of language.

In the age of hunters it is impossible for a very great number to live together. As game is their only support they would soon exhaust all that was within their reach. Thirty or forty families would be the most that could live together, that is, about 140 or 150 persons. These might live by the chase in the country about them. They would also naturally form themselves into these villages, agreeing to live near together for their mutual security. (Smith 1978 [Feb. 22, 1763]: 213)

Smith's (1767: 437–78) consideration of the origin of language begins in similar fashion. He imagines two people meeting on an island and having to communicate with each other. How would they speak? What part of speech might come first? While language was in the long run perhaps rather less important to him than either his economic or his jurisprudential ideas, it was nevertheless of early concern, and scholars agree that he lectured on such notions as early as the 1740s and 1750s. This does not necessarily mean that he was thinking of what much later became known as prehistory. Rather, these were *hypothetical* people, invented for heuristic purposes by a philosopher.

Preceding Smith, the historian Sir John Dalrymple was actually clearer on early society. Dalrymple was also quite clear that he was thinking in what we might regard today as evolutionary terms:

The first state of society is that of hunters and fishers; among such a people the idea of property will be confined to a few, and but a very few moveables; and subjects which are immovable, will be esteemed to be common. In accounts given of many American tribes we read, that one or two of the tribe will wander five or six hundred miles from his usual place of abode, plucking the fruit, destroying the game, and catching the fish throughout the fields and rivers adjoining to all the tribes which he passes, without any idea of such a property in the members of them, as makes him guilty of infringing the rights of others, when he does so. (Dalrymple 1758: 75)

What is obvious from these economically based accounts is that hunter-gatherers were perceived as possessing a social contract, an incipient notion of property and a notion of appropriate rules of behaviour within their quite basic social formations. Many other Scots in the late eighteenth century were to hold similar views, and from them we derive our first modern understandings of society based on subsistence without livestock or cultivation. Hunting and gathering may seem 'natural' enough to us today, but such notions had to be rediscovered both ethnographically in the Americas and Africa, and more theoretically and generally later during the Enlightenment of eighteenth-century Europe. Only then could Europeans of the time take in the idea of these means of subsistence as a basis for building human societies. Prehistory, in other words, sort of had to be invented.

Homo Sapiens genetic and cultural evolution

The timeline shown in Table 3.1 illustrates genetic and social or cultural evolution from the earliest stone tools, among advanced australopithecines, to the dawn of writing. The dates are, of course, approximate. A similar timeline, but restricted to the last 500,000 years, is given in Barnard (2012: 139). It is represented here in this book, with some very minor changes, as Table 3.2.

Perhaps the most striking thing about the timeline in Table 3.1 is that it shows clearly the considerable overlap between biological and cultural evolution of the human species. Even if we assume an emergence of language rather early, around 50,000 years ago, the overlap is still there. My view is that there has been a much longer evolution, both biologically and culturally (Barnard 2008a, 2009, 2011: 132–41), which culminated in what is sometimes known as the 'faculty of language' or 'language faculty' (see Hauser *et al.* 2002; Pinker and Jackendoff 2005). I do not differentiate here between the faculty of language in the narrow sense, that is, the property of recursion, and the faculty of language in the broad sense, including things that language shares with other psychological phenomena. For me, as for Pinker and Jackendoff, recursion (embedding one unit into another of the same kind, such as short sentences within larger sentences) is an important aspect, but it is not the only one of significance. However, I do disagree with Pinker and Jackendoff (2005: 202) that 'language is a complex adaptation for communication which evolved piecemeal': it is much more than communication (Barnard 2013), and it did not exactly evolve piecemeal. Whether it coincided with the evolution of complex technology, such as spear-throwers or atlatls, is a matter of debate. Recent research suggests that it may have, and that there has been a long and continuous evolutionary development of microlith technology, and with the microliths hardened by heat treatment. A date of 71,000 BP has been recorded for such microliths, notably some found at Pinnacle Point on South Africa's Indian Ocean coast (Brown *et al.* 2012).

Some may say that there may have been an even longer evolution of brain to reach the point where language became possible or likely, but the evidence from archaeology that the mind was language-ready seems pretty conclusive to me (e.g., Henshilwood and Marean 2003). Early language entailed the need to communicate something, and religion and art seem to have been required as well (see Aiello 1998; d'Errico 2009). If the brain could take it, these things were there as elements for language to use, to fashion as needed for collective

Table 3.1 Homo sapiens *genetic and cultural evolution*

2,600,000 BP	The first stone tools (among australopithecines)
2,400,000 BP	Appearance of the genus *Homo* (*H. habilis*)
1,800,000 BP	*Homo georgicus* migration to Georgia
1,800,000 BP	*H. erectus* migration to the Arabian Peninsula
1,800,000 BP	Appearance of *H. rudolfensis*
1,800,000–1,500,000 BP	Controlled use of fire by *H. ergaster*
1,200,000 BP	Appearance of *H. antecessor* and possible FOXP2 mutation
800,000 BP	*H. antecessor* enters Europe
600,000 BP	True hunting and gathering, as opposed to scavenging
600,000 BP	*H. heidelbergensis* enters Europe
400,000–300,000 BP	Wooden spears in Germany and England
300,000–30,000 BP	Development of Mousterian culture by Neanderthals
270,000 or 170,000 BP	Possible ochre use in Zambia
260,000 BP	Hafted spears in Zambia
200,000 BP	Traditional date for anatomically modern *Homo sapiens*
160,000 BP	Appearance of *H. sapiens idaltu* in Ethiopia
160,000 BP	Earliest fishing and use of red ochre
290,000–140,000 BP	Presumed date of Mitochondrial Eve
125,000 BP	Maximum point of the Eemian Stage interglacial
90,000 BP	Y-chromosomal Adam
83,000 BP	Possible engraved ostrich egg shell in Namibia
74,000 BP	Eruption of Toba followed by population bottleneck
71,000 BP	Complex and continuing microlith technology in South Africa
70,000–60,000 BP	*H. sapiens* migration from Africa to Asia
68,500 BP	M168 mutation (carried by all non-African males)
60,000–48,000 BP	Habitation of Australia
50,000 BP	Traditional date for the emergence of language
50,000 BP	Beginnings of the (African) Later Stone Age
42,000 BP	'Neanderthal flute'
41,000 BP	Denisovans in the Altai Mountains
35,000–20,000 BP	Habitation of the Americas
32,000 BP	Aurignacian culture in Europe
28,000 BP	Gravettian period in Europe (complex tools)
25,000 BP	Baby-carriers and clothing
25,000 BP	Cave painting
25,000 BP	Neanderthals die out or are absorbed into *H. sapiens*
18,000 BP	*H. floresiensis* on Flores

understanding of the use of tools, for transmission of ideas to the young, for reflection through symbolism and later mythology (Donald 1991: 201–68, 2009). Donald talks of mimesis, including the pre-linguistic, symbolic activities such as ritual activities and dance. These, he argues, were part of the evolution towards modernity in pre-mythic, pre-linguistic times, and he attributes them to *Homo erectus*. In short, everything points to a co-evolution of cognition along with religion and art.

Table 3.2 *Humankind's most recent 500,000 years*

500,000 BP	heyday of *Homo heidelbergensis*
400,000 to 300,000 BP	split of Neanderthals and *H. sapiens* (according to Stringer)
400,000 or 300,000 BP	early wooden spears (Germany and England)
320,000 BP	possible ritual burial in Spain
300,000 to 125,000 BP	*H. heidelbergensis rhodesiensis*
270,000 or 170,000 BP	possible ochre use in Zambia
260,000 BP	hafted spears in Zambia
250,000 to 100,000 BP	behavioural modernity (according to McBrearty and Brooks)
200,000 to 130,000 BP	evolution of modern humans in Africa
160,000 BP	Herto site, Ethiopia (*Homo sapiens idaltu*)
120,000 BP	Sahara covered by rivers and lakes
100,000 BP	modern humans in Middle East
100,000 to 80,000 BP	shell beads in Algeria
83,000 BP	possible engraved ostrich egg shell in Namibia
80,000 to 60,000 BP	behavioural modernity (according to Mellars)
77,000 BP	ochre use in South Africa (Blombos Cave)
77,000 to 72,000 BP	Still Bay industry
74,000 BP	Toba eruption (approximate)
70,000 BP	possible carved rock cave entrance, Botswana
70,000 to 60,000 BP	possible Out of Africa migrations
66,000 to 59,000 BP	Howiesons Poort industry
65,000 BP	Neanderthal burial at Kebara, Israel
60,000 or 40,000 BP	modern humans in Australia
55,000 BP	pressure flaking techniques
50,000 BP	behavioural modernity (according to Klein)
42,000 BP	'Neanderthal flute'
40,000 BP	modern humans in Europe (Cro-Magnon)
40,000 BP	ritual burial and cremation in Australia
40,000 to 35,000 BP	figurines and beadwork near Danube
39,000 BP	Campi Flegrei eruption, Italy
35,000 BP	evolution of modern human brain (according to Stringer)
35,000 BP	possible domestication of the dog
35,000 or 20,000 BP	modern humans in the Americas
25,000 BP	cave painting
18,000 BP	*H. floresiensis* on Flores

Source: adapted from Barnard 2012: 139

Citing material from the archaeology of Neanderthal burials, Steven Mithen (2009: 125–8) rejects the idea that Neanderthals had language, but argues that the speciation event that separates them from *Homo sapiens* does involve the invention of two systems of aural communication: music and language. The latter entailed a cognitive fluidity, he claims, that led directly to the ability to conceive of supernatural beings. This is also a point taken up in some detail by archaeologist David Lewis-Williams (2010: 139–206) in his book *Conceiving*

God, where he argues that religious experience, religious belief and religious practice all have a neurological basis. In intensified form, this leads to hallucination and ultimately to shamanism, to Eastern and Western religions as well as to the pictorial representations we have in prehistoric rock art. There are also parallels here in neuropsychologist Steven Brown's (2000) notion of musi-language, which is a hypothesized bridge between music and language. Both, according to Brown, have a common evolutionary source, a musical proto-language visible in both infants and adults, and in both males and females. Psychologist Geoffrey Miller (2000a) sees this as a biological adaptation, one that helps in acquiring a mate: though this may be stretching the model.

My own view is that it is useful to distinguish between being evolutionarily ready for language and actually having it. Both can be difficult to prove, and the former particularly so. The great palaeo-anthropologist Phillip Tobias, comparing the skulls of six *Homo habilis* fossils, noticed a protuberance in what is known as Broca's area. This is the part of the brain that governs speech in humans, and which, along with Wernicke's area, which governs comprehension, is essential for language. His discovery suggests at least a trajectory towards the evolution of language, far earlier than often imagined (Cavalli-Sforza 2001: 174–5). The implication of this discovery, then, is not that *H. habilis* could actually use language, but simply that the species was, in a sense, on the way to becoming language-ready. In modern humans, both these areas are located in the left hemisphere of about 97 per cent of the population. Strangely, the less-dominant right hemisphere aids in the understanding of ambiguity in words, whether in sign, speech or writing (Harpaz *et al.* 2009). New discoveries are still being made, for example the discovery that, within Wernicke's area, what is known as Brodmann area 44 is involved in phonological fluency and Brodmann area 45 in semantic fluency (Porter *et al.* 2011).

None of this is essential for an acceptance of Chomsky's (e.g., 1996, 2012) view of language as innate, but it does make the idea more plausible than one might think. Rapid evolution, possibly across species boundaries (between Neanderthals and humans, at least), of an ability to communicate, and to think independently, to invent, to influence, to record the world pictorially or whatever, gives us a reason for language. It also might help to explain too how languages come to be so complex. Chomsky (1986: 30) suggests that linguistic evolution may come down to a chance mutation in one individual, perhaps 100,000 years ago. Perhaps it could, but knowing the exact date is less important than knowing that our species or its precursor was ready.

An ethnographic interlude

Archaeologists tend to think primarily in terms of material culture: the stuff that is left behind in the archaeological record. An alternative perspective is that from social anthropology, where the emphasis is more on symbolic aspects of culture, the non-material stuff which is there in equal measure but in fact more open to observation, because it is still with us. Let us therefore look more closely at the linguistic implications of these aspects of culture.

First, there is language itself. The one thing we can be sure of is that the earliest kind of fully developed language, no matter what its antecedents, was that articulated by members of the genus *Homo*. I say 'articulated', rather than 'spoken', in deference to the possibility that gestural language preceded spoken, at least at some point early in the history of language. Many proposed dates appear in the more speculative writings, some as early as the time of *Homo habilis*, 2,300,000 to 1,400,000 years ago. Deacon considers such ideas, at least in passing, in *The symbolic species*, but opts to emphasize instead the significance of the evolution of symbolism through ritual and communication in an evolving mind (see Deacon 1997: 401–10). My own view is that spoken language did come, if not that early, then at least at some point early in the evolution of the genus *Homo*. This is not least because of the likelihood that pre-*Homo sapiens* had some form of spoken communication, if not language then at least a proto-language with vocabulary and perhaps some grammatical conventions. Obvious sources include the findings of D'Anastasio *et al.* (2013) on the implications of findings on the Neanderthal hyoid bone, and Dediu and Levinson (2013) on further implications for Neanderthal linguistic capabilities. Beyond those pieces of evidence, most of what I say here comes from my own general knowledge of hunter-gatherers, a knowledge acquired through a few years of field research and few decades of reading ethnographies. All hunter-gatherers alive today have fully developed spoken language, of course, albeit language in varying degrees of complexity. Some also have gestural communication, for example in forms of sign language used in hunting. This is never a substitute for spoken language, though, but is used in order to enhance it or to keep silent while on the hunt. Terrence Deacon (1997: 39–46) asks rhetorically: where are the missing simple languages? The answer, possibly, is simply that they do not exist because evolution continued right past them. Neanderthals or Denisovans may have had them, but we should not expect them among any 'primitive' group today. The reason why hunter-gatherers do not fit the bill is that they are all not only adapted, but highly advanced in their adaptation to a hunting-and-gathering way of life. The irony is that the rest of us are too, even though we do not subsist in that way any longer (Barnard 2012: 122–41). The ability to think in language is useful for both symbolic thought and all the cultural baggage that humans carry beyond the Stone Age.

The sort of language most relevant is what Chomsky (1986: 21–4) calls I-language, that which is internal to the person and which enables *thought through language*. This, Chomsky claims, is the essence of cognitive aspects of language. It is less abstract than P-language (its platonic aspect) and more individual than E-language (its external, communication aspect). Importantly, I-language enables both linguistic cognition and the ability to talk *to* or *with* oneself (or one's self). The latter phenomenon is not uncommon among hunter-gatherers, notably among African Pygmy peoples. Among them, individuals may speak for hours without regard either to the presence or the absence of anyone who might be in earshot (Lewis 2009). This is, in a sense, the opposite of communication or of phatic communion: speech for the sake of speech, as opposed to speech for non-communication social purposes ('Hello! How are you? Nice weather we're having ...'). Monologue as understood here is about cognition, not about communication, and not about 'being sociable'.

I say 'language', but we should remember that the plural is what I am talking about. In my experience, no hunter-gatherer ever (or at least almost never) speaks only one language. It is normal for a hunter-gatherer to be able to speak four or five languages, sometimes even more. Hunter-gatherers live in small groups, and often very small groups indeed: 15 or 20 people per group in some parts of the Kalahari, though rather more in the Arctic and Subarctic. Archaeologist Tim Maggs (1967) once used rock art to estimate the apparent group size in Western Cape sites, and he found they had an average of just 13 per group. In the Subarctic, groups can be several hundred in number. A group size of a few hundred has been recorded, though the average seems to be around a hundred in the winter. Summer hunting groups number between 5 and 50, with an average of around 20 (Damas 1969b: 122–3). In the Subarctic, there are small, summer multi-family units of 10 to 20, winter groupings of 35 to 75, and sometimes larger aggregations consisting of more than one band (e.g., Leacock 1969: 9–12). And quite apart from a diversity of hunter-gatherer communities on the basis of geographical limitations, there are limitations in the study of hunter-gatherer communities based purely on the background of the anthropologists who study them. This is borne out, for example, by Mitsuo Ichikawa's (2004) comparative study of Japanese, French and American approaches to the study of hunter-gatherers in central Africa. And if national approaches differ, so too do theoretical ones. This may be particularly true in archaeology (Lane and Schadla-Hall 2004: 155–9), as well as, of course, in linguistics. There are many comparative works and edited collections on hunter-gatherers, and a glance at almost any of them will confirm the great diversity as well as the adaptability of these peoples (see e.g., Burch and Ellanna 1994; Cummings *et al.* 2014).

Groups may be 'isolated' in some sense, but they are in fact interacting, either as individuals move from group to group, or as groups meet for sharing or for trade (which is not the same thing) or as people seek mates. Dialects differ and are ever-changing. I can think of a well-recorded Kalahari language (/Xam) with no speakers alive today, another (N/u) with fewer than 10 and yet another (N!aqriaxe) with around 50. Even in these cases, people are not speaking exactly the same dialect of their language. My own main fieldwork language (Naro) was once, a few hundred, or more likely a few thousand, years ago, acquired by an entire ethnic group, 'the Naro'. Their ancestors, we know almost certainly, were then speakers of a very different language. But although virtually complete, the linguistic shift did not necessarily involve large numbers of people, much less monolingual people. Like the N!aqriaxe today, their children grew up speaking other languages and even acquiring new kinship usages, as their families were always in some way mixed.

The Naro a thousand years ago were not quite 'the Naro' we know ethnographically. They were a small, probably multilingual, community, which must have numbered perhaps 150 or fewer (Barnard 2014: 221). We understand this because of recent genetic evidence, but in my own field (kinship studies) it is plain too: the Naro kinship system has clear elements of both Ju/'hoan and simplified, cognatic Khoe (Naro) structures. This was, in fact, the subject of my PhD thesis (Barnard 1976). Further, I have noticed a similar shift among !Xóõ, or mixed !Xóõ and Naro, who live south of the Naro. At the time I first encountered it in 1975, the nature of the shift was not quite clear to me, though the transition seems to be clear now.

This, then, is the kind of community I imagine to have existed among prehistoric hunter-gatherers: multilingual, with individuals coming from different places and speaking different languages or dialects, mixing and mixing again and again and finally spreading throughout the world. It is perhaps relevant that Khoisan populations have greater genetic diversity than any other population on earth (Behar *et al.* 2008). The first speakers of any languages were probably people much like this, if not this exact set of southern African people or their descendants. Diglossia is likely to have been common, if men and women developed different ways of speaking, different ritual activities or other gender-specific roles. The latter could include, for example, tool-making and hunting methods, as well as ceremonial roles. In my experience, hunter-gatherers do not worry much about translation, because if everyone speaks a set of different languages then each person can use their own preferred way of speaking. Differences in idiolect or even differences in language become possible. For example, I will speak Naro and you will speak Ju/'hoan, but we both understand each other because we both know the other language. Husbands and wives can easily speak different dialects or languages and impart this linguistic diversity to their offspring. We anthropologists or archaeologists may talk of 'teaching and learning' tool-making techniques, rules of sociality, or whatever, but for language in any form it may be better to think in terms of the *acquisition* of it. For Chomsky, acquisition depends on innate skills, and this is exactly what we are talking about. Language is all around, and it is picked up without effort on the part of either a teacher or a learner. Table 3.3 illustrates an example of linguistic diversity: the languages

Table 3.3 *Languages spoken by a N!aqriaxe man*

Language	Language family
N!aqriaxa	Kx'a
G/ui *and* G//ana	Khoe-Kwadi
!Xóõ *(one or more dialects)*	Taa
Kgalagari	Bantu
Afrikaans	Indo-European

spoken by one N!aqriaxe man from Botswana I met in 2011. The extraordinary thing is that his eight or so languages are in five different language families.

Yes, but one might reasonably ask: how difficult is this? The answer is that we do not really know. Penelope Brown and Suzanne Gaskins raise the question of comparative difficulty or languages in reference to Yélî Dnye, a language spoken on Rossel Island, off the coast of Papua New Guinea. It is reported to have 'ninety phonemes including many multiply articulated consonants' (Brown and Gaskins 2014: 192). They add that 'Other languages have sounds rare in the world's languages, like the clicks of the Khoisan languages of southern Africa. We simply don't know how children approach these complex systems or whether they pose major difficulties for their learners.' As one who has learned click languages as an adult, this, it seems to me, is not really the problem. There is nothing intrinsically difficult about producing clicks, or for that matter, click releases as in the series /n!/ (nasalized retroflex click, also known as cerebral, palatal or alveopalatal click) or /ǂkx'/ (alveolar click followed by an (intrusive) k followed by a voiceless velar fricative followed by glottal stop), compared to the grammatical complexities of many so-called 'click languages'. On grammatical complexity, we still do not have a clear idea, since although (in terms of parts of speech) in most cases children do tend to learn nouns first, in verb-friendly languages like Korean or Mandarin, verbs often come first. Throw in vowel harmony, verb classes and many other difficult features, and the difficulties, for either children or adults, are compounded.

After meeting the N!aqriaxe man I reflected on my own early fieldwork conducted more than 30 years before. I had known a number of people with similar mixed backgrounds, as well as families made up of people from different areas and mixed Naro, G/ui and G//ana populations. A group of Naro with Kgalagadi among them interacted with Herero and spoke Naro with the Naro, even though 'superior' groups (like Herero) do not normally speak the language of a lower-status group (like Naro). At Bere the group of !Xóõ I met regularly spoke Naro among themselves, as well as with Naro who lived nearby. This seemed a bit odd at the time, but in the context of later discoveries about language use it seems pretty obvious that this was normal in such small, multilingual communities. There was also a group of ǂKx'ao//'aesi along the

Ghanzi ridge who moved between Ju/'hoan and Naro areas and spoke Ju/'hoan (which is similar to ≠Kx'ao//'aen, the language of the ≠Kx'ao//'aesi). And there were Afrikaners who used Naro, Tswana and Kgalagadi as well as Afrikaans and English. I had truly lived within a *Sprachbund*, though I could really only speak (bad) Naro and English and mutter some greetings.

I imagine a similar situation a few thousand years ago or more. This comes to mind via the recent revelations from geneticists and linguists (Pickrell *et al.* 2012) that Naro did not always speak Naro but switched from a Kx'a language similar to Ju/'hoan to Naro. I have mentioned this before, but it is worth further reflection: 'the Naro' were *not* an ethnic group numbering (as they do today) a few thousand. They were collection of people then speaking several languages, no doubt from more than one place of origin, and the number speaking Naro as a first language may have been only in the tens or hundreds. Their parents were speaking other languages, as were their spouses and possibly even their siblings! I recall here the words of a !Xóõ woman that a spouse is only 'temporary', whereas a brother is 'for life'. It is in the nature of languages that they do eventually coalesce and become one. It is also in the nature of kinship systems.

That is how Naro became a language, and, in retrospect, that is why its kinship system came to be a unique blend of what we would now call Khoe (or Khoe-Kwadi) and Kx'a features. The alternate-generation usage of *tsxõo* and *mama* (both meaning 'grandrelative', that is grandparent, uncle, aunt, cousin, nephew, niece, grandchild) is a case in point. Similarly, Naro are virtually the only other people who practise *xaro*, the gift-exchange system borrowed from the Ju/'hoansi, and *kamane* (Ju/'hoan: *kamasi*), the practice of distributing marriage and childbirth prestations. The latter practice is unusual among hunter-gatherers, in the Kalahari or anywhere else. Both these customs seem to be Ju/'hoan in origin, but they work well for the Naro too. It is also possible that *kamasi* or *kamane* are loan words, as they are not found in some western Ju/'hoan areas of the Kalahari. In any case, *xaro* or *hxaro* (the unpronounced *h* is merely an orthographic convention), in particular, is a valuable exchange mechanism among both Ju/'hoansi and Naro. In Naro, it is termed //'*ãe*, which is a verbal form usually used as a request. For example, '//'*ãe* me your hat', or '//'*ãe* me your stick' (that is, 'give it to me in delayed direct exchange'). It enables the redistribution of material property, exclusive of consumables, throughout the community. It also permits anyone to use the territory and resources of another *xaro* partner, probably its most valuable function, especially as resources in the Kalahari, as indeed in many other hunter-gatherer environments, are so unevenly distributed.

But if the daytime was a time of *xaro* or similar things, what was happening at night? In the daytime, economic transactions and discussions about them were the norm, but the night is very, very different. In her discussion of the significance of fire, Polly Wiessner (2014: 14029) has produced detailed records

Table 3.4 *Ju/'hoan conversation: day and night*

Day conversation	Night conversation
34%: complaints	81%: story-telling
31%: economic matters	7%: complaints
16%: joking relationships	4%: myth
9%: land rights	4%: economic matters
6%: story-telling	2%: land rights
4%: inter-ethnic relations	2%: inter-ethnic relations

Source: statistical data from Wiessner 2014: 14029

of activities in day and night. Her findings reveal that 34 per cent of daytime conversations involved complaints about others, 31 per cent involved specifically economic matters and 16 per cent concerned joking relationships. Only 9 per cent were about land rights, 4 per cent inter-ethnic relations, and just 6 per cent was given over to stories. But astonishingly, by contrast, she records 81 per cent of night conversation as story-telling, mainly stories about the day's activities. Additionally, 4 per cent was myth, 4 per cent concerned economic matters and 7 per cent was complaint. Land and inter-ethnic matters were 2 per cent each. This is shown in Table 3.4.

In other words, night is overwhelmingly given over to the telling and retelling of stories, mostly about those present or known to the people telling them, compared to the revelation of only a very small number in the day. All this was made possible by the introduction of fire to humanity. Additionally, Wiessner makes the point that there are implications here for archaeology, just as archaeological data have implications for sociality (and therefore the use of language). The habitual use of fire enables the expansion of social networks, the presence of beads suggests gift-giving, and the presence of art, including rock art, may imply ritual that brings together social units beyond the band. We do not need to compare the situation at any other point in evolution: Wiessner's results are highly likely to be as indicative of life in the Middle Stone Age as they are of the Ju/'hoansi today. It hints strongly at a rhythmic alternation of two styles of being: night (with fire) and day. Even if the specifics of exchange were different, the use of the night is not altered. The significance of fire to early humanity has long been known, but the anthropological literature emphasizes cooking (see e.g., Wrangham 2009) or the evolutionary significance of cooking through the expensive tissue hypothesis (Aiello and Wheeler 1995). In the latter case, for *Homo habilis* and *H. erectus*, fire and ultimately cooking enabled easier digestion and therefore the expansion of the brain. For both *H. erectus* and ultimately *H. sapiens*, fire had another function. According to Wiessner's findings, it made possible communicative aspects of sociality through *speech*. Signing is important, but speech is possibly more significant because it gives people something to talk about at night. If night is the time for stories, it is also the time when humans learned their full *social* capabilities as communicating animals. The evolutionary result is none other than the full potential of language. There is no doubt that language does exist in part for communication, but it also exists for thinking. These two ideas are not incompatible, but merely throw light on the complexity of the problem.

The interesting thing about current trends in research on the origin of language is that while in the 1990s the emphasis was on speculation, in the first decade of the twenty-first century and since, the emphasis has shifted quite radically towards acquiring and explaining new data (Levinson 2014: 309–11). Stephen Levinson argues that since language is what makes humans a cultural species, it needs to be understood as such, that is, anthropologically. Since biology and culture did not evolve separately but together, more needs to be understood as part of this co-evolutionary process. This is particularly true when we realize that Denisovans and Neanderthals both possessed little difference in FOXP2 except in a gene that binds to it and 'effects its quantitative expression' (Levinson 2014: 312–13). It is perhaps too early to say, but the evidence is pointing to a biological foundation for the precursors of language some 500,000 years ago.

In his incomplete book on the origin and diversification of language, written not long before his death in 1967, the late Morris Swadesh (2006: 214) wrote:

if we go back to the days when prehuman communication was not yet really language, there could be only one system common to our evolving species, albeit with minor individual and subspecies differences. Furthermore, only when a fairly definite and sizable degree of conventionalization had come about was it even possible for different languages to exist. This sort of vindicates the Tower of Babel story, which suggests that, as long as men lived simply, they spoke one language. When they acquired wisdom and yearned to raise themselves to heaven, their language developed local variations and there arose different and mutually unintelligible forms of speech.

This is plausible, except that 'men' here must, of course, include women as well. They were no doubt raising the children. I do not deny that if language is all to do with a chance mutation, we may imagine early language existing only in one family, then one band. However, diversification has to come about almost immediately, that is in just a few generations, as humans separate into communities of diverse, even if changing membership.

A theoretical diversion: Chomsky versus Foucault

Paul Rabinow (1984: 3–7) uses his introduction to the works of Foucault to highlight a fundamental difference between Foucault and Chomsky. Chomsky is a rationalist in the spirit of Descartes. He therefore assumes a fundamental similarity among all human beings. Foucault is the opposite, essentially an empiricist. He does not assume similarity, but difference.

Social anthropology is mainly an empiricist discipline. If we were to allow it a degree of rationality, it would become rather less dependent on data and more reliant on discovery through principle. This opens up the possibility of an anthropological research by means of deduction. If all languages are basically the same, then such an approach is justified. Chomsky's own work is the result. If diversity is almost unlimited, a Foucaldian (or Foucaltian) approach would be more appropriate. Of course, the issue is not unique either to linguistics or to anthropology. In a way, there is a resemblance here to the basis of, for example, law. In England the legal system is based to a large extent on precedent; in Scotland it is based rather more on principle (see e.g., Gloag and Henderson 2001: 1–41). The 'English' system is found not only in England but also in the United States and most of the Commonwealth. The 'Scottish' system is based ultimately on Roman law (or the Roman-Dutch legal tradition), as is the legal tradition of most of the countries of southern Africa. Whatever the specific laws may be, their application in the courts depends on a theoretical understanding of what 'law' is: in the Scottish tradition, one must justify precedent by seeking the principle behind it. Thus, Chomsky's thought (Chomsky 1965) is essentially rationalist. It resembles evolutionist anthropology, which in turn resembles Scots law. Foucault's thought (e.g., Foucault 1970) was, at least in these terms, essentially empiricist. In this it resembled Boasian anthropology, and in turn English law. In short, the theoretical assumptions behind these various systems, whether in philosophy, anthropology or law, share resemblances, no matter how different the subject matter may be.

I am not strongly aligned to either side, but have much sympathy here with Chomsky and what might here be labelled the Chomskyan, principle-based tradition. Ever since the monogenists of the early nineteenth century, social anthropology has held the view that humankind is everywhere the same. Yet social anthropology, and more particularly its American cousin, cultural anthropology, also holds an opposite sympathy with cultural diversity. Herein lies one of the great problems for the discipline. The 'problem' has emerged and re-emerged many times in the history of social or cultural anthropology, and the tension between the two opposites is striking. Those who look at the human race as a whole have obvious need to seek common elements of human nature and to look for commonalities among all 'cultures', rather than to focus on differences, especially if these be superficial. On the question of how language got here, again it depends what we mean by language. Chomsky (e.g., 2004) is quite right: language is a revolutionary occurrence, very possibly originating in a genetic mutation with enabled the emergence of the language faculty. Yet the revolution did not occur merely by chance, nor simply as a logical consequence of gradual evolution. It required social and cultural input, and that, through natural selection, is ultimately what drove evolution.

Back to reality

With these ethnographic facts and theoretical notions at the back of the mind, let us return to the practical questions. But what did early hunter-gatherers do? What kind of lives did they live? And how did they evolve into the speech communities we find throughout the world today?

A clue is apparent in my own archaeological past: consider the arrival of the first diggers at Diepkloof, a rock shelter on South Africa's west coast. I was present when excavations began in 1972. We knew which cave was 'the site', but equally importantly, another cave had to be designated as the one for human waste. No doubt much the same was true of the ancestral hunter-gatherers of a growing population. There was one cave for making tools in, another for defecating in. Cooking could be done on the dry open plain, but near habitation, as indeed it is among hunter-gatherers living today. Or indeed it could be done under cover, as the weather might require. Eventually, people would die, and their remains would require disposal as well. Bushmen bury people under their huts and move on. Australian Aborigines have quite different customs: they require elaborate ceremonies, and rather than abandoning a site, they return to it a few years later to rebury the bones of the deceased. Importantly, these customs imply not only different beliefs about death, but also different notions of taboo.

Yes, it is easy to think of hunter-gatherers as somehow more primitive than herders or agricultural peoples. In a way, they might be, but individual skills are as obvious, if not more so, as among food-producing peoples. Knowledge of the environment is likely to be far greater, in fact. Hunter-gatherers often know the names and uses of hundreds of different plants and how to hunt a large variety of animals. They are not migratory, as often described: rather, it is food-producers, especially pastoralists, who most strongly possess this attribute (see Brody 2000: 87–90). It is a trite saying, but hunter-gatherers *do* know their environments well. They have to. Otherwise, they could not survive, and we post-hunter-gatherers would not be here. Hunter-gatherers therefore spend *less* time, not more time, in work-related activities than do the rest of us (see e.g., Lee 1979).

As Marshall Sahlins (1974: 1–39) pointed out, in comparison to non-hunter-gatherers, the needs of hunter-gatherers are easily satisfied, and they value free time over the accumulation of property. Their chosen lifestyle is not there purely because of social constraints: it is to some extent *chosen*. The rest of us have chosen the accumulation of wealth instead. Of course, this is not all choice, and of course their harsh environments do not easily allow for the development of any other lifestyle. Yet it is wrong to think of them as having no choice in the matter: the constraints they have are cultural as well as environmental, however. What do hunter-gatherers do with their chosen spare time? They play games, they indulge in art, in music and presumably dance, and therefore in ritual, in argument, in philosophical thought, in myth-making and in symbolic expression generally. Why should we suppose it was any different 70,000 or 80,000 years ago at Blombos Cave?

At Blombos, art was no doubt created with red ochre (see Henshilwood and Debreuil 2009). The ochre found there had been moved distances of several kilometres from its natural sources and been carefully stored in prepared surroundings. The purpose of ochre today is essentially for body decoration. This very fact suggests further ritual elaboration and the creation and use of ritual meaning and social differentiation, presumably with the signification of gender and therefore of the symbolic expression of gender (see Knight, Power and Watts 1995), and possibly other social norms as well. Henshilwood and Debreuil (2009: 44–6) regard the presence of engraved ochre at Blombos and other Middle Stone Age sites as evidence for the existence of language in these places. Although this claim has been attacked for the lack of an adequate bridging theory to connect ochre to language or beads to language (Botha 2009, 2012), to an anthropologist (as opposed to a philosopher) a bridge, if a flimsy one, *does* seem to be there. Why construct an edifice of symbolic relations unless language is already either present or in the process of being created? If language was not present at that place and time (more than 77,000 years ago), then at least it seems to have been imminent. The earliest etched ochre found there is 100,000 years old.

From ritual follows belief. From cognition follows language. In other words, language results from the evolution of cognitive capacity rather than from animal communication and sociality. Or, as Ib Ulbaek puts it:

The correct theory of evolution of language, in my opinion, is this: language evolved from animal cognition not from animal communication. Here lies the continuity. Language grew out of cognitive systems already in existence and working: it formed a communicative bridge between already-cognitive animals. Thus, I not only reject the seemingly natural assumption that language evolved out of other communicative systems, but I adopt the far more radical assumption that cognitive systems were in place before language. (Ulbaek 1998: 33)

Ulbaek cites evidence from primate studies, but in essence his theory remains speculative, even though it is probably true. What differentiates humans from animals is an evolutionary trend towards cooperation, reciprocal altruism and sharing. Thus, humans possess a special kind of sociality, one dependent on these things. The idea is not entirely different from Steven Pinker's (2011) tracing of the reduction in violence in human history, except that the timescale is very different. And just as sociality is contingent on interpretation, so too is the very idea of violence (see Stewart and Strathern 2002: 35–51). Its legitimacy depends on the perspective being chosen for review: state violence, for example, in many minds differs from terrorism.

Sociality itself creates the need for rules, not of grammar but of the regulation of sex and marriage. This means that incest taboos were early: they are virtually the one thing that is universal among living humanity. They are the cultural universal that, along with language, distinguishes humans from non-humans. Lévi-Strauss (1969a [1962]) emphasized the diversity of totemic ideas, even to the extent that they do not all illustrate the same set of things. That is why he rejected a simple explanation for either a universal theory of 'totemism' or for the diversity of incest taboos we find around the world. He saw exchange as the basis of human interaction, and this, along with sharing (within the family) is a prime basis of human interaction. From this follows the necessity of a kinship system, to determine, among other things, who is available for sex and marriage and who is not. In both the Kalahari and the Australian deserts, there are precise rules of *to whom* one may speak, *how* one may speak, *how closely* people may sit, and so on. The regulation of incest implies rules of exchange, and the idea of exchange of people in marriage is the very basis of anthropological explanations of society (Lévi-Strauss 1969b [1949]). Also implied are further rules concerning descent, and therefore relations between the generations. I have very little doubt that early kinship was cognatic, but other possibilities certainly emerged in time (Barnard 2008a).

All this, of course, is the stuff of social and cultural anthropology. It is striking therefore that so few social anthropologists are among the contributors to recent collections such as *The Oxford handbook of language evolution* (Tallerman and Gibson 2012a), which has just 3 social anthropologists among 62 contributors, or *New perspectives on the origins of language* (Lefebvre, Comrie and Cohen 2013), with just one social anthropologist (myself) among the 38 contributors. The three social anthropologists in the former are Robbins Burling (though here writing as a linguist) and the team of Chris Knight and Camilla Power. In other words, the former collection includes just one article within the discipline of social anthropology. In their very brief chapter, Knight and Power (2012) attempt to tackle the problem of social conditions for the emergence of language, notably the threshold of the level of cooperation required for language to begin to evolve. As we shall see later, they do this to a great extent through biological concerns though these are followed by social concerns. They argue that a degree of empathy is required, as well as cooperation, a 'deep social mind' and the development of egalitarianism. The latter, in their view, was sparked by female cooperation, shared sexual signals and symbolism, such as cosmetics to mimic menstruation. There is ethnographic material in the latter volume (Debreuil and Henshilwood 2013), as well as a chapter on kinship, specifically on early kinship terms and the evolution of kinship systems and family structures (Bancel and Matthey de l'Etang 2013). My chapter (Barnard 2013), like that of Knight and Power in the earlier volume, concerns social aspects of language origins, though in a rather different sense. I argue that the basis of language as we know it depends on cognitive abilities and the wish to express these through narrative. Narrative is essentially shared symbolic expression, and this seems to explode into levels of verbal complexity far beyond anything a non-human primate can imagine.

In short, from early linguistic expression emerges language, and from that human culture itself. But is that all social anthropology has to contribute to the question of the evolution of language? Heavily implicated are social anthropological issues. These entail anthropological questions as much as they do linguistic questions. A related explanation here lies in what in biology is termed *fitness*. This is the capacity to survive until breeding age and pass on genes to one's offspring, and with them traits that would be of evolutionary benefit to the next generation. Language entails fitness, and it is adaptive in that it is changeable and creative. It is creative because it enables the creation of new ideas, as well as new material aspects of culture. It is difficult to understand this in any other way: fitness, biological advantage and cultural evolution all conspire to increase humanity's capacity to expand the habitable territories of the world and expand into them. They do this through language, which is the attribute that sets humanity apart from other apes.

Language here really comprises a kind of multilingual *Sprachbund* in which men and women may speak different languages, sometimes for different purposes. Language can be hierarchically ordered, that is, it may have different levels of prestige. Communities, or very small linguistic communities within these communities, may be very small indeed. Everyone can speak to virtually everyone else, and languages mix and remix almost without linguistic boundaries being noticed, through the generations. Groups expand and contract, and they spread stories, myths, ideas, technology and cultural traits far and wide, as they have done for millennia. We observe this among living hunter-gatherers to this day, and it is to hunter-gatherer ethnography that we can look and find answers to the early development of language within our species. It is a pity, then, that so few social anthropologists are involved in exploring such questions.

4   How did prehistoric people think?

Prehistoric people, of course, thought the same as any other people today. Or did they? There are, in fact, a number of relevant theoretical notions in social anthropology, including the original affluent society (Sahlins 1974), immediate-return economics (Woodburn 1980, 1982), the giving environment (Bird-David 1990), the foraging mode of thought (Barnard 2002) and universal kin categorization (Barnard 1978), as well as issues such as totemism (Lévi-Strauss 1969a) and the symbolic relations between animals and people (Willis 1974).

Israeli anthropologist Nurit Bird-David's work is especially interesting here. In a short paper in *Current Anthropology* (Bird-David 1990) she argues that the Nayaka, a hunter-gatherer group of southern India, perceive the environment differently than do people in the West. We take from or exploit our environment, whereas they think of their environment as 'giving' to them. This creates an entirely different way of thinking about economic and ecological relations, and one that may be more similar to understandings in prehistory than among non-hunter-gatherers today. In some of her other work, she takes on similar issues. The notion of 'animism' is misunderstood, because it is approached as a strange religious idea and not as a relational notion of personhood, where people and other beings share attitudes to the environment (Bird-David 1999). In a comparative study of Marshall Sahlins's notion of 'original affluence', she (1992) reformulates his theory of economic relations among hunter-gatherers with reference to three case studies: the Nayaka, the Mbuti of central Africa and the Batek of Malaysia. There are also understandings, like the own-kill rule, whereby one does not eat meat from animals one has killed but gives or exchanges them with others (Knight, Power and Watts 1995). All these anthropological ideas have profound implications for the origins of language.

Obviously, linguistic issues are also relevant. For example, there are differences in complexity among the languages that hunter-gatherers speak. Then there is the question of multilingualism, the theoretical consequences of the Whorfian hypothesis in its strong form and the peculiar case of Pirahã (Everett 2005): a South American language said to lack many common 'universals', including recursion. All these anthropological and linguistic issues have implications for the way hunter-gatherers think, and how they might perceive the world differently from non-hunter-gatherers.

But first, by way of background, let us consider briefly the 'linguistic' behaviour of animals.

Animals as examples of 'pre-human' behaviour

I have some sympathy for the views of the amateur philosopher-linguist Ronald Englefield. He begins his posthumous book *Language: its origin and relation to thought* with a preface to introduce Dinah and Sarah, the two black labrador dogs who were 'the constant companions of the author' and who gave him the opportunity of 'observing their ways, studying their language and divining their thoughts' (Englefield 1977: xvi). My own two black labradors (and their late predecessors) have done much the same for me, in inspiring aspects of my own writing. But let me take an example from Englefield. He notes that Sarah would take up a position from which she could observe Englefield. Sarah had no intrinsic interest in Englefield's actions, but she correctly interpreted the ones that were significant to her, namely those suggesting that a walk might be imminent (like his putting on a raincoat). She also obeyed verbal commands (like being told to lie down). Communication and ultimately cooperation follow, and from this, humans are able to achieve the invention of signs which can be correctly understood even by their animals (Englefield 1977: 15–18).

Other developments include steps beyond imperative communication, namely indicative communication (where the agent wishes to make the patient aware of certain facts), colloquial communication (where the two share a common situation) and forensic communication (where ambiguity is anticipated and overcome through explication) (1977: 33–6). Dinah and Sarah understand many actions not even intended as communication but which be so interpreted. For example, they think it their duty to drive cats out of the garden, and they can tell when biscuits are likely. They understand when, during a walk, their master is about to turn left or right. Although Englefield may represent this as if it is 'language', clearly it is not. Labradors indeed often have large passive or receptive vocabularies of several hundred words, but they do not in any sense have language. Language is not just an advanced form of communication, but something quite different and much more complex.

Different breeds of dog possess both innate and learned ability. These different abilities, in a sense, amount to canine 'customs'. A border collie, bred for herding sheep, is often better at playing ball than a labrador retriever, bred for picking up dead birds in wetlands. The collie's interaction with humans reflects both its breeding and its typical forms of play, and of course different individual dogs behave differently from one another. In one instance, a vocabulary of 1,022 border collie 'words', specifically the names for individual toys, has been recorded (Pilley and Reid 2011: 184). Instinctive behaviour can also be used by dog owners, and indeed turned to their benefit.

In Namibia there is a custom practised by goat herders, whereby dogs are raised among the goats from a very young age. The dog grows up perhaps thinking it *is* a goat, and develops herding skills to such a degree that it can be left on its own with a herd and 'naturally' both herd them and protect them from predators. In a sense, such dogs become 'captains' of the herd, and the goats follow their lead. To my knowledge, this custom has escaped the attention of modern science, although I would be surprised if it remains unrecorded anywhere at all.

These examples show that animals learn by means other than by language. But what about humans? In a way, the same is true, except that the acquisition of knowledge about animal behaviour closely follows the practice of learning by observation. In other words, both humans and animals observe behaviour, but only humans have the ability to describe what they have learned. This may seem pretty obvious, but consider the fact that the telling of hunting stories contains elements such as imitation of animal movements and sounds, the building of story-lines based on dramatic intent and the inclusion of these elements within mythology (see MacDonald and Roebroeks 2013: 112–14). The observation of animals is, as it were, part of the story. Mythologies across the globe are replete with stories of animals, either in their own right, just as animals, as characters symbolized through animals, or as more generic figures such as tricksters. The evolution of human understanding is an evolution of the understanding of animals. As mythology shows us, the two are indistinguishable.

Animal grammar, then?

The most common animals for comment are certainly higher primates. The most famous of non-human primates is probably Kanzi, a male bonobo taught by Sue Savage-Rumbaugh to use a customized keyboard containing lexigrams, symbols that stand for words. His most commonly used forms of grammatical relations involve combinations like *agent-action* (such as 'carry-person') or *entity-demonstrative* (such as peanut-that) (Savage-Rumbaugh and Rumbaugh 1993: 99–101; see also Beaken 2011: 76–7). For Kanzi, the lexigram often comes first, followed by either another lexigram or a sign indicating some kind of action.

However, in linguistics, theorists frequently emphasize the dawn of full sentences rather than grammatical relations such as these, and there exist any number of theories about the need for language in the first place (see also Carstairs-McCarthy 1999; Hurford 2007, 2012). For example, early humans needed to communicate in order to hunt more effectively (hunting theory). This enabled them to exchange information, not only about hunting but about related activities too: trapping prey, making tools for killing prey and so on. Another possibility might be that early humans required communication about vegetable foods (foraging theory). Views like my own have been labelled narrative theory: language began in order to express views on origins or on supernatural phenomena. Or, according to the Machiavellian intelligence view, primates in general can recognize social relationships and things like familial relations, alliances and dominance hierarchies. Language grew from this. In the gossip view, language evolved among humans in order for it to replace grooming, which is much more common in other primate species. Gossip is efficient because it takes less time, and information about friends and foes can be exchanged with more than one person at a time. In memetic theory, cultural elements (memes) replace genes as adaptive mechanisms for coping efficiently with environmental change. As Heine and Kuteva (2007: 6–9) explain, all of these positions are essentially Darwinian, as indeed are alternatives, such as exaption theory (things evolving through natural selection for one function are appropriated for another) or spandrel theory (a related idea, in which structures acquire function as an accidental by-product of Darwinian evolution).

Consider also the work of the Chilean cyberneticist Humberto Maturana (e.g., Maturana and Varela 1992: 205–38). Maturana views language less as a thing, and more as a process. The linguistic domain lies in the area where communicative behaviours and ontogenic behaviours coincide (Figure 4.1). While other animals (such as birds, or the dogs described earlier) may exhibit linguistic behaviour, according to Maturana and Varela (1992: 210), only humans possess language. Language exists because of a coordination of action within a social system: 'We operate in language when an observer sees that the objects of our linguistic distinctions are elements of our linguistic domain. Language is an ongoing process that only exists as languaging, not as isolated items of behavior.' In other words, we describe language as a 'thing', and employ the word language as a count noun, whereas in reality it is neither. This can be seen in Figure 4.1.

As a process, language is visible, or literally audible, and all around. It is not quite this way among non-human primates, though. As Lawrence Barham and Peter Mitchell (Barham and Mitchell 2008: 178) have explained, 'Human societies differ from those of apes in repeatedly using favoured places as camps for sleeping and socialising, including the sharing of resources (reciprocity). Even if individuals do not forage as a group, they come together as a group, often at a central place, to consume at least some of their collected food.' Barham and Mitchell go on to point out that, with the addition of controlled fire, *Homo erectus* could extend the use of such places, nesting or sleeping in trees, and increased the gender-based division of labour. This might easily have increased exchange practices and even have favoured the dream-related stages of sleep. The latter are 'linked to enhanced memory, creativity, and visual-spatial

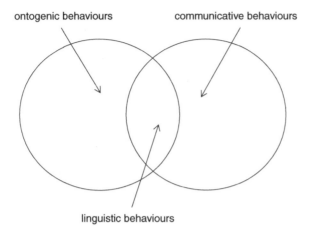

ontogenic behaviours　　　　communicative behaviours

linguistic behaviours

Figure 4.1 Linguistic behaviours

Source: adapted from Maturana and Varela 1992: 209

awareness', leading to the utilization of a wider geographical range and innovative changes to the physical, as well as the social, environment (2008: 178–9). They infer a limited vocal capability for early *H. erectus*, so clearly we are on the right track for language. And as we have seen in Chapter 2, *H. ergaster* or *H. erectus* apparently had at least some linguistic capability by the time members of the species left Africa to cross into Asia.

Denisovans, Neanderthals and *Homo Sapiens*

Among the most intriguing finds of recent times is the finger bone (along with some teeth) of a small, brown-skinned, brown-haired girl. These were found in Denisova Cave, in the Altai Mountains of central Siberia. They date from around 80,000 BP (Meyer *et al.* 2012). Despite the meagre amount of physical material, the genetic detail proved enormous, and from it a huge amount can be deduced. Through analysing the 'missing evolution' of the genome, the geneticists who studied these finds managed to determine that the population was relatively uniform. It was also widely dispersed across Asia. The Denisovans interbred both with Neanderthals and with *Homo sapiens*, and their genetic heritage is dispersed particularly in Melanesia. About 4.8 per cent of the present-day Melanesian population is traceably of Denisovan descent, and there is a fair amount in Australian Aboriginal populations as well. The important thing about Denisovans in relation to language is that at least eight genes relevant to nerve growth and the development of language have undergone changes since the time of the Denisovans. What this means, very simply, is that Denisovans apparently lacked the ability to create language as we know it, although they may have been able to produce some kind of communicative speech or gesture. They were effectively, in some sense, pre-linguistic though otherwise human-like beings.

Neanderthals were, however, rather different. They bred both with *Homo sapiens* and with Denisovans, but a crucial question for the anthropological sciences in general is to account for the transition from the increased brain size of Neanderthals to a brain which is actually smaller. Neanderthals had larger brains (1,200 to 1,740 cc) than *Homo sapiens* (average, 1,450 cc), but this does not mean that they were necessarily any brighter. The answer is not difficult, though. What is needed in order to enable the smaller brain size of *H. sapiens* is an 'external memory store', in other words, complex language. Mike Beaken (2011: 131) puts it this way: 'The point where human brains stop increasing, must be the point at which language is firmly established as a social practice.' What is interesting here is not whether Neanderthals possessed language or not, but rather Beaken's assertion that language as a social practice had, among Neanderthals, already taken place. This is possible, but we do not know whether language was being utilized to its full capacity. Beaken presents his theoretical perspective as *materialist*, but it could equally be characterized as social, in the sense that advances are seen as developments in society as much as specifically in the significance of property.

We do not have any idea whether Denisovans had language either, since we have no skulls and no fossils at all apart from a few bones. We presume, however, that from what archaeological evidence there is, that Denisova Cave was the home of ancestors of *Homo sapiens*, *H. neanderthalensis* and Denisovans, not only at different times but at least occasionally at the same time. From mtDNA evidence, we know that there was interbreeding among these species. The date of the relevant fossils found at Denisova Cave is about 41,000 BP, but the material culture around seems to have been slight. What is most surprising is the fact that all three populations seem to have shared the cave and exchanged genetic material. This is astounding if it indicates the possibility that they could *communicate* with one another in spite of significant genetic differences among them. There is a growing popular literature on the Denisovans, but the most important work is by Johannes Krause *et al.* (2010). No doubt there will be more to come by way of analysis, with or without findings from further excavations.

What is clear is that humans are in nature hunter-gatherers. It is not the general importance of a materialist (much less a Marxist) perspective that is significant, but a recognition that our hunter-gatherer past is still with us. However old or young language is, there is no doubt that it emerged and evolved among hunter-gatherers, and most probably among Neanderthal as well as among *Homo sapiens* ones at that. Denisovans, in contrast, may have been locked in a linguistic *H. heidelbergensis* existence (whatever that might be), but we simply do not know. Beaken emphasizes the social, and with it the community that shares a language and its 'collective consciousness', which may be one take on the question, but we are still very short of an answer on language. What kind of language, and could there have been communication among the three species? There is no relevant *H. heidelbergensis* material present with which to seek answers on their cognitive skills. However, as Beaken reminds us:

Consciousness is the creation of a community. It is the sum of its actions, each action giving rise to an associated meaning that exists in the collective consciousness of all its speakers. This means that each speaker has access, through the system of signs and their meanings, to all the experience, knowledge and wisdom of the other speakers of the language. (Beaken 2011: 32)

It follows that when the collective consciousness is lost, so too is collective knowledge. A common view at present is that Neanderthals became extinct as a result of pressure from a 'brighter' species, *Homo sapiens*. An equally plausible view might be that the smaller population sizes of the isolated Neanderthal communities, as well as changes in climate, threatened the viability of culturally accumulated Neanderthal *wisdom*. For that matter, the genetic evidence points to population diversity and possibly a rather larger population of Denisovans than there were of Neanderthals! The Denisovans were probably a *Homo heidelbergensis* offshoot, but they paralleled Neanderthals in their evolution: it is an accident that they were left behind in the fossil record (see Stringer 2011: 196).

The capacity for the linguistic brain to store information is significant for evolution because it enables a group to share knowledge, history, folklore, song, ritual and a host of other things. Both speech and gesture are more effective than individual thought for any number of other things. Teaching and learning take on new meanings when gesture is replaced by speech. Gesture can simply be supplemented: when the audience is looking the other way, when one's hands are in use for other things than signing, or in the dark, when one runs out of signs, if signs are ambiguous or simply because speaking requires less energy than signing. Beaken (2011: 131) suggests that this happened perhaps between *Homo erectus* and *H. sapiens* evolution, earlier than in Neanderthal times. Lieberman (e.g., 2006) points to an array of anatomical and neurological features that may be involved, although the exact timing within the evolutionary sequence is not as clear as one might have hoped. To return briefly to Englefield's (1977) labrador dogs, and more particularly my own, it seems to be a characteristic of the breed (or maybe of all dogs) that they understand both hand signals and speech. Hand signals are hardly language, but they are at least very similar in that they are both manual, gestural mechanisms that can be used for communication within a community: be that within a species, or across a species boundary. If we were to put a date on the transition from signing to speaking, I would look to an early one. Gordon Hewes (1973), the father of gestural theories of language origins, talks of gestural origins in a context of primate communication. Others look to the descent of the larynx prior to the separation of Neanderthals and modern humans (e.g., Lieberman 1984). In other words, in spite of similarities between sign language and spoken language, the ability to speak and produce at least more or less the sounds of modern humanity is a precursor to language, at least as we understand the idea in its early stages. For this reason, some writers do distinguish 'sign' from 'gesture': 'Sign *is* language, in the fullest sense of the term, and gesture is not' (Fitch 2010: 437). Human language, whether spoken or signed, is quite different from simple gesture.

As to the equation of Neanderthals with sophisticated thought, the case gets stronger all the time. According to Neanderthal expert João Zilhão (2014: 202), 'the evidence for body painting and the use of personal ornaments sufficiently demonstrates that Neanderthals possessed cognitive capabilities identical to those of Modern Humans and evolved symbolically organized cultures in Europe at about the same time as evidence to that effect first appeared in Africa'. Among evidence he cites is ritual burial (in Israel) dated to between 130,000 and 100,000 BP, a cemetery in France dated between 75,000 and 60,000 BP, abstract notches not unlike those at Blombos, though not as old, and so on. The sites he mentions are all clearly Neanderthal, though from different stages in the evolution of the species and of the changes in climate throughout Europe in Neanderthal times. Stephen Shennan (2001) and more recently Adam Powell, Stephen Shennan and Mark Thomas (2009) have demonstrated that innovative behaviour increases as population rises, and that this is true in both Africa and Europe. Neanderthals evolved culturally in the Mousterian, as groups moved to the northern European plains between 60,000 and 40,000 years ago. They became a distinct population, separate from *Homo heidelbergensis*, before this, some 135,000 years ago. Could these peoples have evolved language at this time? Would such advances not entail more sophistication concerning things like knowledge of plants as well as stone tools? Is this where modern human behaviour begins?

Richard Lee (1979: 479) once noted that the Ju/'hoansi of Botswana and Namibia recognize 105 edible species of plant, although 75 per cent of their vegetable diet is made up of just 14 per cent of these species. Of course, they have distinct names for most of the species they eat, and they know when and exactly where most of them are found. They are familiar with similar numbers of animals, and they know their habits as well as they know their habitats. The Ju/'hoansi are not primitive either linguistically or even otherwise: ecologically, they are highly sophisticated, knowledgeable vegetable utilizers, even though they eat a much higher percentage of meat than do most humans on the planet today. And as meat eaters, they are sophisticated too in relevant symbolic domains. Like most hunter-gatherers, their systematic knowledge contains beliefs about animals that we in the West might think of as superstitious or as indicative of a false consciousness. Yet nevertheless such beliefs form part of that sophistication itself. The fact that 'we' do not attribute beliefs about the rain, about the power of the eland or about the ability of the lion or the snake to 'travel' the sky is not really the point. In the minds of these hunter-gatherers, they do or at least they seem to. It is in the nature of humanity that we all can think symbolically (see James 2003; Barnard 2012).

To think symbolically, the significance of the eland is particularly interesting here. Camilla Power sees the Eland Bull Dance of female initiates among the Bushmen as central to early culture. In the dance, a man mimicking an eland bull (often the grandfather of the initiate) 'chases' the girl around a dance fire. This happens at the time of the girl's first menstrual period, and as Power (2015: 53) puts it, 'this dance is the most likely candidate for humanity's longest continuous religious tradition – at a guess, 70,000 to 100,000 years old'. Chris Knight (personal communication) adds:

I prefer the more generative thesis that gestural, ritual and other non-verbal metaphor is logically prior, actually giving rise to symbols and grammar ... To be a metaphor, an expression has to count as a false statement, at least on the face of things. The listener then has to discern some honest communicative intention in that surface falsehood. That's why so much trust is involved, much more than anything conceivable between animals as competitive as wild-living apes. The Eland Bull Dance is a wonderful example, in the sense that a young woman's actual identity (biological identity) is systematically reversed. Ritually, everyone insists that she is what she is not, and because they do it collectively and in a sense coercively, the fiction becomes true, becomes an institutional fact.

The ancestors of today's hunter-gatherers have lived in southern Africa for longer than any other population group has lived on earth. Other populations, including both Neanderthals and Denisovans, are mixed, both biologically and culturally; Africans are not mixed (at least not to the same extent) but are in a sense 'pure' *Homo sapiens*. Famously, Richard Lee and Irven DeVore (1968a: ii), in the frontispiece to *Man the hunter* and in their introduction (1968b: 3–4), noted that in 10,000 BCE the world's population was 10,000,000, and all of them were hunter-gatherers. By the year 1500 CE the world's population was 350,000,000, of whom some 3,500,000, or about 1 per cent, were hunter-gatherers. By 1900 CE, with a world population of 3,000,000,000, only 0.001 per cent or around 30,000 were hunter-gatherers. That tiny handful of human beings lived only in isolated areas of Africa, Australia, Asia and the Arctic, whereas once they had inhabited virtually every part of every continent. Lee and DeVore add that for more than 99 per cent of its existence, our species has lived solely by hunting and gathering alone. Only the last 10,000 years or so of human existence has

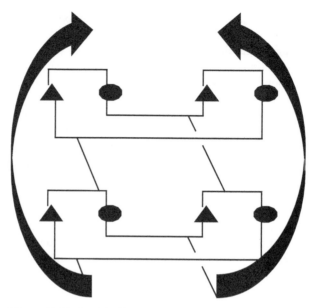

Figure 4.2 Kariera kinship structure

been spent in domesticating plants and animals, using metal or harnessing any form of energy beyond the human body. In 1968, only 6 per cent of humanity had ever lived through cultivation or pastoralism and a smaller number in industrial societies. In short, 'the hunting way of life has been the most successful and persistent adaptation man has ever achieved' (1968b: 3).

A final question: did Neanderthals marry? Clive Gamble (2008: 39–40) considers this question in light of a number of related issues, namely Nicholas Allen's theory of tetradic society, relations of sharing and a notion of incest avoidance. Tetradic structure is the presumed early kinship pattern in which society is divided into four units, equivalent to father, mother, mother's child and father's child. It is like the classic Kariera model in Australian kinship: father marries mother, mother's child marries father's child. Four 'sections' are needed because there is an alternation of generations. I (a male ego) am in the same category as my father's father, and my wife is in the same category as her mother's mother. This is illustrated in Figure 4.2. In each generation the male marries the female, and the children are those of the generation below. Only one brother and one sister are illustrated, because all same-sex siblings are equivalent. That is, the top left triangle is both 'me' and 'my brother'. Since the generations cycle indefinitely, it is also 'my son's son', and so on.

If Neanderthals had marriage they could indeed have invented such a structure, but I think that such a structure is unlikely for them. The prospect is intriguing, but it is unlikely simply because it is commonly assumed to have been a late development within Australia. What it does do, though, is regulate incest with the fewest possible number of generations (two generations), with alternation between them. It is possible, however, not to alternate generations, if kin categories become recognized. In other words, if we grant them language they do not need to alternate generations. They can name them instead. Or indeed they could simply invent moieties, which are also found in Australia and are common elsewhere, particularly in South America. As to whether or not they had language, Gamble's (2008: 35) conclusion is that they did, or more specifically they possessed a means of communication based on socially focused gossip, rather than primate grooming or vocal chorusing (in the case of *Australopithecus*) or metaphor and technical communication (in the case of modern humans). In his view, they had pair-bonding and they had in-laws too, but they did not quite have marriage.

How do anthropologists think?

For the benefit of both anthropology itself and readers from other disciplines, a reflection on some of the constraints imposed by anthropology will help to understand both its limitations and its potential.

Anthropology is by no means a unified discipline. In a sense, it is not a discipline at all but a collectivity of theoretical perspectives, each of which directs thinking within different paradigms: linguistic anthropology or anthropological linguistics, biological anthropology or physical anthropology, social anthropology or cultural anthropology and prehistoric archaeology. Linguistic anthropology does generally adhere to a notion of belonging to a wider discipline of anthropology, and its definition is complicated by its ambiguous history (Enfield, Kockelman and Sidnell 2014a). The term linguistic anthropology seems to be older than anthropological linguistics and has been in use since the late nineteenth century (Duranti 2003: 327). It has been championed especially by Dell Hymes (e.g., 1964), who indeed had a strong preference for that term over anthropological linguistics. Within linguistics more generally, theory since the 1950s has tended to follow the various permutations of transformational and generative grammar, including most recently (since the 1990s) the so-called minimalist program (see Chomsky 1993). Before that, linguistics was based on descriptive and structuralist approaches related to social (or cultural) anthropological work in the field. This book is not the place to outline the enormous complexity of linguistic theory in general. Rather, it is useful to consider instead simply the main trends in evolutionary linguistics, especially since Chomsky himself has until very recently (see e.g., Hauser *et al.* 2002; Chomsky 2012: 103–7) been so reluctant, or at the very least sceptical, to consider the origin of language as an area of interest within linguistics.

Biological anthropology need not concern us that much here, at least inso-far as it might have an impact on anthropological theory. Biological anthro-pology is of course theory-driven, but perhaps not quite in the same sense as these other branches of the (broadly) anthropological sciences. However, one area of interest, if not particularly convincing to me or to anthropologists in general, is some of the work of Tecumseh Fitch (2004). He sees a biological origin of language through his theory of 'mother tongues'. The idea is that, as in W. D. Hamilton's (1964) Darwinian model and Robert Trivers' (1971) theory of reciprocal altruism, individual mothers favour their biological chil-dren. That favouritism is then extended to other members of the kin group, and that depends on people believing what they are told. In short, altruism seems to evolve first, and it depends on trust. Biology and evolution come in, since the human brain evolves slowly and time is available for evolution to occur. Ultimately, symbolic thought emerges and enables communication for plan-ning ahead (Gärdenfors 2004: 237). This is necessary, of course, for the evolu-tion of sociality and society.

Importantly, genetics has in recent decades joined the much older con-cerns of palaeo-anatomy and prehistoric archaeology in some departments, especially in the United States, but ideas from these disciplines have yet to penetrate social anthropology in Europe. Neuroscience also has had minimal impact within anthropology generally, although there is hope here for its influ-ence through future realignments. In social anthropology, theory is really quite simple and tends to follow a sequence of historically grounded traditions. There exist about seven basic perspectives, each of which differs, often very markedly, from the others. These 'isms' are pretty stable, unlike the perspec-tives within linguistics. They are listed below in the order of their historical development (see also Barnard 2000).

1. evolutionism
2. diffusionism
3. relativism
4. functionalism (including structural-functionalism)
5. structuralism
6. interpretivism
7. post-structuralism and postmodernism.

Evolutionism became the dominant perspective in the 1860s or so, with the related dominance of Darwinian theory in the natural sciences. I like to tell my students that we can date the science of anthropology to around 1871, which marks a number of significant events: these start with the founding of the Anthropological Institute, with Sir John Lubbock as its first president. Also in that year we see the publication of *Systems of consanguinity and affinity of the human family* (Morgan 1871) and the two volumes of *Primitive culture*

(Tylor 1871). Lubbock's (1874 [1870]) own *Origin of civilisation* came out only the year before, and several other important anthropology books were published around that time or in the 1860s. *Origin of species* (on general ideas in Darwinian thought) was published in 1859, with *Descent of man* (bringing humans into consideration) in 1871 (Darwin 1859, 1871). Darwin was a Fellow of Lubbock's Anthropological Institute. Evolutionism in anthropology emphasized humanity's progress from simple to more complex forms, and it held that similar processes occurred around the world. Different schools of thought gradually emerged within evolutionism.

The important thing to note is that evolutionism stressed the sameness of humanity, while its opposite, diffusionism, assumed a lack of invention. Ideas were invented once and spread to other places either by diffusion or by migration. Whereas evolutionism was at first largely anglophone, diffusionism became the dominant perspective in the German-speaking world (e.g., Schmidt 1939 [1937]). There were exceptions in the former case (e.g., Perry 1923), but they did not last the battle with the Malinowskian functionalism and Radcliffe-Brownian structural-functionalism that began in the 1920s. The national associations are important given the later events of the twentieth century, but German anthropology was greatly affected. Although Father Wilhelm Schmidt and his colleagues (many of whom were priests) escaped Austria and moved to Switzerland for the duration of the Second World War, their brand of diffusionism was not passed on to students.

The next generation was decidedly dominated by the British functionalist tradition (of either Malinowski's or Radcliffe-Brown's sort), which from around 1922 emphasized long-term fieldwork and the use of the native language for it, rather than interpreters. This was useful for that tradition, although it did mean a growing isolation from evolutionist concerns. The reluctance to consider any form of evolution still dominates in the majority of British departments, where neither students nor their teachers have much understanding of the importance of interdisciplinary explorations, for example, in language origins. It is useful here to divide British departments into two factions: those with a unified anthropological vision (for example, University College London) and those with a narrower social anthropological focus (for example, the University of Edinburgh). The best general source on British anthropology is Kuper's *Anthropologists and anthropology* (1973 and subsequent editions).

Relativism became the dominant perspective of American anthropology from its very beginnings in the 1890s, with Franz Boas (e.g., 1940), and indeed it continues to dominate much thinking there even today. It holds that cultures differ, but that none is 'better' than any other. Essentially, it involves a rejection of the importance of either evolution or diffusion. In North America, Boasian relativism and later offshoots like interpretivism and postmodernism have held sway ever since functionalism (e.g., Radcliffe-Brown 1952) became the dominant perspective in the United Kingdom until the rise of structuralism there. It is based on the importance of ethnographic field research and held that it is useless to speculate about the origin of things when what is important is to understand society as it exists today. What both Boasian relativism and particularly Malinowskian functionalism share is the necessity for fieldworkers to learn the local language and to use it in their fieldwork. Both traditions retain this today, after more than a hundred years of study (in the case of the Boasians) and nearly a hundred (in the case of the Malinowskians). In a sense, then, both are more language-focused even than linguistics. This is indeed one reason the Whorfian hypothesis came to be so strong within relativist circles: practitioners had all learned and worked in some of the world's most exotic languages, and they brought their linguistic insights to bear on the deep cultural problems they studied.

Structuralism (e.g., Lévi-Strauss 1963) was initially French but came to dominate British thinking too around the 1960s, with the search, in anthropology as in linguistics and many other fields, for *relations between things* as the key to understanding *things themselves*. Ultimately, three sorts of structural anthropology came into being. In France, practitioners generally followed Lévi-Strauss most closely, and therefore agreed with his programme based on the idea that humans everywhere are the same. In a sense, this kind of thinking is not unlike Chomsky's: all languages are basically the same, so let us simply explore English as our example. In Lévi-Strauss's case, though, considerable effort was given over to comparative interests.

In the United Kingdom, practitioners tended to concentrate on explaining one thing at a time: a structural analysis of a British wedding, a structural analysis of the Sistine Chapel ceiling, and so on. In the Netherlands and Belgium, there was an in-between approach that concentrated on ethnographic regions: central Africa, the Kalahari Basin, and so on. The idea was to identify a common regional cultural structure and to compare in detail within the region. The emphasis on 'national traditions' here, though, may be misleading: my own early work (e.g., Barnard 1992) and Kuper's (e.g., 1982) is in regional structural comparison, even though neither of us is in fact either Dutch or Belgian.

Interpretivism came about the same time and was one of several approaches that evolved by rejecting ideas of function and structure in favour of 'interpreting' culture. Both structuralism and interpretivism see the world through linguistic analogy (see Lévi-Strauss 1963: 29–97), but the nature of the analogies differs significantly. Whereas structuralists hold that cultures possess 'grammars' of thought that anthropologists need to work out, interpretivists hold that cultures require 'translation' so that people from other cultures can understand them. In both the American (Geertz 1973, 1983) and the British (Evans-Pritchard 1956) traditions, interpretivism became popular. Geertz's interpretivism, though, is quite different from Evans-Pritchard's in that Geertz's sees a greater degree of abstraction in what he is interpreting. He comments on the diversity of sets of symbols and remarks, in his treatment of religion, that symbols form complexes (Geertz 1973: 91–4). Similar views have been expressed by Terrence Deacon (2003: 118). Finally, postmodernism is in essence a radical form of relativism. It argues that there can be no grand theory of anything and it was largely developed beyond the boundaries of social anthropology (but see Clifford and Marcus 1986).

In archaeology, there are, of course, many national traditions, and the field has often been weakened by the tendency for scholars to follow colonialist and nationalist political agendas. However, there are at least three clear theoretical trends in the discipline (see e.g., Johnson 2011).

1. historical particularism
2. processual archaeology
3. post-processual archaeology.

The first is historical particularism, which takes ideas from evolutionist and diffusionist thinking in social anthropology, but generally without much concern for theory in any real sense. Boas's life-long project remains a good example. Cultural traditions progress and borrow from other such traditions, and to some extent it is possible to construct the history of an ethnic group. Then from the 1960s onwards, adherents of the 'New Archaeology', otherwise known as processual archaeology, developed an approach based on hypothesis-testing. Lewis Binford's article 'Archaeology as anthropology' (Binford 1962) and a great deal of his subsequent work (for example, 1978) established this as a major perspective. This, mainly American, school considered themselves similar to researchers in the natural sciences and ultimately to the social anthropology of the time. They sometimes rejected the notion that cultural traditions of the past can easily be equated with later modern ethnic groups, though Binford (e.g., 1983) always maintained that his interest in modern hunter-gatherers was in order to understand the past. Many archaeologists today do so for much the same reasons: hunter-gatherer complexity cannot be understood simply by speculation (see Cummings 2013: 1–12). This school was followed by the post-processualists, from the 1980s onwards (see Hodder 1985). The post-processualist school, mainly British in the beginning, was essentially relativist. They rejected the search for objective truth and held that archaeology involves instead subjective interpretation. (See also Trigger 2006 [1989]: 386–483.)

In summary, anthropologists bring a diversity of ways of thinking to the problems of 'culture' and 'society', and each generation rejects what has gone before and starts again. Actually, this is not all that different from approaches hunter-gatherers take in finding solutions to environmental and technological difficulties and opportunities. Or is it? Two things are very different. The time frame for the evolution of hunter-gatherer society is, of course, much longer. And the evolution of hunter-gatherer society required the development of technological responses to food shortages. Yet, actually, hunter-gatherers experience these much less than pastoralists or agriculturalists. Richard Lee (1979: 250–80) tells us that Ju/'hoansi spend only two or three hours a day in obtaining food. Wiessner (2014) reminds us that the evolution of communication among such peoples occurred mainly at night, through stories (and probably when gesture had to give way to speech). And Lévi-Strauss (1968: 351) suggests that there is no reason to believe that ancient hunter-gatherers were any less philosophical than people of later times.

Biological needs and cultural responses

The great ethnographic fieldworker and founder of the 'modern' functionalist tradition in the United Kingdom was Bronislaw Malinowski. Towards the end of his life, Malinowski (1944: 91–119; see also 1953: 75–90) proposed a theory of seven biological needs and their respective seven cultural responses. Neither his students nor anyone else paid that much attention to this unusually theoretical endeavour. Nevertheless, the idea is worth a little reflection. This is not because of its correctness, but because the idea of such a scheme does, at least, link purported cultural phenomena to their supposed biological basis. Malinowski's proposed scheme is illustrated in Table 4.1, with the categories slightly modified to add details of his explanations (see also Barnard 2000: 68–70).

Most of Malinowski's suggestions here are fairly obvious. My own list of biological needs would be rather shorter: *food and drink*, *sex* and *talk*. For *Homo sapiens* Middle Stone Age hunter-gatherers, food and drink would include mainly meat, fat, salt and honey as the most desired, along with water. Sex is obvious. Talk is obvious too. Yet what is important about talk is its enabling, not only of conversation and lecturing to a crowd, but also of the facility to teach, to ask questions and indeed to create an oral literature of some sort. Much of this is indeed implied in Malinowski's lists: cooperative behaviour suggests communication. Among cultural responses, several involve communication too. These include rules of commissariat, the organization of kinship and the family, defence of the community (protection, in his original list), economic activities and knowledge transfer (training, in the original – including the teaching of artefact manufacture and of social conventions and morally correct behaviour). Most of these, of course, do involve talk as well as communication.

Talk is fundamentally what distinguishes *Homo sapiens sapiens* hunter-gatherers from their *H. erectus* ancestors. Even if we grant *H. erectus* or *H. antecessor* (forerunner of *H. heidelbergensis* or *H. helmei*) proto-language,

Table 4.1 *Malinowski's seven basic needs and their cultural responses*

Basic needs	Cultural responses
1. metabolic processes	1. rules of commissariat
2. reproduction of the community	2. kinship and the family
3. bodily comforts	3. shelter
4. safety	4. defence of the community
5. cooperative behaviour	5. economic activities
6. growth and maturation	6. knowledge transfer
7. health	7. hygiene

Source: adapted from Malinowski 1944: 91–119

they presumably would have no ability to communicate to the degree that we do. Lorna Marshall (1961), another ethnographer of the Ju/'hoansi (whom she called the !Kung), caught the essence not only of Ju/'hoan life but of the hunter-gatherer lifestyle in general when she entitled her seminal article: 'Sharing, talking, and giving'. Sharing, talking and giving are the elements which make up hunter-gatherer sociality in advanced human cultural entities. Together, they also enable social evolution to the degree necessary for the exploitation and control of the harshest environments of Africa and beyond. It is clear from much of Malinowski's own work that it is the social aspects of both language and communication that were important to him, and in particular what he termed phatic communion (Malinowski 1953). This is the small talk, such as greetings, talking about the weather and other forms of ritual communication, whose significance is more in communication itself than in what is said. Phatic communion is also one of the six functions of verbal communication as defined by the great structural linguist Roman Jakobson (1999); see also Hébert 2011). The other functions of verbal communication are: referential, emotive, conative, meta-lingual and poetic.

Each of Jakobson's six elements expresses a relation between the message and another person or object. The referential gives the context (as in 'The ball is round'). The emotive shows the emotional state of the speaker ('Wow, what a prize!'). The conative is similar, but in reference to the hearer ('Come and sit down'). The meta-lingual provides definition ('What is that?'). Finally, the poetic simply focuses on the message for its own sake. Perhaps relevant here too is C. G. Jung's (for example, 1964: 45–56) distinction of four psychological functions: sensation, thinking, feeling and intuition, each with the potential to be associated with either an extraverted or an introverted attitude to reality. The self-proclaimed functionalist Malinowski, even more than either Jung or Jakobson, talked incessantly about functions. Yet the concept of 'function' in the writings of each theorist is quite different. This is not merely because they come from different disciplines, but because the nuances conveyed by their usages of the term reflect something deeper in their intended meanings. In other words, language itself stops short of expressing the deeper meanings it can convey. Exactly when it came to have this ability is not really possible to say, but my own experience of speaking with hunter-gatherers suggests to me that all modern humans, and not just food-producers, are quite capable of using language in ways that are well beyond responding to the needs of biology. Cognitively, hunter-gatherers are as fully modern as anyone else.

After Malinowski, and indeed even before him, anthropologists in general began to look for supposed cultural universals in order to explain the unique features of humans over other animals. I do not hold much store in their findings any more than is the case with Malinowski. This is not because they were wrong but because there was rarely anything new to learn from such a broad question. Looking to hunter-gatherers specifically often provides a clearer answer (see Barnard 2012: 134–6). Those seeking human universals, for example Clyde Kluckhohn (1953, 1959), George Peter Murdock (1945) or Donald Brown (1991), have tended to emphasize aspects which, frankly, are trite if not superficial. An exception to this, however, is Brown's (1991: 130–4) commentary on language.

A very significant portion of UP [Universal People] culture is embodied in their language, a system of communication without which their culture would necessarily be very much simpler. With language the UP think about and discuss both their internal states and the world external to each individual … With language, the UP organize and respond to, and manipulate the behavior of their fellows. (1991: 130)

Furthermore, language allows people to think in abstractions, to represent things and processes which are not immediately present, to gain prestige, to express humour, to mislead and to use symbolism. Grammar, like other aspects of language, is nearly always more expressive than it needs to be, and through grammar and through kinship terms and the categories they represent, we can provide not only meaning but social context well beyond biological requirements. In this, humans differ from all other animals, even those who make tools, signal to each other or recognize family structures and rules of correct and incorrect behaviour.

Beyond grammar, therefore, there is *culture*. I have long since given up using this word in the plural, since the notion of counting 'cultures' and identifying exactly who belongs to them is so complicated (see also Kuper 1999). Nevertheless, it is useful to think here in terms of levels of complexity: phonological complexity, syntactic complexity, semantic complexity and, beyond that, cultural complexity. Every social anthropologist will be familiar with Marshall Sahlins's (1976) *The use and abuse of biology*. Essentially, this little book was an attack on sociobiology, written in its heyday (the 1970s). Sahlins (1976: 3–16) makes the point that sociobiology can only ever represent a tiny fraction of what it means to be human, and that beyond that lies the whole of human culture (or cultures): indeed, the whole of anthropology. It was attacked by its reviewers (e.g., Alexander 1977) for misrepresenting sociobiology, but even if we accept the criticisms, its central argument remains: anthropology covers an enormous corpus, and its subject matter represents a diversity not found in many theoretical realms.

Ecological and cultural models

The challenge of culture

Many, both in archaeology and, to a lesser extent, in social anthropology, adhere to formal, ecological models to describe such things as optimal foraging strategies and other forms of behaviour related directly to hunting-and-gathering activities. Ultimately, these are Darwinian in their foundation. Examples include the work of Robert Kelly (2013 [1995]), Robert Bettinger (1991, 2009) and Bruce Winterhalder and Eric Alden Smith (1981). As noted earlier, Kelly, in particular, has emphasized diversity in hunter-gatherer economies. For example, he devotes one chapter (2013: 241–68) specifically to non-egalitarian hunter-gatherers such as the various peoples of the Northwest Coast of North America. And even within this category there is diversity: Tolowa and Yurok of the southern coast of this area lacked elaborate notions of prestige. Farther north, among Wakashan and Salishan linguistic groups, status was much more important generally, but nevertheless differed among the groups. Farther north still, Tlingit, Tsimshian and Haida possessed yet more complex forms of social organization and chiefly hierarchy, which again differed from group to group. Such diversity has enabled Kelly to resist attempts to pigeonhole hunter-gatherers as having a single type of economy or foraging strategy. Yet still, the assumption remains that hunter-gatherers broadly are economically efficient and seek the most advantageous behaviour for their ecological circumstances. In other words, while there may be no single 'original' form of foraging practice, there was nevertheless one that worked in each circumstance, and hunter-gatherers sought it through cultural evolution and adhered to it according to local circumstances.

Recent work has continued this theme. For example, there are the authors of *Information and its role in hunter-gatherer bands* (Whallon *et al.* 2011). As its title indicates, the focus of this work is on band-level organization and the accumulation and transfer of information. Case studies include, among others, the Western Desert of Australia, the Kalahari, central Africa, Tierra del Fuego and Patagonia, the Arctic and Mesolithic Europe. Diversity is virtually guaranteed, given the geographical and climatic differences in the cases. However, the present book takes quite a different approach. While hunter-gatherers plainly differ a great deal in many, many respects, there is nevertheless common ground among them. A few years ago, I outlined ten broad attributes which I claimed are typical of hunter-gatherer societies (Barnard 1999: 55–9), and I stick to that view. The ten attributes include (1) a large territory, (2) band organization, (3) a lack of social hierarchy, (4) gender differences in subsistence and ritual, (5) mechanisms for the redistribution of food, (6) universal kin categorization (everyone placed in a kin category), (7) symbolic structures that define relationships between humans and animals, (8) a symbolic order based on binary oppositions, (9) symbolic relations both within and between levels (animal, human, cosmological, etc.) and (10) a degree of flexibility in social and symbolic relations. Not all of these are present in every hunter-gatherer society, but they are widespread among hunter-gatherers and relatively uncommon among nearly all non-hunter-gatherers.

Beyond the question of diversity versus similarity lies yet another problem. This is the problem of identifying the ways in which hunter-gatherers perceive their own place in nature. A key to that question is whether indeed they perceive themselves as apart from nature or part of it. A common understanding today is that hunter-gatherers do not maintain a dualistic view of the problem (nature/culture or nature/society), but see themselves inseparable from nature itself (for example, Descola and Pálsson 1996). Others, such as Tim Ingold (2000: 40–76, 89–110) and Nurit Bird-David (1990, 1999), have argued similar views on the basis of both their own and classic ethnographic observations. Recently, the 'common sense' understanding that animals do not really want to be killed and do not, in fact, stand in a social relationship with their hunters has gained greater acceptance (e.g., Knight 2012). My view is that the question is largely ethnographic but depends too on the degree of agency one wants to grant to, not merely individual people, but to whole 'cultures' in telling people what to think. That said, it is evident from my own ethnography (e.g., Barnard 2002) that hunter-gatherers can 'think' differently from non-hunter-gatherers, or at least articulate their thoughts in terms that 'we' may find awkward to accept. In other words, it is difficult to decide which side to support. John Knight's solution is to separate the flesh-and-blood animal of the hunt from the spiritual being which is the 'animal' of Descola, Pálsson and the others.

This debate highlights yet again what is a fundamental problem in anthropology and archaeology writ large. Do we follow ecology blindly, or do we accept what our informants tell us (or how we imagine them to have thought in prehistoric times)? Wherein lies ethnographic truth? The beauty of language is that not only does it not solve this problem, it confounds it. If language is for communication alone, it communicates strange thoughts indeed. One team who do emphasize communication for its social significance is the team of Daniel Dor and Eva Jablonka. In recent articles (e.g., 2010), they argue a general theory of stages of evolution in which *Homo erectus* became more and more genetically adapted for language, and with it, culture. I have no problem with this view, except that it still does not explain peculiarities such as animals seeking to be hunted, or economic transactions that are plainly counterintuitive. Culture is not always adaptive, and explanations of the ways in which it is not adaptive are as interesting as explanations of the ways in which it is.

Inverse mafisa *versus optimal foraging*

Let me take one more specific example. What it shows is the power of culture over the purely economic. Of course humans operate optimally much of the time, but my contention is that when we do not, then something else may well be overriding economic strategies. That is why culture is such a powerful force and needs to be explained.

The example I have in mind is the contrast between optimal foraging and what Thomas Widlok (1999: 113–19) has called 'inverse *mafisa*'. The latter is a Hai//om custom which operates rather in the reverse manner of the Tswana practice of *mafisa*. In the traditional Tswana practice, found in Botswana, a pastoralist would leave his cattle or goats with a client to look after for him. Sometimes, especially in more recent times, such clients would be members of San or other minority communities. In return for looking after the animals, the client was allowed to take milk and to eat the remains of animals that died under his care. Often the patron, upon his return, would give his client a calf or two in payment for his service. Thus the poor acquire wealth at the expense of the rich. However, in 'inverse *mafisa*', the reverse is true. In this case, common between relatively well-off Owambo in northern Namibia and poor Hai//om semi-hunter-gatherers, the opposite occurs. Here, in order to hide his livestock from fellow hunter-gatherers, the Hai//om leaves his animals (usually goats) with Owambo agro-pastoralists. The latter are allowed to keep any offspring of these animals, and thus the rich get richer. There is no economic benefit to the poor, but only social benefit as what 'wealth' they have is hidden from view.

Optimal foraging theory is the theory advocated by Winterhalder and Alden Smith (1981), among others, that grants hunter-gatherers an agency that recognizes their ability to act with economic rationality. This means not only that they happen to do so, but that they calculate costs and benefits and choose to act rationally. The best example of this is one of the five mathematical models proposed as possibilities for hunter-gatherer behaviours in Bettinger's (2009: 21–46) *Hunter-gatherer foraging: five simple models*. The model is called 'optimal foraging with constraints' or 'linear programing'. In Bettinger's lead example, a group of Alaskan foragers has to choose between fishing for sockeye salmon or hunting beaver. In my view, the element of conscious choice and possible discussion of the merits of different subsistence strategies would not often be a real issue for hunter-gatherers. However, in this case, it might well be. The salmon lie in one tributary, and the beaver in another. The salmon are by far the better bet if an abundant and cheap source of protein is what is sought, but the beaver would be favoured if the acquisition of furs is the significant factor. The hunters have only limited time, so they must choose between the two, quite different, potential resources.

Obviously, in Bettinger's example, economic rationality is assumed. In Widlok's, it is not: cultural values take over from rationality. 'Inverse *mafisa*' benefits the already well-off, and puts more rather than fewer livestock in their possession. The real choice, then, is between economics and culture, possibly a pervasive reality for humankind in general. Perhaps the problem with culture, then, is precisely its seeming economic irrationality. Inverse *mafisa*, like patrilateral cross-cousin marriage (Lévi-Strauss 1969b: 438–55), may have a limited lifespan, but its existence at all illustrates the conundrum that culture is, and culture and language are obviously connected in a way that makes this not only possible but utilitarian. It is as if language enables not only the advantageous but the disadvantageous too. There is nothing peculiar in this. The existence of witchcraft (see Evans-Pritchard 1937) has the same effect too, as generations of anthropology students have long been told.

Hilary and Janette Deacon (1999: 101–2) summarize behaviours that connect Middle and Later Stone Age hunter-gatherers. These include family foraging groups, strong kinship ties that allow groups to aggregate and disperse, intensive hunting, the management of plant resources by utilizing fire, and the ability to communicate by using symbols, including the symbolic use of colour and the exchange of artefacts. There is archaeological evidence for all of these through these periods, and certainly the development of language as commentary, and not just for asking questions or giving orders, is strongly implied. Language, then, needs what we might call a true 'sociobiological' reason for existence, though not in the sense of E. O. Wilson (1975). The emphasis must be on the social results at least as much as the biological roots.

5   Narratives of the every-day

Narratives as most people use them, most of the time, include stories, descriptions of recent and long-ago past events, discussions of future plans, and so on. Through means such as these, humans have advanced their understanding of the world to a degree that would have been quite impossible without them.

In cognitive psychology, both experimental work (e.g., Morrison and Conway 2010) and theoretical studies (e.g., Nelson and Fivush 2004) have suggested a clear relation between the acquisition of vocabulary and the laying down of autobiographical memory. Both are necessary for individual cognitive development, which in turn creates a propensity for the co-evolution of language and cognition. In order for memory to exist, one must have words to describe things. These begin to proliferate at the age of about six months. In order to describe, one must have rules for doing so. In other words, one needs a grammar as well as a vocabulary. Grammar, and with it early memories, can appear by the age of three years. Morrison and Conway (2010: 23–4), among others, distinguish the age of acquisition of words from the age of encoding of those words, and, therefore, episodic memory from a slightly later development (a few months later), namely, autobiographical memory. The latter suggests what they call *retrievability*, the ability to remember the association between the word and what it represents: 'the problem lies not in forming memories but in representing them in long-term memory in a way that renders them retrievable' (2010: 23).

The answer to the problem of everyday communication among hunter-gatherers, I am afraid, does lie in some complicated arguments.

Language and thought

Much is dependent on communication with the 'self', but communication with others, in other words, *talking*, must also be implied. In other words, the evolution of language requires elements of both the former (as Chomsky 1986 would have it) and the latter (see Knight and Power 2012). Indeed, the usages here date only from the 1970s, and are open to revision and debate among psychologists. It has been argued that talking enabled, for example, the communication possible for humans to sail to Australia by 48,000 (or 60,000) years ago (see e.g., Davidson and Noble 1992). Sea-level changes (a fall of more than 100 metres) did mean that this was easier than it would be later, but even then, hopping from island to island was a difficult prospect. In the late Pleistocene, from that time until 10,000 years ago, Australia was colder and drier than it is today. The Holocene climate of the last 10,000 years is quite different: both warmer and wetter (Lourandos 1997: 5). Archaeologist Scott Cane (2013: 25–6) claims a very early arrival, possibly 70,000 years ago, as a result of the Toba explosion. This is conceivable, because of the low water level at that time, rather lower than the island-hopping routes favoured by the majority of experts. Language no doubt did assist the relatively rapid spread of humans throughout the world, and the transfer of the cultural abilities of *Homo sapiens sapiens* from generation to generation. To what degree language was in place at that time is difficult to say, but plainly it was in place at the time of the earliest (permanent) migrations. Although there is evidence of later contact and trading between the islands of present-day Indonesia and Australia, the acquisition of language across such a route and distance (nearly 100 kilometres) would seem unlikely. In turn, language gave rise to new ways of thinking and, certainly, new ways of interacting within societies. In other words, language made possible more advanced forms of sociality. This was, of course, among hunter-gatherers and specifically hunter-gatherers who could both talk to themselves and talk to each other at that time.

There do remain doubters, mostly about modern thinking and its exact relation to the evolution of enhanced working memory. Evidence for the latter, in the archaeological record, has been 'dated', for example, by the psychologist-archaeologist team of Frederick Coolidge and Thomas Wynn (2009: 245) to only 32,000 BP. However, as in the old archaeological adage, absence of evidence is not evidence of absence. Coolidge and Wynn (2009: 214–45) are sceptical about the idea of Neanderthals being mute and *H. sapiens sapiens* loquacious, and about the implications of such simple reasoning to explain the ability of humans to sail (with their spouses) to Australia (and to use language both along the way and while they were there). They are also sceptical about the symbolic nature of ivory figurines, Blombos beads and so on, and, above all, of the implications of these for the assumption they definitively indicate the presence of language. We do not really need to take sides on this question. The more important point is that one will eventually need to explain to others, and perhaps to one's self too, what these things are for. There is no reason not to assume some kind of co-evolution of creative design, adornment and language. Indeed, the rapid development of these things suggests many things evolving at the same time. There is also clear evidence that Neanderthals had jewellery, in the form of a necklace or bracelet found in

Croatia made from the talons of white-tailed eagles 132,000 years ago (Anon. 2015). This is 80,000 years before the arrival of *Homo sapiens* in Europe.

Yet what kind of language was there at the beginning? What level of complexity? And what sort of grammar are we talking about? It is puzzling to me that so much ink is spilled on things that did not lead to language at all and are hardly even analogous. Birdsong is an obvious case in point. Yet even primate communication lies only on the edge of what might be relevant. Many things had a selective advantage, and a great deal may have been required throughout long periods of evolution. That is why grammaticalization theory (e.g., Heine and Kuteva 2007) lies on the right track. Some psychologists and linguists work with children to decipher logical steps that they observe among them. Linguist Barry Blake (2008: 278–9), for example, notes that the syllable consonant–vowel is found universally, and therefore assumes it to have occurred first. And these can be double: think of the kinship terms *mama*, *papa*, *kaka* (Bancel and Matthey de l'Etang 2013). Syntax cannot exist without words, so words must precede syntax (Blake 2008: 279–81). Location words, Blake argues, must be early, then hierarchical structures (one phrase inside another), in other words, recursion, and so on. However clever they may be, chimpanzees have not yet hit on this or developed the necessity to do so. They may paint, if given the utensils to do so, but they lack art, and therefore they lack grammar.

Francesco d'Errico and his colleagues (d'Errico *et al.* 2003) note that a number of discoveries relating to the use of pigments all point to the origins of symbolism. These include discoveries at Twin Rivers in Zambia, dated to between 400,000 and 260,000 years ago, and at Kapthurin in Kenya, dated to the Acheulean to Middle Stone Age transition of about 200,000 years ago or earlier. These are in addition to work by d'Errico, Henshilwood and others at Blombos Cave in South Africa, most famously etched ochre dated at around 75,000 BP. Which, if any, of these, indicate language remains debatable. I, for one, favour an interpretation that places symbolic thought earlier than language, that is, not requiring language, but certainly related to it where the two are in conjunction. And therefore, we can speculate that pretty immediate co-evolution is likely. Whatever the exact date or the neurological precursors, humans were, it seems, on course for the invention and subsequently the spread of this tremendously useful evolutionary advance. And ultimately, it was not communication itself that was important, but the ability to communicate with an expanding vocabulary, complex grammar and narrative purpose.

In short, language and thought evolved at approximately the same time, and probably there was a relation between the two. Much ink has been spilled on the question of whether there is a language instinct (e.g., Chomsky 2002, 2005; Pinker 1994) or not (Sampson 2005; Evans 2014). Very simply, it may not matter as much as it has been thought and, like Paul Postal (2005), I am fairly agnostic on the issue. It is not so much whether language is instinct-ual, but whether humans are prepared for it when it happens. This is not quite the same thing as instinct. It is more like being ready for the invention of the bicycle once one is invented (see Ingold 2000: 374–6). One is biologically programmed for it, whether or not one has learned how to ride it: both innate ability and training are involved, to be sure. Yet instinct alone does not make one a cyclist, any more than living in a French-speaking speech community makes one speak French. Perhaps nearly, but not quite. Julie Tetel Andresen (2014: 108) explains the crucial difference between Chomsky and Pinker like this. In essence, Pinker

began with a commitment to arguing against Chomsky's evolutionary views while upholding Chomsky's linguistic views. Pinker originally undertook the task of (attempt-ing to) account for the Chomskyan view of language within the framework of contem-porary evolutionary theory. The Pinker/Chomsky divide gives us the first fold in the multilayered continuity/discontinuity dichotomy, one that might have been easily over-looked in the opening description of continuity theories. To repeat: continuity theories propose that the emergence of human language *can be told in terms of evolutionary processes* that have operated on the kinds of communicative display systems found elsewhere in the animal kingdom.

In other words, Pinker and Chomsky are (sort of) asking different questions, and their disagreement stems from this. On the question of whether there are evolutionary antecedents (say, among primates) to the development of lan-guage among humans, both Chomsky and Pinker answer 'no'. On the question of whether language can nevertheless be explained through Darwinian prin-ciples of natural selection, Chomsky answers 'no', and Pinker answers 'yes'. In the latter case, that is simply because language confers such great survival value on the species.

In any case, I am in agreement with Chomsky and the 'innate instinct' side on the specific question of the likelihood of some sort of genetic mutation, per-haps FOXP2. We do not yet know the details of how this might have opened up the faculty of language, and the suggestion of innateness is still rather vague. As Christine Kenneally suggests:

Language has to be partly innate, simply because human babies are born with the abil-ity to learn the language of their parents. While this can justifiably be called a language instinct, there is no one gene compelling us to produce language. Instead, a set of gen-etic settings gives rise to a set of behaviors and perceptual and cognitive biases, some of which may be more general and others of which are more language specific. (Kenneally 2007: 201)

But what precisely does this mean? Pinker and Jackendoff (2005) would seem to argue that the gene sequence of the mutated FOXP2 makes it uniquely human. On the other hand, Hauser *et al.* (2002) see basic biological grounds

for a broad understanding of the language faculty and do not consider this specific gene in their assessment of the problem.

All that said, the strongest argument against Chomsky's view seems to come
from primatology. In particular, Klaus Zuberbühler (2013) puts the case for
the idea that language evolved gradually through communication skills, rather
than through cognition. In other words, individual developments create unique
means of expression, and these, of course, become culturally understood within
a communicating community. The significant point here is that there were
non-linguistic elements in the beginning, which became linguistic after the
evolution of mental capacity and larger brains. Monkeys in the Taï Forest of the
Ivory Coast, for example, think differently, and communicate differently, from
those on Tiwai Island in Sierra Leone. Their calls are not absolutely unique for
they are formed in combinations of two to seven calls in a 'semantic' sequence.
This being the case, why should monkeys be able to do this and not humans a
very long time ago? The implication is that human evolution worked in similar
ways: we learned to reason as we learned to communicate. Slowly!

Some writers, like Evans (2014: 198–203), have sought to see a difference
between biological universals such as perceptions of colour and linguistic ones
such as Universal Grammar. The former is conditional on a number of things,
like the ability of language to reflect what we see. It is also dependent on
the original description and experimental findings, which are fairly weak, of
early studies of colour perception. Berlin and Kay (1969) famously argued that
perceptions of basic colour exist in a scale from few colours perceived (white
and black) to more (the addition of red) to more still (the addition of green or
yellow), and so on, up to a maximum of 11. But are they testing here innate,
cross-linguistic, neurological universals, as they had argued, or a kind of cultural complexity? I am not sure it is as easy as Berlin and Kay had imagined
to make this distinction, or as obvious as it seemed to Chomsky (2002, 2011)
simply to assert that all languages are basically the same. The evidence for
one or the other is always nuanced, more complicated than assumed. More
specifically, on the notion that all languages possess Universal Grammar, this
is refuted by Evans (2014: 101–6) in fairly simple terms: first, the notion that
overt correction of grammatical errors is not necessary is confounded by the
evidence. In fact, children take years to learn a language, and they *do* make
mistakes. Secondly, there is no evidence for the kind of neurological mechanism that would be required to correct grammatical errors. Such a mechanism
would have to be the same for all languages, so any language that did not fit
would have to be unlearnable!

Nor does Pinker's (1994: 12) analogy with the spider web quite work. Pinker
agrees with Chomsky that language is an instinct, and he likens it to the spider's ability to spin a web without ever having seen it done before. Personally,
I think Ingold's bicycle is a better analogy. The ability to ride a bicycle contains

both instinctual and learned behavioural mechanisms. It is quite different from a spider's ability to spin a web. A creature born to be a spider would spin a web. Peter the Wild Boy discovered in a forest in Hannover in the early eighteenth century, on the other hand, would not, *did not*, learn to speak until he was taught (Monboddo 1774 [1773]: 172–4). Language is not an instinct, but it *is* like riding a bicycle.

What lies behind the very question of linguistic relativity is the problem of whether or not language precedes thought. There are three views here (see Andresen 2014: 186–90). (1) Enlightenment thinkers, following John Locke, held that thought came first. Before there was a faculty of language, there was a faculty of thought. Humans developed thinking, this view maintains, in order to communicate perceptions and thoughts to others. People invented words to describe things and built language on this basis, which is essentially a *social* basis. (2) The second view, that language precedes thought, derives ultimately from Wilhelm von Humboldt and the later German romantics. In this view, symbols emerge, and grammar is the means to put these into effect. If individuals then think through language, it follows that language, in a sense, is imposed upon them and their collective consciousness. That is why the romantics came to be obsessed with the idea of the 'nation' or the (national) linguistic community. Language, in other words, fosters a collective soul. Saussure was also aligned with this position, in the sense that he held that language provides an organizing principle for human thought. (3) The third view is associated more with the early German romantics, and in our times with writers such as, from a linguistic understanding, Jerry Fodor (e.g., 1983) and later Steven Pinker (1997), and from a yet more evolutionary perspective, Terrence Deacon (1997). It may seem more complicated, but in essence it holds simply that language and thought co-evolve. Also, language itself evolves within a child as he or she acquires the ability to speak and think, and within a speech community as language comes to meet the needs of those who speak it.

The importance of ritual

The notion that ritual, and therefore communication through ritual, is fundamental to the origins of language was first proposed by anthropologists Chris Knight (1998), Roy Rappaport (1999), Jerome Lewis (2009) and others. We have already seen this with reference to the Eland Bull Dance of Kalahari Bushman groups, and evidence from central Africa points in this direction too. The acquisition of language, however it was accomplished (through a FOXP2 mutation, through rapid natural selection, through slow evolution, etc.), led ultimately to kinship structures, incest taboos and other cultural features that are not possible without language. One of my goals here is to decipher what exactly happened to create the propensity for narrative, and to explain its spread among humans from prehistoric times to the historical era. Language enables the existence of various narrative forms, as well as simile and metaphor. As I have noted earlier, it enables the power both to gossip and to deceive, which themselves are unique properties of human communication systems (see also Dunbar 1996). Narrative also allows the construction of sophisticated cosmological ideas such as those found among the living and recent hunter-gatherers of Australia, Africa, Asia and the Americas. Despite their concerns over points of detail, mainly archaeological thinkers (such as Coolidge and Wynn 2009: 214–22) speculate on a number of cognitive attributes of language that they see as evolving at least within the last 100,000 years. They are not, and need not be, too specific about the timing: a heritable mutation that leads to greater phonological storage capacity, recursion and enhanced working memory is required. It is up to neuroscience to explain in more detail when this was, and whether or not we can attribute this development just to *Homo sapiens* or, for example, to *H. neanderthalensis* as well.

Hunter-gatherers, as we have seen, can speak languages in four or five different language families, each sophisticated, different from the others and grammatically complex (see also Lucy 1992: 25–68). However, in a way, the reverse has also been documented in work by Daniel Everett (2005, 2012): language with no recursion, and very little grammatical complexity. There is little doubt that languages differ from each other quite profoundly, but there is also little doubt that even 'simple' languages enable their speakers to communicate far more meaning than is required by technology alone. Even if Everett is right about Pirahã being a language without recursion, it is only one of thousands of languages that have been spoken in South America. The fact that the Pirahã possess language without recursion still makes them not only unusual but extremely unusual, if not unique. It does not prove that the absence of recursion is in any way normal. What is normal is the ability to speak many languages, all with recursion, in a socially complex and linguistically evolving community.

As with other groups in the Kalahari, the female initiation ceremony of the Naro takes place when a girl reaches menarche. There are many descriptions of it in the ethnographic literature. I encountered such a ceremony in 1974, early in my fieldwork with the central Naro (Barnard 1980: 117–18). They told me that its meaning was lost in time, or more literally that they did it simply because the 'old parents' did it, or because God wills it. Beyond that, they could not explain it. A few years earlier, Mathias Guenther (1986: 278–81) found much the same among the eastern Naro, which he elaborates on, though not through indigenous explanation but rather through the theoretical ideas of Arnold van Gennep and Victor Turner. In the 1920s Dorothea Bleek (1928: 23) seems to have found a similar situation among the western Naro, and she leaves it unexplained. Likewise, George Silberbauer (1963) among the closely related G/ui, who comments on its relation to marriage. To my mind, and I think to theirs as well, no Naro or G/ui could really explain it because it required no explanation. Its meaning was not 'lost', rather, it lay literally beyond words. It is worth recalling that Naro are not a linguistically ignorant people, but a people who possess 26 words for 'talk' or 'talking' plus another seven words for 'tell'. We have, for example, 'talk' (*kx'ui*), 'talk about' (*/hóà-kx'am*), 'talk at the same time' (*!gàbàkú*), 'talk too much' (*!nabè sa tsi ko gone*, literally, 'you are chasing a giraffe'), etc. (Guenther 2006: 242, 256–7; Visser 2001: 209–11). It is not as if they had no words for their concepts. Rather their concepts simply needed no words, because the 'words' here are entirely embedded in the actions. Perhaps it could be the same with the Pirahã. Or perhaps the Pirahã simply prefer metaphor to speech.

The initiation ceremony of the Naro is elaborate, but its meaning is, it seems, beyond words. Words are there to explain myth, they are not there for ritual. The anarchist philosopher of science, Paul Feyerabend (1978: 142–3, 156), once said that his aim was *not* to establish the truth but to force his opponent to change their mind. Although on the surface quite ridiculous, this proposition is also rather profound. The person with the greater persuasive powers is also the person with the greater ability to lead, to change opinion or to seduce. He or she is therefore one who possesses the greater powers of Darwinian fitness. There is, if anything, a greater likelihood of such power of persuasion to be present among hunter-gatherers than among herders or cultivators. In an ordered, anarchical society, in the sense of an order existing through local autonomy, the ability to persuade and not prior ownership or inherited status is what is important. For this reason, as well as because we know that language did evolve solely among hunter-gatherers and no one else, it is to hunter-gatherer ethnography that we must look to find clues about the prehistory of language.

And by drawing our attention away from always seeking the truth, Feyerabend reminds us, though without knowing it, of another vision of truth well known to anthropologists. By nature, anthropologists seek to understand someone else's truth, and not simply rest on their own truth. Once in a seminar I was confronted by a participant who wanted to know why I was studying the strange ideas of Lord Monboddo. He asked why I was not studying the ideas of someone more important, like Linnaeus. Yet my concern with Monboddo was never that he was *important*, but rather that his ideas were *anthropologically interesting*. The fact that Monboddo was wrong in beliefs such as his view that Basque is mutually intelligible with Scots Gaelic and with Inuktitut, that the Orang Outang is a variety of humanity, that slavery was acceptable because it was part of ancient tradition or that naked exercise (along with a diet consisting entirely of raw vegetables) is good for you, is beside the point. It just made him all the more interesting.

Eats, shoots & leaves

Speaking of raw vegetables, there is no linguistic reason to expect hunter-gatherers to speak a different kind of language from non-hunter-gatherers. Where we find related languages being spoken both by hunters and by non-hunters, the lifestyle of the hunters is usually at the root of both. There is no particular evolution of language from a hunter-gatherer form to an agro-pastoralist form, since there is little or no difference between languages according to means of subsistence. The Khoe-Kwadi languages of southern Africa illustrate this well.

Naro and G/ui are Khoe languages spoken by former hunter-gatherers. (Khoe is now regarded as a subgroup of Khoe-Kwadi, though no one speaks Kwadi any longer.) As we have seen, the ancestors of the Naro were at one time Kx'a-speakers, related to the Ju/'hoansi. Khoekhoe is a Khoe language spoken by both traditional hunter-gatherers (the Hai//om) and traditional herders (the Nama and the Damara). The Hai//om may at one time also have spoken a Kx'a language. The grammars of all these languages are both complex and extremely similar. Whatever their origin, the grammatical and lexical material they share fulfils the task of creating myth, explaining God (all these peoples are monotheistic) and so on. The rituals practised by them lie beyond this in a non-linguistic realm of expression. The Khoekhoe rituals may be pastoralist in origin, or they may not be (see also Barnard 1988). Beyond that specific question, we can assume that language in general was created by the hunter-gatherers of tens of thousands of years ago, and not by Neolithic agro-pastoralists, Iron Age warriors, or philosophers or writers. Until we understand how hunter-gatherers behave, how they think and how they speak, we cannot understand what language truly is. Hunter-gatherers have lived until very recently on every inhabited continent, and the diversity of their languages is well known.

But at this point let me take two languages spoken by non-hunter-gatherers and consider the implications of what we find. My examples here are Navajo and Khoekhoe. Both are spoken by traditional sheep-herding peoples, one North American and the other African. The former is well known as being among the world's more grammatically complex languages. It is also one of great precision: 'excessively literal, little given to abstractions' (Kluckhohn and Leighton 1974 [1946]: 273). Clyde Kluckhohn (a psychological anthropologist) and Dorothea Leighton (a psychiatrist) interpreted this linguistic fact as a reflection of Navajo thought processes, which they regarded as very different from those of English-speaking people. The language also enables more complicated uses of puns than English, where two meanings of the same phrase reflect not imprecision but rather awareness of both meanings at the same time. For example, there can be a play on the phrase *ha'át'íishą' nílí* (meaning both 'what is flowing' and 'what clan are you'), when embellishing a story about the clan of a man standing by a river. Or jokes can be made on the basis of the fact that *hodeeshtał* means either 'I will sing' or 'I will kick him'. Yet the time period of diffusion is occasionally represented in linguistic expression, and this can contradict the notion of precision in Navajo thought. For example, both metals and knives came to the Navajo at the same time and replaced flint; thus metal, knife and flint are all represented by the word *béésh* (1974: 279).

In Khoekhoe, the usage is similar, and we find similar expressions, if without the deliberate ambiguity. For example, we find (in traditional orthography): '*khoikhoib*, the man of men; ... *khoisi*, friendly, human; *khoisis*, humanity, friendliness, kindness, friendship, or *khoixa* and *khoixasis*, kind and kindliness; *khoisigagus*, marriage, intimacy, friendship; *khoixakhoib*, most intimate friend ...' (Hahn 1881: 17). In place of the ambiguity which enables puns in Navajo, we find etymological correspondences like /*aus* (feminine), meaning blood or fountain, and /*aub* (the same word in the masculine), meaning snake or flowing, which are recalled in superstitions and folklore (1881: 53). Theophilus Hahn, the missionary, ethnographer and later librarian who grew up speaking Khoekhoe, knew well the details of such usages and their reflections in Khoekhoe religious belief.

While it is likely that aspects of both Navajo and Khoekhoe language and belief reflect their cultural background as herding peoples, nevertheless their relationships to hunter-gatherers are apparent. The Navajo are an Athapaskan-speaking people of Arizona, related to the other Athapaskan groups, who live in western Canada. The latter are traditional hunter-gatherers, as no doubt the ancestors of the Navajo once were as well. The Khoekhoe are a Namibian and formerly also a South African people, related to the Naro, G/ui, Shua and other Khoe-speaking San groups who live in Botswana. The latter are all hunter-gatherers and probably have been for the last couple of thousand years, even if before that they were in contact with the ancestors of the Khoekhoe. In other words, in some respects, it makes little difference whether we are talking about hunter-gatherers or about non-hunter-gatherers. Both have the propensity to use very complex grammars and sophisticated forms of expression. The point is that, in general, these must have preceded the transition from hunting and gathering to food production.

Concepts that may seem strange in the West are often widespread elsewhere. For me, the interesting thing is whether they are common among hunter-gatherers (implying they might be ancient) or not. One danger in social anthropology, though, is that well-known peoples become models of what is normal and therefore that generalizations about them become extended to other peoples of the same 'type'. For example, *xaro* or *hxaro*, is 'a regional system of reciprocity for reducing risk among the !Kung San' (Wiessner 1977, see also 1982). It is also found among a few neighbouring hunter-gatherer peoples, though normally called by its verbal form //'āe. Through this custom, people give and receive non-consumable gifts, and possessions are redistributed throughout society. But *xaro* is not found among San peoples generally. It may be useful for San to have this custom, but it is not specifically a hunter-gatherer custom. Northern Kalahari pastoralist peoples have similar customs too (Barnard 2008b: 67–9).

For anthropologists and other intellectuals there are further problems. I mean here not problems of modern technology, like cell phones or computers, but problems in the use of abstract words. For example, in my department a debate was recently held on 'the value of value' in anthropology. One of my colleagues defended the proposition: 'Value is nothing but a series of disconnected homonyms. The concept has no utility as an anthropological analytic or as a comparative frame.' Even though a Naro or a Pirahã who speaks English as a second language may know what this means, I doubt if he or she could translate it into Naro or Pirahã in such a way that Naro or Pirahã who do *not* speak English could understand it.

In the beginning, there were languages

Multilingualism as the norm

It follows from my assumption of multilingualism that there was no single, original language. Language was diverse, and languages were numerous, or at least not single, almost from the beginnings of speech (or even of speech and gesture). It is also possible to envisage language including both gesture and speech from its early use, perhaps even with a gender distinction. However, I find that kind of gender distinction unlikely. Much more likely is interbreeding or ultimately intermarriage between groups, each using different dialects. Some of these dialects, as certainly in later times, would be very different, but the effect within communities would not be problematic. This is because our common assumption of monolingualism is what is problematic.

Imagine this scenario: James's mother speaks Greek and his father speaks Latin. Their children grow up understanding both but speaking a mixture, perhaps developing a gender-specific diglossia: Greek to their female relatives and Latin to male relatives. A generation later, children choose to use only the higher-status language. The only thing for certain is that 'language' exists, not that it has any particular properties of grammar at a language-specific level. It acquires those later, as it develops in the mind of the child or children. One does not need to possess 'a language' in order to have the propensity to use languages. One simply needs to possess the capacity to learn them. Which one or ones a person learns is a different matter.

Non-literate people generally do not speak just one language: they speak several, and they are capable of moving from a language to the next, and sometimes from one symbolic system to the next. They do this through a kind of comparative method, of which they need not be completely aware – or aware of at all. Nevertheless, it encourages people to take on a degree of cultural awareness, though again, one that they need not fully realize. Just as a native speaker has no necessary awareness of the grammar of the language he or she speaks, so too is cultural awareness intuitive. However, both 'culture' and language are fluid. Both change constantly. The linguist and specialist on creoles John McWhorter (e.g., 2005, 2011) has developed an explanation to account for the relative complexity of languages. His hypothesis is controversial, but it is also basically simple. Languages mix and pidgins appear. Rapidly, these acquire grammatical complexity and in a generation or two they become creoles. Then more gradually their grammars and vocabularies take on further complexity. And eventually, these complex languages come into contact with other languages, and they become simpler. This is what has happened to English since the Norman Conquest and to the Romance languages in a similar period. Or, the cycle repeats completely: pidgin to creole to complex language and on to another creole. McWhorter's hypothesis explains both why some languages are more complex than others and how languages develop and *lose* complexity. Along the same lines, Salikoko Mufwene (2001) argues for an 'ecological' approach to language evolution. He argues that creoles develop in the same way as other languages, and that even North American English can be explained as a product of language contact (Mufwene 2001: 81–105). For these thinkers, the evolution of creoles is a natural occurrence. As Derek Bickerton (1981: 5) puts it: 'children of pidgin-speaking parents have as input something which may be adequate for emergency use, but which is quite unfit to serve as anyone's primary mother tongue'. The parent, he adds, 'knows no more of the language than the child (and pretty soon will know less)'.

McWhorter (2003: 93–129) describes three levels of language mixture: words, grammar and intertwining. His general thesis is that the processes that create these forms of mixture are inherent in language itself. In spite of attempts by scholars such as Joseph Greenberg and Merritt Ruhlen, he argues, it is impossible to reconstruct the language of Adam and Eve. McWhorter (2003: 302–3) speculates, though, that the first language had no inflections or tones but only the bare minimum of grammar required for communicating. Tense was kept simple, and words were interchangeable without change (see also Aitchison 1996: 107–22). McWhorter's conclusion is:

our closest living approximation to human language as a lily ungilded is not words like *tik* [Proto-World 'finger'] and *aq'wa* [Proto-World 'water'] but the grammars of certain creole languages largely unknown beyond where they are spoken. In the languages that today get the most press – a dozen or so in Europe, plus Chinese, Japanese, and Arabic – the structure of the first language remains only as shadows and vestiges, the rest long since obscured by morphings and random accretions upon the foundational rootstuff.

The living languages most like the parent of all six thousand are spoken in places as little known to most of the world as Surinam, islands off the west coast of Africa, and Papua New Guinea. (McWhorter 2003: 303)

The alternative view is worth brief consideration too. This is the proposition that cooperation among humans is facilitated through sharing an 'accent'. That is, that speaking rather alike encourages people to work together to a greater extent and thus aids sharing and the building of regional networks for exchange and the like. That view has been advocated by Emma Cohen (2012). It is not necessarily always in opposition to McWhorter's hypothesis, but these two views nevertheless do seem to stand logically at opposite ends of a spectrum. Humans either get along together because they have some commonality in language, that is, they belong to the same community and share the same language. Or, they speak exactly the same dialect and therefore communicate more readily than they might with people who speak differently. Either way, in a multilingual setting, there is always choice, always a degree of complexity. Cohen's view is a good explanation of the degree and form of sociality within a speech community, whereas McWhorter's is a better explanation of how languages change and acquire agreed meanings.

The alternative to either is to grant significant status to ritual in giving meaning. This could explain the continued existence of the Eland Bull Dance, something I frequently asked about in the Kalahari though never found a clear answer. Chris Knight may be right that ritual precedes language and aids in giving it meaning through agreed rules. For this to happen, both the initiate and other participants must accept the elements of the dance as metaphor. This could indeed imply that priority should be given to metaphor for the origin of language, something hinted at in philosophical definitions of metaphor as literal falsehood: 'Generally, it is only when a sentence is taken to be false that we accept it as a metaphor and start to hunt out the hidden implication' (Davidson 1979: 40). The same is true in linguistics, as argued by Stefan Hoefler (Höfler) and Andrew Smith (Hoefler and Smith 2009; Smith and Höfler 2014): metaphor precedes grammaticalization. It also calls to mind any number of metaphors:

> He's a real pig.
> She is a beacon of light.
> That's a red herring.
> She is an eland.
> He is an Eland Bull.

Further examples of change and multilingualism

I have been involved in a research project on language loss. I witnessed, for example, the choices people make in deciding which language a husband and wife will use to their children. In our survey of language use in Khekhenye, in Botswana, out of a majority originally G/uikhoe- or G/ui-speaking community, 206 speak to their children in Kgalagadi, 57 in G/ui, 14 in Tsasi, a few in Tswana and only 2 in N!aqriaxe. N!aqriaxe is a very rare Kx'a or Northern San language spoken in southern Botswana, well away from the area in the north of the country where other K'xa languages are found. In the past, communities were small enough that individuals could maintain social relationships and speak more than one language: in this case, languages in three different families: Kx'a, Taa and Khoe-Kwadi. Today they add Kgalagadi (in the Bantu family), and either the G/ui or Kgalagadi peoples may now dominate the other groups politically. Individuals who can speak languages in four different language families are, of course, not stupid, but they often are illiterate and undereducated. In the past, they shared access to wild game. They apportioned access to melon patches, the only source of water in the dry season. According to my informants, in the case of the N!aqriaxe language, even the word for 'band' implied sharing, and the practice was widespread. The word is !òa. Today it means to distribute meat, to give and take things, to give water and to share space.

Languages are lost perhaps because children communicate with each other, specifically in big communities. Among hunter-gatherers, bands of 25 to 35 are typical, although communities or band clusters may be rather larger. Yet even in such communities, more languages, not fewer, can be spoken. Linguistic diversity creates a degree of cultural diversity, and with it, both cultural creativity and cultural exchange. Of course, words pass from one language to another, but Khoisan became recognized by linguists as a *Sprachbund* only very recently. Multilingualism existed as a theoretical issue in the time of Benjamin Lee Whorf (who lived from 1897 to 1941), but it has not received that much discussion since then. To my mind, it deserves a rethink in light of the multilingualism that we now know characterizes small communities on several continents (see also Lucy 1992). This is true for anthropology as well as for linguistics.

In their conjecture on the future of language, Margaret Mead and Rhoda Métraux (2005 [1966]) noted that globalization creates powerful peoples and politically (and economically) weak peoples too. They argued that languages employed by the former tend to take over and swamp those of weaker groups. For this reason, they favoured moving towards a language of a weaker nation, ideally a language spoken by a smaller group, not politically important, and with a simple grammar and few phonological difficulties. The irony is that the earth's most longstanding linguistic traditions (like Khoisan, possibly) are anything but simple. Mead and Métraux rejected artificial languages (like Esperanto) in favour of natural languages, because the latter were developed though the elaboration of cultural as well as linguistic considerations. But

whose cultural considerations? The rich elaboration of expression is a product of the evolutionary development of languages and would not be there if
the world opted just for simplicity. And as McWhorter shows, the fact that
languages seem to develop again and again from pidgins is no barrier to their
potential ultimate complexity.

The question of group size demands a rethink too, especially in light of
McWhorter's hypothesis of language change. It is perhaps no accident that
Mandarin Chinese is a 'simple' language, French and Spanish have a slight
degree of complexity, and San languages are more complicated still. In other
words, there is no reason to assume that hunter-gatherers should speak simple languages; there is every reason to assume that they speak languages of
great refinement, with grammatical specificity and rich vocabularies: vocabularies often quite different from those of neighbouring languages. There is
every reason too to assume diversity among hunter-gatherer languages, both in
that hunter-gatherers differ linguistically from their neighbours and that their
speech communities are often very small indeed. It is possibly no accident
either that among the largest speech communities in the Kalahari is Ju/'hoan,
along with very similar neighbouring dialects !Xũ and ≠Kx'ao//'aen: some
60,000 people in all. One example, of course, is not sufficient here. Further,
we do not know anything about the size or duration of, say, the Blombos community in prehistoric times or the linguistic changes that took place there over
time. All we know is that trade (for ochre) existed between Blombos people
and their neighbours and trading partners many kilometres away. They could
have spoken the same language, but I rather doubt that they did. It is not unreasonable to suppose that languages evolved, mixed and evolved again throughout the times Blombos Cave and nearby areas were occupied, and that this set
of multilingual communities was indicative of a co-evolution of culture and
language among hunter-gatherers as they developed in both cultural and linguistic spheres.

The situation described by Daniel Nettle and Suzanne Romaine
(2000: 86) may hold clues: they reflect on language diversity in Papua New
Guinea. In one lowland area, the average number of languages an adult male
speaks is five. That is a lot of languages! Everyone knows the vernacular, and
many know the languages of neighbouring groups as well. This is especially
true where fewer languages are spoken. Consider this, among their examples.
On New Britain a linguist was left in the company of a six-year-old boy. The
boy was collecting plants, and told the linguist their names in each of four
languages. He knew not only about botany but also about how to name and
describe plants to people who spoke the languages all around him.

Such examples may be anecdotal, but they are indeed indicative of the global trend, although Papua New Guinea may be a particularly striking area. The
median number of speakers per language there is only about 1,000, and the

mean is 3,752 (Nettle 1999: 71). In any case, Nettle makes the point that language diversity on a worldwide scale is to some extent simply a matter of latitude: the number of speakers a language has, in both Africa and the Americas, can be correlated with the length of the growing season. Near the equator, language communities tend to be small and geographically limited. At higher latitudes, with greater seasonal difference, language communities are larger and spread over bigger areas. This has an effect on kinship and other social institutions, as well (Dunbar 2008: 146–7).

The great cause of linguistic change was the adoption of cultivation and the domestication of animals. The Neolithic Age was the source of language loss in a big way, not because languages were simply forgotten but because population explosion and consequent migrations caused some languages and language families to take over vast territories. The Indo-European and Bantu language families are obvious examples (see Nettle and Romaine 2000: 104–7). This is in spite of early farmers being *less* well nourished, and (particularly in the Americas) anaemic, with a narrower range of foods in their diet, especially proteins, as well as having shorter life spans, longer working hours and so on. Yet what the Neolithic also brought was the ability to grow more food and to sustain larger populations than hunting and gathering ever could. This is the paradox, but it is rarely considered as a major factor of change by evolutionary linguists. There was, of course, neither a single Neolithic Revolution nor a slow Neolithic transition. In a way, there was both. Between 12,000 and 7,000 years ago, at least seven separate centres of activity (one in Papua New Guinea, two in China, one in the Middle East, one in North Africa, and one each in Mexico and Peru) gave birth, fairly rapidly, to agriculture (Tattersall 2008: 113). The domestication of animals occurred in most places at roughly the same time, and these transitional periods followed closely behind the end of the last Ice Age at the beginning of the Holocene epoch. Yet despite the views of some commentators, none of this had anything to do with the evolution of language. Language was in existence already, and had already evolved to a point virtually identical to that before this transition. We know this through comparison of the very similar languages of hunter-gatherers and agricultural peoples.

The linguistic relativity hypothesis

Whorf (1956a: 85) famously compared English to Hopi, and argued that the latter is the more sophisticated: better to explain ideas in nuclear physics, for example, than English. It does not matter whether one agrees with his argument or not, or indeed whether it is really true or not. The fact that it exists at all is the issue. Some languages are better for some things than other languages are. No language can be best of every language for every purpose: they have

Table 5.1 *Hanunóo pronouns: 'traditional' distinctions*

kuh first singular	**tah** first dual	**mih** first plural exclusive
–	–	**tam** first plural inclusive
muh	–	**yuh** second plural
yah	–	**dah** third plural

Source: adapted from Conklin 1969: 54

each evolved for expressing what is needed to the people who speak it, understand it and think in it (see also D'Andrade 1995; Levinson 2003).

In fact, more important than worrying about the relation between semantic complexity and nuances of meaning or which language is more sophisticated is capturing meaning in a language's own terms. Pronoun systems are not arbitrary but often coherent and logical. Their logic, though, may differ from more familiar examples like English or Latin, the latter often imagined to be logical, such as when we think of tense structures. English, like other Germanic languages, has only two natural tenses (past and present), whereas we often represent it as having, like Latin, six tenses (past, present, future, past perfect, present perfect and future perfect). 'He was' and 'he is' are natural, whereas (according to my grammar teacher long ago) the future perfect 'he will have been' is a concoction made up by the addition of 'helping verbs'.

Among the more extreme examples of the use of such folk classification is that in Hanunóo, spoken in the Philippines and described by Harold Conklin (1969 [1962]: 41–59). Instead of trying to explain 'missing' categories of the 'traditional' system, illustrated in Table 5.1, Conklin describes the pronoun system according to the internal structure of Hanunóo pronoun usage itself. This is what is shown in Table 5.2. Thus the eight Hanunóo pronouns meaning 'they', 'I', 'we', 'you', 'we two', 'we all', 'he, she' and 'you all' are described in terms of the properties *minimal membership, non-minimal membership, inclusion of speaker, exclusion of speaker, inclusion of hearer* and *exclusion of hearer*.

In Conklin's words,

If a close examination is made of the distinctive contrasts involved, not in terms of labels but in terms of actual, minimal, obligatory differences, a more satisfactory, economical, and semantically verifiable solution is reached. The necessary and sufficient conditions for defining each of the eight categories depend on the regular intersection of six components which comprise three simple oppositions. (1969: 55)

As the two tables show, it is the emically relevant distinctions that illustrate the more elegant solution to the question of representation. Conklin notes too that other languages in the Philippines, namely Tagalog, Ilocano and Maranao exhibit similar semantic relationships. So, we can perhaps speak of a regional structure of pronoun systems here, not entirely unlike the one for kinship

Table 5.2 *Hanunóo pronouns: emically relevant distinctions*

dah	M̲SH
yuh	M̲SH
mih	M̲SH
tam	MSH
yah	MS̲H
muh	MS̲H
kuh	MSH̲
tah	MSH

M means minimal membership; M̲ means non-minimal membership

S means inclusion of speaker; S̲ means exclusion of speaker

H means inclusion of hearer; H̲ means exclusion of hearer

Source: adapted from Conklin 1969: 55

structures I once proposed for Khoisan (Barnard 1992). This kind of search for the local understanding is normal in social anthropology, and especially in the study of kinship systems, where the purpose of focusing on the detail of local usage, without regard to its being better or worse than Hopi, or English, is virtually the only method that is acceptable. Whether an analysis captures 'God's truth' or merely represents 'hocus-pocus' as the best we can do, is a related problem (see Tyler 1969: 343–432). In other words, in our search for the best possible description, are we after psychological reality, or rather are we after the most economical representation of the system? The two are not necessarily the same.

Take one final example here: the words for 'society' and 'sociality' in Japanese versus the words for these in English. The word for society in Japanese is *shakai*. The word for sociality is *shakaisei* (Kazuyoshi Sugawara, personal communication). The notion of sociality assumes the existence of a concept of society. However, some anthropologists claim that sociality evolved first and society only later. Of course, one might be able to say this in Japanese, but the idea does not sit well in the language. The sentence, 'True hunter-gathers have not yet evolved a concept of *society* but have only *sociality*' is almost impossible to express literally in Japanese, or at least would not carry quite the meaning it does in English.

The sign not arbitrary?

Standing above the town of Paarl, in South Africa's Western Cape Province, is the Afrikaans Language Monument (*Afrikaanse Taalmonument*). As far as I know, it is the only monument in the world dedicated specifically to a language rather than to a people or a person. But Afrikaans is not just any language. Its history is bound up with that of the 'white' people who speak it, and, of course, the 'Coloured' and 'black' people who use it as well, not only in South Africa but also in Namibia and several other African countries, and even beyond Africa, such as in Argentina. It is said that the concave and convex shapes that make up the monument represent the various influences, including Khoekhoe, Malay, Portuguese, several Bantu languages, French, English, German and, of course, Dutch. The point is that Afrikaans is not simply a kind of Dutch: it is a language in its own right, with its own grammar and a rather mixed vocabulary. When exactly it became 'a language' is, nevertheless, not an easy question. Officially, it acquired that status in 1925, but it was in use long before that, and certainly indeed with more than one dialect. It emerged as long ago as the seventeenth century, from a mixture of several dialects of Dutch then spoken in South Africa (Ponelis 1993). All languages are, in a sense, mixed languages. Just as there is no 'pure' human being, there really are no pure languages either.

One of Ferdinand de Saussure's (1974 [1916]: 65–70) most famous pronouncements is that the sign is arbitrary. By 'sign' he meant simply the relation between a word (the signifier) and what it signifies. By 'arbitrary' he meant simply that there is no *natural* relation between the word and the object signified by it. If I speak French I say *la chat*. If I speak German I say *die Katze*. If I speak English I say *the cat*. There is nothing natural about any of these words and the animal they represent. That said, others use the word 'sign' in different senses, and Saussurian thought has been criticized for confusion of the fact that Saussure himself seems to have meant slightly different things at different times by this term. Of course the sign is arbitrary in the sense that Saussure intended its meaning. The fact that philosophers, linguists and, in particular, specialists in semiotics have debated what it should mean is beside the point.

The discipline, or theoretical perspective, of structural anthropology is based on the metaphor that culture is a science of cultural (that is, non-linguistic) signs, related to each other in similar, if not always arbitrary, ways. For example, red in a political context signifies 'left wing', while in a traffic light it signifies 'stop'. The contexts, like the meanings, are unrelated: one cannot predict the meaning based on these alone. That is the beauty of language: meaning goes beyond the merely literal. This is nowhere more true than in the study of mythology, which we shall explore in the next chapter.

6   Mythological narratives

According to the great scholar of ancient mythology, G. S. Kirk (1970: 8), 'For the Greeks *muthos* just meant a tale, or something one uttered, in a wide range of senses: a statement, a story, the plot of a play.' What in southern Africa are usually assumed to be myths, as opposed to some other sort of narrative, have a similar definition: no distinction is made between them and any other kind of story. Plato was among the first to use the term myth in writing. For him too, *mutholgia* simply referred to the 'telling of stories' (Kirk 1970: 8). And Kirk (1970: 280–5) ends his exploration of the functions of myth with a brief assessment of theories of origin. He stresses the dynamism of mythology and the gradual evolution of narrative structures. Kirk, in fact, sees the acquisition of symbolic meaning almost as incidental. He also points to the diversity of forms of meaning in myth, and for the Ancient Greeks this seems to have been characteristic of the genre.

My own view is not entirely dissimilar, except that I disagree with Kirk's emphasis on the diversity of mythologies. Like Lévi-Strauss (e.g., 1978), I prefer to see the unity of meaning across the continents, even where the elements of narrative and the stories themselves differ in specifics. Kirk discusses Lévi-Strauss's structural approach at some length, but Kirk's concern is more with myth in literate contexts, including myth in ancient Mesopotamia, Greece and India. Lévi-Strauss always saw myth quite differently, not only as a property of pre-literate culture but also one property among three others: mathematical entities, music and natural language.

Languages are said to be 'embodied' where sound and sense intersect. Music is 'language without meaning' and 'myth is overloaded with meaning', producing 'structural patterns coded in images' (Tilly 1990: 45–6). Music and myth are 'by-products of a structural shift which had language as its starting point' (Lévi-Strauss 1981 [1971]: 647). In other words, from language, all else emerges. It is telling that language is Lévi-Strauss's starting point, and indeed that it is in the four volumes of his great work, the *Mythologiques*, that his fame rests. Yet it is not necessarily literally true that language was invented before myth, or indeed that language preceded music. Some writers, such as John Blacking (1973), would begin with music and from that imagine that all symbolic culture is so derived. The extent to which music and language evolved together is debated. Steven Mithen (2005), at least, considers this possibility, though he does reject the notion that the 'singing Neanderthals' possessed language or its evolutionary accompaniment, religious thought (see also Mithen 2009). It is a possibility that Lévi-Strauss seems to have imagined as well, and some of his work on myth is indeed written using musical metaphor, *as if* he were writing about music rather than about myth (see also Osmond-Smith 1981).

Neanderthals probably communicated with sound or by gesture, perhaps both. We know rather little about their social organization except that they did bury their dead, though without grave goods (see Tattersall 2008: 89–108). We do know that in the later period of their existence they lived alongside speaking humans, though, and that they had contact. They could indeed have been the first to invent stories that became the world's first myths.

The meaning of myth

The idea of mythology

Mythology, as the term is used today, often signifies much more than G. S. Kirk thought. It is the most complex form of narrative, to be sure. This is not merely because it possesses such power over everyday events, but also because it usually entails rich, and often metaphorical, description and explanation. It is in fact significant that mythological systems have contributed greatly to the richness of language. The linguistic elements of myth enhance creativity, and even if the essence of language is the spoken, at some point in its history, signing was probably more dominant than speaking. Writing, of course, only came much, much later. Mythology exists on every continent, and myths invariably contain complex linguistic elements: sentences within sentences within sentences, animals acting as if people, animals symbolizing other things, deception and logical contradiction. One does not need such things in order to build a pyramid or a cathedral; yet one does need them in order to create a myth. In other words, mythology may lie at the root of all language. Kirk (1970: 42–3) remarks that structural theory in Lévi-Strauss's writings is one of three important developments in the modern study of myth, the other two being, first, the recognition of the significance of myth in 'primitive societies' generally by Sir Edward Tylor, Sir James Frazer and Emile Durkheim, among others, and second, the discovery of the unconscious by Sigmund Freud.

In this chapter we examine, in part, Lévi-Strauss's work on South American and North American mythology, and also his theory of structural relations among parts of given myths. Yet it is wise not to neglect other notable anthropologists, linguists and religious studies scholars who, since the nineteenth century, have written on the subject. Important, for example, are the writings of the Bleek family (e.g., Bleek and Lloyd 1911), who recorded more than 12,000 pages of /Xam folklore (including what is usually regarded as mythology). The question of human universals is also raised, in the context of the linguistic separation of the continents, and therefore the seeming unlikeliness of any diffusion of the myths themselves (which are often quite similar) from Australia to South America or vice versa. This is something Lévi-Strauss commented on in *Totemism* (1969a).

The Bleek family are less well known than some of these other writers, but because it is so rich and extensive, their corpus offers a significant test for theories of myth. It also tests the boundaries of the idea of myth as a distinct genre. Like other Bushman groups, the /Xam did not clearly distinguish myths from legends from stories generally. For this reason, it may be more appropriate to refer to *narrative* more broadly, with myth a special case within this category. The fact that in southern Africa, at least, hunter-gatherers so often merge mythical ideas with other forms of narrative and do not distinguish the two lends weight to the nebulous nature of mythological ideas.

'Myth', with the exact meaning we generally give it, is not a concept found everywhere. Yet myth-like structures, with metaphor, allusion to deities, semi-deities and heroes, unusual deeds that take meaning from opposition to other deeds, and so on, are found on all continents. This universality of the genre is important. Myths and other narratives are passed down from generation to generation, along with great amounts of accumulated knowledge acquired, of course, by individuals within their respective societies. Together, both narratives and practical skills constitute what makes us human. This may be *less* true for humans living in the last 10,000 years or so in the Middle East or Europe, but it is certainly true of *Homo sapiens sapiens* over the majority of its 200,000 year existence. With narrative comes the ability to create, and to understand through speech, hearing and learning, the symbolic world. Symbolism is crucially important in the development, if not the absolute origin, of language. It is the symbolic world, understood through language, that has enabled humans to build up the classification systems through which we understand what lies beyond language. These systems, in turn, regulate vocabularies, grammars and the means of communicating them to and with others. These others thereby acquire both linguistic competence and some practical use to make of it. And through this, we collectively have acquired our skills at manipulating the many hundreds and ultimately thousands of words that enable us to classify things.

Lévi-Strauss (1963: 213–18) argued that myth is crucial to classification. Myth entails the ability to manipulate characters (real or fictitious) in space and time. Through such manipulation, tales emerge and intermingle in a truly human universal of creative activity. The fact that such creative activity is not readily apparent is simply that it has not been a focal point of empirical research. Language, as we know, exists not *just* for communication. It also entails creative endeavour, teaching children and others, learning skills and classification of the world. It implies the reasons for learning and classifying, and these are embedded in social structures. It is a method for the same, and a shared method at that. The fact that myth is part of social structure, of course, has implications for the development of kinship systems, social institutions like marriage and parenting, and belief systems like totemic thought and understandings of the cosmos. In brief, practically everything is enabled through language.

The irony is that this shared method of transmitting knowledge should exist amidst the diversity of 'culture' (including the diversity of languages) that is found on this planet. Language is partly a means to express culture, and in this both exemplifies and creates what culture is for: the passing on of ideas and the formation of new ideas. In a sense, then, the existence of language enables both greater complexity of thought and the enhancement of thinking. In other words, it has an impact on cognition. All this really stems from the development of language as a means to classify, and this was Lévi-Strauss's main interest in it. In prehistoric times there must have been an interplay between the development of systems of classification and the evolution of language itself. Anthropologists tend to take classification almost for granted: it is what humans do, and it is fundamental to culture. To imagine that language evolved separately or independently from culture is simply not plausible. In a sense, much the same can be said of cognition and even of myth. They all go together and provide meaning, each in the realms of the other.

Reflections on a Seechelt myth

In *The view from afar*, Lévi-Strauss (1985 [1983]: 101–20) moves beyond classification to reflect on the relation between ecology and his own version of structural anthropology. One of his examples is a myth told by the Seechelt, a Salish-speaking people of south-western British Columbia (see Lévi-Strauss 1985: 110–13). The distribution of the myth is wide, in that it occurs not only among the Seechelt but also among indigenous peoples from the Columbia River in the south to the Fraser in the north. In the usual, most widespread, telling of the myth, there is a trickster who asks his son or grandson to climb to the top of a tree and take the feathers of the bird nesting there. The trickster uses magic to make the tree grow, leaving our hero stuck at the top. The trickster then takes the hero's form and seduces his wives. The hero manages to return to earth and forces the trickster to fall into a fast-flowing river. The trickster floats downstream and is saved by a group of supernatural women who keep the salmon prisoners. He tricks them and frees the salmon, who then migrate upstream each year, and there the people catch them and eat them.

Lévi-Strauss remarks on the fact that the usual version of the story, for example the Thomson River story, reflects objective, economic reality. However, the version presented by the Seechelt is quite different, and it reflects their own peculiar ecological circumstances. Everything, apparently is backwards. At the beginning of this version of the story, the father, not the son, falls into the river. A woman rescues him. He blames his son, whom through magical means he sends to the sky. There his son meets two old women and tells them that there are salmon nearby. Grateful, they help him to return to earth. Why these differences? Essentially, it is because the Seechelt have no salmon in their territory. While it may be possible that they got the story wrong, it is equally likely that the salmon have to be in the sky because they do not exist on earth, or at least not in the lands known to the Seechelt. They did catch salmon, but only in rivers far from their own country, and often after heated battles. In Lévi-Strauss's view, in mythic thought the poles are reversed: sea becomes sky and lands nearby become lands far away, and the empirical becomes the imaginary.

Myth, then, is not really quite 'reality' at all, but something a little different, though equally logical. The true 'reality' is that the same logical relations among things exist in both. In language, the brain does not actually hear sounds but phonemes, and through them relations between contrasting sets of sounds. Language and mythology, according to Lévi-Strauss, function in the same way. Meaning is embedded *in the relations between things*, not in things themselves. This is crucial to understanding Lévi-Straussian thought in general. It can, in a way, also explain how and why grammar exists: grammar regulates such relations, subconsciously. It does this through rules of 'agreement' among parts of speech.

Dancing your prayers?

In the early days of religious studies, as we commonly understand the field, a fundamental debate emerged. The original theory was that religion began with animism. This was the idea that an object could possess a soul, and therefore that the soul was separate from the body. This notion was argued through, in particular by Edward Tylor in the second volume of his *Primitive culture* (1871). According to Tylor, the most primitive examples of humanity believed in this separation between soul and body, and only later did humankind gain notions of spirits and deities.

Tylor had a long and distinguished career at Oxford, where he was eventually appointed Reader and later Professor of Anthropology. His friend and successor at Oxford was R. R. Marett, who was appointed Reader in 1908. In *The threshold of religion* (1909), Marett argued, against Tylor, that there was an earlier stage than animism. This earlier, pre-animism form of 'religion' entailed magic, and no distinction between body and soul. Its fundamental force was *mana*. This term *mana* in Melanesia and elsewhere in the Pacific identified a sacred but impersonal phenomenon. It could be likened to luck. The force was said to be present in both plants and animals. Marett's concept of religion or 'magico-religion', then, was a wide one. Marett looked to faith, feeling and ritual more than Tylor, who saw all religion more in terms of doctrine.

Like Marett, our contemporary Karen Armstrong (for example, 2006: 3–4) argues the case for religion as action. Through it we derive both myth and ritual, neither of which is obvious or simple in its spiritual 'truth'. The fact that all three of these writers come from entirely different personal religious backgrounds (Tylor, a Quaker-evolutionist; Marett, a Darwinist; and Armstrong, a Roman Catholic) is interesting, but not entirely relevant to their views on this matter. Something else is going on. Each has sympathy with the 'primitive', but their respective visions of the 'primitive mind' are quite different. Their sense of the relation between religion and language differs too. Armstrong (2006: 4) expresses that relation correctly, in my view, when she says: 'Myth is about the unknown; it is about that for which initially we have no words.' Marett had long argued that in the history of religion dance precedes prayer, though never specifically that words came into being only with the latter. For this reason, historians of anthropology often claim that Marett's theory of religion was that primitives danced their prayers, whereas later peoples had words to express them.

Whatever the place of religion in relation to language, it is good to remember a different configuration: the relation of religion in structural-functionalist thought (as in Radcliffe-Brown 1952) in social anthropology. Radcliffe-Brown never made this explicit, but he and his followers saw religion as one of the four *systems* comprising the many *institutions* that make up society. The other three are kinship, politics and economics. Each institution has a place in these. For example, the institution of marriage figures mainly within the kinship system, although it also has functions within political, economic and religious systems. Language is nowhere here, but it is useful to think of it in this context. Language also has a place within the configuration including kinship, politics, economics and religion.

Theories of myth and the purpose of language

The greatest nineteenth-century theorist of mythology was the Indologist F. Max Müller. His writings contain many gems, several of which have at least a grain of truth. 'It is the essential character of a true myth that it should no longer be intelligible by a reference to the spoken language', Max Müller (1881b [1856]: 376) wrote. Further, mythology is but 'the dark shadow that language throws on thought' (1881c [1871]: 590), and comparative philology is the very thing that can enlighten this shady area we call myth. While such views are not commonly held by later thinkers, nevertheless they do highlight possibilities in the interplay between mythological thinking and linguistic expression.

In a way, though, Max Müller anticipated both Freud and Lévi-Strauss in their respective concerns with the unconscious and with language. Freud did not invent the idea of the unconscious, but he popularized it. This is especially true in his monumental, if belatedly acknowledged, work, *The interpretation of dreams* (Freud 1913). Dreaming is the prime example of the unconscious at work. Dreams can be primarily linguistic expressions, or they can be otherwise: visual, for example. They are also fundamentally individual, while reflecting also collective representations or indeed a *collective unconscious* – an idea attributable to Adolf Bastian, Lucien Lévy-Bruhl, C. G. Jung and Claude Lévi-Strauss alike.

The existence of myth highlights the purpose of language more generally. As the theoretical linguist Jean-Louis Dessalles (2007: 28–9) explains, one of the most innovative features of language is that it enables creatures to explain things that are *unexpected*. In his view, this is part of what distinguishes language from primate communication, but I would add that it is also what enables the inventive capacity that is afforded by mythological systems. My view echoes other parts of Dessalles's (e.g., 2007: 42–4) argument, and in particular his comments on the theory by William Noble and Iain Davidson (1996: 214) that language appeared as a result of human behaviour, and not directly from human biology. Noble and Davidson note that language allows for the 'invention of the supernatural', as well as for the investigation of the mind itself and for the creation of a 'past'. All this, in Dessalles's view, is bound up with a cultural revolution at least twice as old as the 40,000 years suggested by material evidence, if not necessarily as long ago as my own suggestion of a symbolic revolution 130,000 or 120,000 years ago (Barnard 2012: 12–14). All this points to a beginning of language, bound up with symbolic thought, mythological explanation and cognitive development, and coterminous with the evolution of humanity itself.

Dessalles (2007: 76) also argues that the notion of a cultural invention of language is 'untenable', and that the faculty of language is part of human nature and has been for some 100,000 years. Ingold's example of the bicycle in Chapter 5 is similar: the faculty for riding a bicycle is not the same thing as the invention of the bicycle. The exact date for the invention of language does not seem to interest Dessalles that much, but the fact of the biological propensity to communicate through language does. I think a symbolic revolution could certainly have taken place before the origins of language as we know it, but this would not render Dessalles's position problematic. It would simply mean that the trajectory of both biological and cultural evolution was leading exactly in the same direction, and simultaneously. In other words, it is not as if we have to choose between biology and culture: they go together and have long done so, throughout human evolution. To paraphrase Dessalles, language is simply a (very) fortuitous evolutionary curiosity. It enables new forms of thought, easy communication and forms of artistic expression, that is, it enables myth, religion and so on. These trigger a seemingly endless path towards greater and greater cultural sophistication. At one level, myth obscures meaning, but at another, it brings it to light. Language, Dessalles (2007: 77–91) says, is not simply a necessary outcome of evolution, nor a slow and gradual process, nor a product of human intelligence, nor the necessary outcome of past evolution. Nor indeed is it just an 'evolutionary curiosity'. Rather, its existence has to be explained through its function, which is to tell myths, to make up stories more generally, to create grammar and to use it.

Lévi-Strauss explores this apparent contradiction especially in his book *Myth and meaning* (1978: 25–33), though also in earlier work such as *Totemism* (1969a) and *The savage mind* (1966). A mythical mind knows this contradiction instinctively, whereas an anthropological mind can recapture this understanding by playing with the binary oppositions, the metaphors and the symbolic meanings that lie behind the readily apparent meanings. The myth-makers may have been illiterate, but they were not stupid. They set out to blur these distinctions on purpose, just as they do today in the Americas, in the Kalahari, and in Australia, as well as in other parts of the world where mythological thought still prevails. *Myth and meaning* is a very short text, originally a series of radio talks he gave for the Canadian Broadcasting Corporation. The intended audience is clearly the general public, and the language he used was English, not French. The talks therefore come alive well to the English-speaking reader: Lévi-Strauss avoids the intellectual complexity often characteristic of his French writings, as well as the long and grammatically cumbersome sentences common in those. Yet, while the writing is simple, the subtleness of the meaning is less so. It also has to carry the weight of the mythology of the First Nations (as original Canadians are commonly called within Canada). The characters described are often animals, but they symbolize humans and human emotions and actions. They also represent human social relations in action, for they possess human form and behave and *speak* as if human. For me, this is what is most significant: language is not a mere ordering of reality. It is reality *reordered*, in mythical time.

In essence, this reordering requires great cultural complexity. Cultural complexity, in turn, means building cooperation between individuals through the sharing of goals and through inter-subjectivity, that is, a shared theory of mind (see Gärdenfors 2013). That is what is necessary to evolve language. This is more complicated than it might seem, since it means that in order to possess language one must share not only simple communication but also a mental capacity to put oneself into another person's mental state. Even if chimpanzees can share emotions or empathy (Preston and de Waal 2003), they cannot quite do this and certainly cannot explain what they are doing: 'Humans can not only know what someone else knows – that is have second-order knowledge. They can also have higher-order knowledge and belief about, as witness: "of course I care about how you imagined I thought you perceived I wanted you to feel". This capacity forms the basis of joint beliefs, which collectively are often called collective knowledge' (Gärdenfors 2013: 146). Ultimately, this concerns the creation of religious belief. Religion is 'cultural', but (like music and language) it is also 'innate' (Boyer 2001: 54, 150–4). It evolved in the brain as part of a desire to shape the world as humans wished it to be. If it is natural and innate, as Boyer suggests, then it forms part of human cognition itself. In its nature, it is also shared. It comes to the fore within language, and even within ritual when it comes to be spoken about – as well as within many other cultural contexts (see also Boyer 1994: 185–223).

The skate and the South Wind

Take, for example, this explanation of the myth from western Canada of how the skate was trying to dominate the South Wind, and along with Lévi-Strauss ask why this was. According to Lévi-Strauss: 'Well, this story never happened. But what we have to do is not to satisfy ourselves that this is plainly absurd or just a fanciful creation of a mind in a kind of delirium. We have to take it seriously and to ask ourselves the questions: why the skate and why the South Wind?' (Lévi-Strauss 1978: 21). Obviously, we have to play the game. The explanation is there if we want to find it, but we can only do so if we choose, ourselves, to adopt the stance of a mythological mind.

Some background is necessary, though. The time of the myth was a time before humanity existed. Animals and humans were not distinct but were creatures with part human and part animal form. The winds blew all the time, and they made it difficult for the creatures to fish or to gather shellfish, these being the activities that provided not only the bulk of subsistence but also the culturally important items of subsistence. Thus the creatures were in a quandary. But eventually one creature, the skate, managed to subdue and capture the South Wind and made him promise to blow sometimes, but not all the time. We are not told the exact details of the capture at all, but we are given hints: Lévi-Strauss reminds us of the characteristics of the skate. Its underside is slippery, but its back is rough. Seen from the side, it is very thin, but seen from above, it is large and highly visible. You could not easily shoot it because it would display its thin form, nor catch it because it would show its slippery surface. These characteristics enabled the skate to demand that the South Wind behave himself and blow less often.

To Lévi-Strauss, the characteristics of the skate are reminiscent of binary properties in cybernetics. This explanation is not essential, yet it does explain a crucial part of Lévi-Strauss's thinking: what is important is that we see mythological thought as a framework quite different from ordinary thinking. I think a better analogy is perhaps with the later Lévy-Bruhl: 'there is not a primitive mentality distinguishable from the other by *two* characteristics which are peculiar to it (mystical and prelogical). There is a mystical mentality which is more marked and more easily observable among "primitive peoples" than in our own societies, but it is present in every human mind' (Lévy-Bruhl (1975 [1949]): 100–1). Lévi-Strauss never really changed his theoretical perspective. Lévy-Bruhl, however, came to see the universal in what he had previously regarded as primitive thinking. That dichotomy is, in a sense, already there too, some years later, in Lévi-Strauss's thought. It is not that there once was a primitive view that becomes less primitive through social or biological evolution, but that this primitive form of thought exists within everyone. C. G. Jung (and others) called this form of thought the collective unconscious.

As Jung put it: 'The collective unconscious – so far as we can say anything about it at all – appears to consist of mythological motifs or primordial images, for which reason the myths of all nations are its real exponents. In fact, the whole of mythology could be taken as a sort of projection of the collective unconscious' (Jung 1971 [1933]: 39). Jung, in fact, attributed this collective unconsciousness to a time before the beginnings of humanity. Although this idea seems quite far-fetched, the allusion does capture the notion that we should be thinking of very early, even pre-mythological, notions that become formalized linguistically once language appears on the scene. It is as if the human mind were already there: anticipating language even before it came on the scene. It may seem trite to suggest it, but the beginnings of both language and myth may lie very early in the human mind, and probably with the Neanderthals too, as much as with *Homo sapiens sapiens.*

Finally, Jungian archetypes

Just as Sir Edward Tylor (e.g., 1871) felt that dreams were important in the very origin of religious ideas, so Jung argued that they were the foundation of consciousness. This foundation, however, in a sense preceded consciousness itself, since both dreams and religious ideas were first formed within the unconscious mind. Jung (e.g., 1959 [1948–54]) amplifies Tylor's reasoning. Jung speaks of, for example, the meaning of the word 'spirit', its existence in dreams and in fairy-tales, the identification of self with cult heroes and with groups. He finds parallels in the development of individualism, and in personality traits. He finds power in the 'mother-complex', with echoes of eroticism. Magical practices and rituals are in the mix too. The trickster that figures prominently through the mythological systems of the world is given prominence for Jung's thinking too.

What is all this about? For Jung, the collective unconscious is a layer of meaning that is shared among humans. It is not specifically individual, since the individual, like Chomsky's I-language, exists almost independently of collective thought. For Jung (1959: 3), collective thought 'is not individual, but universal', whereas personal thought is a 'more or less superficial layer of the unconscious'. He speaks of primordial images existing at the dawn of the human species (1959: 12). However, and although his text is primitivist, unsubstantiated by clinical practice and so on, he does make an intriguing theoretical point in all this. Humans do think via languages, and not independently of them. Tricksters do not exist in nature, though mothers certainly do. The fact that the two concepts can be spoken of in the same breath suggests that they are alike in their form (see Samuels 1985).

Jung first introduced the concept of the collective unconsciousness as early as 1919, and his ideas were developed through later years. The representations of archetypes are just that: representations of things that are difficult to put into language. Language is perhaps almost a contradiction of linguistic intention, it seems, as well as a means to express thought.

Anthropologist Martin Edwardes (2010: 12–13), writing on the origins of grammar, provides a simpler explanation of why language exists and how it has evolved.

If we wish to discover why language evolved, a good starting point is to look at what we use it for today. It is unlikely that, when it began, language was as versatile as it is now; but somehow in the current wide range of uses we may find clues to the original purpose.

On the broadest level, language can be viewed today as occupying two particular niches: cognition and socialization. The cognitive uses for language can be summarized as problem-solving and planning ...

We can also consider language in terms of what we use it for socially. Some of these uses have implications for cognition; but it is in socialization, and not in cognition, that we can see them as solutions to evolutionary needs.

His conclusion (2010:13) reads:

So if we want a plausible evolutionary explanation for grammar in language, we should concentrate our search on the social process of information sharing. The question of why we need grammar is tied to the question of how a social structure evolved requiring the exchange of complex information, and what that social structure was.

On this he is quite correct. The evolutionary trick, though, is in how to transform the requirement for information into meanings that can be both understood and acted upon socially. At some point in evolution one might easily imagine simple grammar, leading to more and more complex usage. But was there a community sitting around, trying to make simple meanings out of archetypes? For me, the magic of grammar is in how it can make meaning out of virtually anything. And yet it does this within a social structure. At the risk of conflating universals, such as Jungian archetypes, with utter specifics, such as the grammar of some particular language, I imagine an almost contradictory scenario. Language did not evolve in just one speech community but in several at the same time.

And then there were languages

The truth is: in the beginning, there were languages. Just as the same myths in South America cross language and language-family boundaries, so too do words and metaphors. It is wrong to assume a common origin for all languages, because it is language itself, in the abstract, which was shared in the beginnings of human society. My belief is that humans have virtually always spoken more than one language. This does not mean that there are no universals, like *mama*, *papa* and *kaka* (the last, meaning variously mother's brother or another close kinsman), for these could easily have crossed from one language to another as humans began to recognize both their close kin and the idea of kinship. Their universality (see e.g., Bancel and Matthey de l'Etang 2013: 69–77) might indicate a shared origin and multilingual communities as much as it might imply a single, original language. The latter is apparently the view of Bancel and Matthey de l'Etang (see Figure 6.1), but the very fact of the existence of such common terms as *mama*, *papa* and *kaka* is at least as likely through borrowing as it is through a point of origin. In other words, I do not take issue with the idea of common origins, but rather with its implications for understanding linguistic diversity. Probably, diversity has always been the norm, whether vocabulary passes from language to language or not. Diffusion is far more likely in multilingual communities than it is in monolingual ones.

The idea of a single origin for language does not necessarily exclude reinvention after this point. It simply means that to think *mainly* in terms of some specific point of origin misses the point. Language did evolve, but really only in the sense that it continues to evolve and re-evolve through repeated cycles of simplification and renewal through changes in usage. As McWhorter (2014) argues, the fact that a language does not have a word for something does not mean one cannot be thinking in that language. In a way, this is a problem both for Whorfian thinking (the focus of McWhorter's recent critique) and for the Chomskyan emphasis on I-language. It also echoes the contradictory ideas of Johann Gottfried Herder: language, in a sense, both assumes the existence of society and imagines humanity without it. Herder put it this way: 'The wild man, the solitary hermit in the forest would have had to invent language for himself, even if he never spoke it. It was an agreement of his soul with itself, an agreement as necessary as the fact that the man was a man' (Herder

(a)   (b)

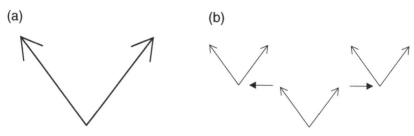

Figure 6.1 Two models to explain where words and languages come from
6a. is the implication of Bancel and Matthey de l'Etang (2013), while 6b is my preferred model

1772, quoted in Stam 1976: 123). As Herder's critic, philosopher James Stam, explains, 'The origin of language is not so much invention as discovery, man's discovery of the world about him. If natural cries and exclamations are expressions of inward feelings, an activity whereby the internal becomes external; language learning is the activity whereby the external is made internal, the appropriation of the outer world within the human soul' (Stam 1976: 123).

It is the same with myth. Myth plays on oppositions, the resolution of contradictions simply through their exposure as contradictions. It is less that language has an origin but more that it, in a way, feeds off itself once it exists. There remains, however, one problem. The most erudite and wide-ranging writings on mythology, such as those of Lévi-Strauss (e.g., 1981) and of Michael Witzel (2012), all assume a great spread of time in the life of a given myth. This is especially true in the case of Witzel (2012: 57–9), who comments on the time depth: 40,000 or 60,000 years. How can myths be preserved for such a long period? How can they be preserved in spite of migrations, environmental factors, indeed changing environments, across seas and continents? And all of this among non-literate peoples, who pass myths one person to the next, one generation to the next, through changing linguistic environments as well as varied natural environments? And of course, mythology, or at least some myths, may be much older than this: as old as language itself.

One possible solution to the problem of the age of myth is to accept the suggestion of a very early start for it at the point of human dispersal. Assuming a very small population, reduced to just a couple of thousand by Toba about 74,000 BP (Wells 2007), this is not unlikely. The earliest myths would have been, in Witzel's terms, Pan-Gaean myths. These are the myths of the creation of humans by a distant sky god, and of the origin of death. There is a parallel here between Witzel's *The origins of the world's mythologies* and Vico's *The first new science* (2002 [1725]). Both see the evolution of mythology and religion on a very grand scale. After the migrations from Africa, we see the evolution of Laurasian mythology which spread from a source in south-western Asia to the rest of Asia and onwards. Witzel looks to the gods, to semi-divine heroes, then humans, violence, the analogy of the universe as a body, the notion of decay and sometimes of primordial incest. These elements, he claims, are widespread in the mythologies of the world, though not found in some of the earliest places to be inhabited, such as Australia, Melanesia and Africa (Witzel 2012: 1–35). As for Gondwana, early habitation was quite different, and therefore also mythological memory was different. Witzel treats this in the latter part of his book.

Gondwana was first colonized by Africans, and its mythological systems do not contain the story-line invented by Laurasians, with, for example, an emphasis on gods, heroes and so on. In a sense, this is the mythology I am most familiar with, since it is the mythology recorded by the Bleek family (for example, Bleek and Lloyd 1911), and that mythology is still with us today in the tales of the Bushmen or San. Their mythological world does not begin with the creation of the world because it takes that for granted, and the emphasis is much more on tricksters who outwit humans. Invention lies within this mythology too, as when the trickster represents the Bushman against outwitting the Afrikaner.

Witzel's ingenious (if sometimes fanciful) theories aside, there must either be something extraordinary about mythology in its ability to withstand such factors as massive migrations or enormous changes in language use. The persistence of the symbolism carried with mythology is also implicated, as indeed is the continuation of the languages that carry all of this through many hundreds of generations. Of course languages change relatively rapidly, whereas mythological truth is much, much slower to change. And although it is not literally true to see a sanguine origin in myth, nevertheless it is as if mythological thought is somehow in the collective mind, or brain, of our species. Lévi-Strauss (1969a: 155–64) praised Radcliffe-Brown (1951) for having discovered a collective mind in seeing the same mythical forms in both Australia and the Northwest Coast of North America, and therefore being on the verge of inventing structuralism. However, it is also conceivable that Radcliffe-Brown had merely discovered a Pan-Gaean myth: the relation between mythical Eagle or Eaglehawk and mythical Crow on these two very distant and seemingly mythologically unrelated continents (a proposition that both Radcliffe-Brown and Lévi-Strauss would have rejected). The two similar birds symbolize similar attributes and sets of kin relations on the two continents.

The prehistorian Paul Taçon (2009: 70), who has worked extensively in Aboriginal Australia, explains and with a quasi-theological twist:

My view is that the world was changed forever by the increased contacts and interactions that occurred among archaic humans across Africa, Asia, and Europe, since at least 160,000 years ago. Further periods of intense migration and contact followed, one of them occurring between fifty thousand and thirty thousand years ago. These contacts would have radically changed group worldviews, regardless of their nature. Whether populations were replaced by invaders 'out of Africa', different groups interbred and/ or there was an exchange of ideas, material culture and technology, the result of contact for all inevitably would have been a changed view of the world and one's place in it. Perhaps in those moments that followed revelation occurred and religious thinking as we know it began to blossom.

Of course we do not know whether this represents what actually happened, but the sentiment is clear. Intense and long-lasting social interaction coexisted for a very long period, and from an era when languages were being invented (and reinvented). Religious ideas, whether theistic or otherwise, were present both in human consciousness and in society. Myth, as well as material culture, was no doubt present as well.

Three possibilities are all present in explanations of myth: (1) myth is a universal property of the human mind, (2) it entails human invention and coincidence or (3) it is passed by diffusion from a common source. Arguments about the origin of language fit the same pattern. In specific instances, there may be room for choice, but ultimately the big theories do require big decisions and a choice among the options.

7   Sexual selection and language evolution

So what does it mean to be human? Well, the ability to tell a story, to narrate, is an important part of what it means to be human. If narrative is going to be truly useful it will have to be involved in choices, and none more important than the choice of mate. This is important for Darwinian reasons, and it helps us understand why language has grown and improved its ability to express to the extent it has done over the last few tens or even hundreds of thousands of years. Certainly this is more likely than a Bronze Age origin of complex grammar, as Mary LeCron Foster (1999) has argued. Foster sees a seven-stage evolution, from australopithecine communication through imitation, to early *Homo* sets of semantic associations (for example, enclosing, inward and female, or projecting, outward and male) to the development of communicative systems needing to express things over distances, and so on. Finally, according to Foster, there is proper grammar in the Neolithic (12,000 years ago and later) and 'language as we know it' just 3,000 years ago. To my mind, this is far, far too late, even if we concede the influence of farmers on foragers late in the evolution of language. Southern and eastern Africa never went through any Bronze Age, but certainly Africa went through a period when myth, metaphor and very complex grammar occurred, and in spite of the need for people to travel any great distances from their place of origin.

Hadza and Bushman hunter-gatherers have lived in their present locations for millennia, and /Xam, in particular, has developed a very complex grammar, including verbal particles to show things like duration and completion of action, continuous action and repetition (Bleek 1928/9, 1929/30). The sentence in which South Africa's motto is contained has about five degrees of recursion, and it occurs in a traditional piece of folklore probably dating from many centuries ago, and definitely not recent. Certainly, there is no reason to attribute it to anyone other than the hunter-gatherers of South Africa who had lived in the Cape area for many millennia. They are now culturally extinct, though related ethnic groups remain nearby. The motto, incidentally, is *!ke e: /xarra //ke*, usually translated as 'Diverse people unite', or more literally meaning something like 'People who are different, joining together' (see Barnard 2003, 2013).

In *The mating mind*, Geoffrey Miller (2000b: 341–91) has written on the importance of mate selection in the evolution of language. This is likely to have been far more important than any Neolithic or Bronze advances in technology or food production. Part of Miller's case is that humans evolved, along with the capacity to develop more sophisticated forms of language, as a product of mate selection. This 'Scheherazade effect' emphasizes the significance of narrative as an evolutionary device. Just as the mythological Scheherazade stayed alive by never finishing her story, so too lovers offer intrigue and words of promise. She (or he) who can tell a good story is a better catch than someone who cannot. Perhaps the story of Scheherazade is not as far-fetched as at first it may seem? If the mythologists of Venezuela or Brazil can spin a myth out to several days in the telling, as often they do, then so too can a mythical Persian queen.

Story-telling, in other words, is a form of sexual display. Or as Miller puts it in another publication:

Human culture does not make much sense as a set of survival adaptations shaped by natural selection. Too much cultural behaviour, such as art, music, ritual, ideology, myth, humour and story-telling, seems so expensive in terms of time, energy and practice costs, and so useless for survival ...

This pessimism is misplaced because it ignores the astonishing revival of Darwin's sexual selection theory in biology over the last two decades. That revival has not been taken seriously by cultural theorists, but it seems to offer their best hope for a fruitful connection with human evolutionary psychology. Human culture makes a great deal of sense as a set of courtship adaptations shaped by sexual selection through mate choice. (Miller 1999: 88–9)

Miller encourages us to look beyond what he regards as the subjective meaning of courtship practices to an objective one of the costs and benefits of Darwinian fitness.

From sex with Neanderthals to compassion: linguistic selection?

Along with sexual selection, we might envisage what we might call linguistic selection, in other words, the propensity for people to choose mates with whom they want to converse. There are many ways to explain this: the desire to make love with a great poet or orator, the wish to use one's own dialect in preference to another or simply the need to find someone who talks the same as oneself. Changes in mobility within historical times, and more recently inventions enabling motorized and air travel, have obviously facilitated contact between speech communities. It is worth some reflection, though, that in prehistory, transport was probably, in general, one way. Of course, early humans returned regularly to their base camps. However, it took early humans and their ancestors a number of generations to accomplish any permanent distance at all. Humans went to Australia, and humans went to South America. It is telling that

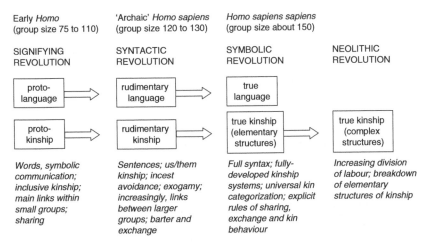

Figure 7.1 The co-evolution of language and kinship

Source: adapted from Barnard 2011: 133

in the latter case there is cranio-metric as well as genetic evidence for a relationship between the inhabitants of the southernmost tip of South America and those of their cousins in Baja California (González-José *et al.* 2003).

In my work on the co-evolution of language and kinship (for example, Barnard 2008a) I considered such issues, at least implicitly. Yet if we take a broad sweep, and look at communication from our earliest *Homo* ancestors to the present, we can see clear relations between the evolution of linguistic phenomena and kinship structures. This is illustrated in Figure 7.1. Here I simply combined work by Aiello and Dunbar (1993) on primate group sizes and their implications for social structure with the work of Calvin and Bickerton (2000) on the evolution of language. I then considered the implications for the evolution of kinship structures.

From initial phases of symbolic communication there emerged an inclusive kinship pattern (Barnard 2011: 132–41). I speculated that social interaction was mainly within small groups, like hunter-gatherer bands, and sharing among kin was the norm. In the domain of kinship, incest avoidance and rules of exogamy will eventually have emerged. When this happened, exchange between groups likely became the norm. Later still, among *H. sapiens*, fully developed syntax and elementary structures of kinship will have come into being. Incest avoidance at this stage was probably regulated by positive rules of mating and, ultimately, marriage: 'One must marry someone of category X'. Kinship systems among modern hunter-gatherers are typically universal, that is, everyone in society is classified according to kin category. In such a system, there is no such thing as 'non-kin'. Rules of kin behaviour, like rules of syntax, would have become increasingly complex. Then in the Neolithic, such truly complex behaviour becomes 'complex' in Lévi-Strauss's peculiar sense of that term (1969b). In other words, 'elementary' positive marriage rules are replaced by 'complex' negative ones: 'One may *not* marry one's sister'.

Exactly when all this happened we do not know. The irony is that we know the details of the evolution of kinship structures thanks to a wealth of ethnography from around the world, and thanks to Lévi-Strauss's theoretical work. The latter coincides almost exactly with the first use of radiocarbon dating in archaeology, although unfortunately neither language nor kinship can be dated by such methods. My gut feeling is that linguists have been too conservative in their estimates for early language. On several grounds, I have proposed around 130,000 BP as a possible date for early symbolic thought (Barnard 2012: 12–14). Language presumably followed this, but a date *after* the migration of a significant group of non-African *Homo sapiens* out of Africa seems impossible. Migration dates of around 125,000 BP have been suggested (Armitage *et al.* 2011), although this is on the basis of the presence of stone tools in the Arabian peninsula. That population, of course, may have died out quite quickly. Genetic evidence over recent decades (e.g., Soodyall 2006) all points to an exodus by 70,000 BP, and this is certainly consistent with the hypothesis of a Toba-induced volcanic winter, around 74,000 BP, and a subsequent population bottleneck in eastern Africa.

An alternative view is that of Chris Knight and Camilla Power (2012). Knight and Power talk of social conditions for the emergence of language, but it is clear that their theory is not actually based on sociology or social anthropology, but mainly on biology. Social factors, though, do include the evolution of egalitarian society from primate hierarchical structures. This happened, they say, through resistance against being dominated: 'reverse dominance' or 'counter-dominance'. Female alliances also played a part, through the evolution of sharing practices. They see the emergence of language as part of this social configuration, but also part of biological pressures such as the consequent development of social intelligence. Ultimately, 'the full transition to language and symbolic culture' (2012: 349) is triggered by the invention of menstrual taboos, cosmetics and the breakdown of promiscuity. In my view, Knight and Power's solution to the problem is ingenious, but it is not entirely convincing. Rather, it takes too many steps, and each step in evolution must work precisely and in the right order. As much as I admire the work of Knight and Power, this particular solution remains dependent on the acceptance of their general theory of the significance of menstrual taboos as the starting point for the evolution of symbolic thought.

A slightly different narrative is presented in Knight's (2010) article, 'The origins of symbolic culture'. Here he emphasizes the fact that symbolic culture is made up of false signals, often with no obvious Darwinian explanation. Since the prevalence of the 'human revolution' scenario (Mellars and Stringer 1989), Knight suggests, four new and less Eurocentric positions have appeared. *First*, as Francesco d'Errico (2003) argues, there is the case for thinking in terms of the symbolic capacity of several species evolving at the same time: *Homo heidelbergensis*, and from them, Neanderthals and moderns. *Secondly*, there is the evolutionist, as opposed to revolutionist, view of Sally McBrearty and Alison Brooks (McBrearty and Brooks 2000; McBrearty 2007). This view downplays the idea of a 'human revolution' in favour of the gradual evolution of material, cognitive and symbolic behaviour. Symbolism and language are both part of this flexible and creative package. *Thirdly*, there is the view that the human revolution was a product of modern human speciation. This view emphasizes the significance of symbolism, and ultimately language, in ordering human life in the African Middle Stone Age. Symbolic thought was not an extra appendage to human life at that time but was becoming fundamental to it. Christopher Henshilwood (Henshilwood and Dubreuil 2009) and Ian Watts (2009) hold this position. *Finally*, Richard Klein (2009, see also Klein and Edgar 2002) maintains a position quite opposed to this one. While accepting the advances made in the Middle Stone Age, he argues that the development of cognitive modernity did not occur until the Later Stone Age (or Upper Palaeolithic). It was due to a mutation in the brain, and this led to language.

Of these, I suspect that Knight's sympathies lie rather more with the views of Henshilwood and Watts than with any of the others. That is my view as well, although I am less inclined to accept Knight's emphasis on female solidarity through the symbolism of cosmetics. That said, it is nevertheless worth thinking about the implications of Klein's argument too. As I stated earlier, a great deal here will depend on exactly what we mean by 'language'. What would happen if we were to grant a form of 'language' to, say, Neanderthals? This is a serious and interesting question, especially in view of the greater evidence afforded to us by recent genetic studies, including the uncovering of both Neanderthal and Denisovan genomes.

The Neanderthal understanding of syntax and morphology might be rather different from ours (see, for example, Comrie 1989). However, this does not mean that they had 'no language'. Quite on the contrary, if indeed they had the same FOXP2 mutation as *Homo sapiens sapiens*, then they almost certainly had a form of language and of grammar. A quite recent book edited by John Bengtson (2008) highlights the problem. Some contributors (Lieberman 2008; Zegura 2008) concentrate on species mixing and therefore the likelihood of the genetic acquisition of a vocal apparatus similar to our own about 50,000 years ago, with the possibility of language at some point earlier. Ofer Bar-Yosef (2008) examines the possibility of an earlier evolution of language and the diffusion of stone tool techniques, perhaps between *H. sapiens sapiens* and *H. Neanderthalensis*, at some point in the early Palaeolithic. Paul Whitehouse

(2008) argues the case for an episodic rather than gradual evolution, with both rapid innovation and periods of stability. His argument is based in part on the virtually instant acquisition of Nicaraguan Sign Language after 1977. It is also based on the notion of alternating genetic bottlenecks with slower periods of evolution among late *H. erectus*, as well as later among *H. sapiens*. This later period was between 200,000 and 100,000 years ago. These events allowed late early-linguistic humans to participate in, and indeed to forge, their own evolution, which in turn allowed us to become what we are as a unique species. This was presumably during Sir Grahame Clark's (1969, see also Barnard 2012: 23–7) Mode 3 of stone tool technology, the African Middle Stone Age, which was the time of flaked tools made from prepared cores.

In yet another development, historian of science Robert Proctor (2003: 213) begins his paper 'Three roots of human recency' with this question: 'When did humans become human? Did this happen 5 million years ago or 50,000 years ago? How sudden was the transition, and is this even a meaningful question?' He continues, noting that: 'No one knows whether speech, consciousness, or the human aesthetic sense is a fairly recent phenomenon (ca. 50,000 years ago) or 10 or even 50 times that old.' The problem is of interest not least because it has an impact on our perceptions of the necessity (or otherwise) of linguistic communication and the means of transmission of technical and environmental knowledge. It also has a potential impact on whether there once was a Proto-World, Proto-Human or Proto-Sapiens, the universal language once spoken by a small group and from which all languages spoken today are presumed to be descended. Of course, Neanderthals could have spoken something else – as implied in Chapter 1. Given that the standard 'historical method' of reconstruction in linguistics has a time depth of only about 8,000 years (see Nichols 2002: 2–3), there is not much at all that can be said about longer reconstructive efforts. There may be more imaginative alternatives, though, as indeed Nichols (1997) herself once proposed in the context of long-term Australian-New Guinea comparisons.

Communication between *Homo sapiens neanderthalensis* and *H. sapiens sapiens*, in any case, could only ever have been minimal. Wynn and Coolidge, though, seem to suggest a lot more. They speculate quite provocatively:

1. Neandertals had speech. Their expanded Broca's area in the brain and their possession of a human FOXP2 gene both suggest this. Neandertal speech was probably based on a large (perhaps huge) vocabulary: words for places, routes, techniques, individuals, and emotions …
2. Many of these words existed in stock sayings, also held in long-term memory, much as the idioms and adages in modern language …
3. Speech depended heavily on environmental and social information to disambiguate word clusters …
4. Neandertal speech regularly used questions, commands, exclamations, and perhaps directional reference (indicatives). The differences may have been marked

with 'aspect' words, or morphological rules. But the difference might also have been delivered through context or change in tone of voice, or even gesture.

5. Neandertal speech was capable of describing new situations, as when they juxtaposed terms for animals and places that they had not combined before (Wynn and Coolidge 2012: 131–2)

Wynn and Coolidge (2012: 130) note that the differences between Neanderthal and *Homo sapiens* speech must have been greater than that between any pair of *H. sapiens* languages (they prefer the usage *Homo sapiens sapiens*), and they point out that both subspecies evolved separately over hundreds of thousands of years.

The 'evolution of compassion' argument put forward by Penny Spikins, Holly Rutherford and Andy Needham (2010: 314–17) is relevant here. These authors speculate on an *initial* stage involving only a brief response to stress, such as hugging. There is, of course, no archaeological evidence for this stage, but it is not unlike what is observed among chimpanzees. They place it between 6,000,000 and 1,800,000 BP. A *second* phase is arguably when compassion was extended into long-term care, and for this there is some, if minimal, archaeological evidence. They date this at 1,800,000 to 300,000 BP, roughly the time period of *H. erectus* and *H. heidelbergensis*. The *third* stage is one of cooperation, including cooperation with someone else in hunting activities, as well as self-sacrifice and the development of close-knit groups. They date this at 300,000 to 50,000 BP in Europe, with the development of mortuary practices and an assumption also of grief among both *H. sapiens sapiens* and *H. sapiens neanderthalensis*. Finally, from 120,000 BP in Africa and 40,000 BP in Europe, there is an extension of compassion towards strangers and animals. There is also a widening of social networks and indeed the development of language as we know it among *H. sapiens sapiens* (see also Marwick 2003). In short, what is suggested here is a kind of co-evolution of compassion and language, each assuming advancing stages of the other. This seems entirely plausible to me, although nevertheless the degree of speculation required is quite considerable.

And along with compassion, there is a need for more effective control over inter-individual communication. By 'inter-individual' I mean not only I-language (the internal or cognitive aspect of language) but also a requirement that speaker and hearer agree on what they are talking about. In other words, that they use the same expressions for the same phenomena. In short, that they are *speaking the same language*. This is, in a sense, a linguistic extension of the emotion of compassion. In order to speak with someone else, one must be able to feel for them: compassion comes first, one could argue, and language follows. In my view, it makes sense to see this aspect of evolution, like many others, in terms of co-evolution: compassion and language evolve together, each enabling greater facility with the other. Rather like Geoffrey Miller in our own time, the great Danish linguist Otto Jesperson (1922: 434) regarded court-ship as the source, but in reality, a complex origin of language seems rather more likely than any single source (see Aitchison 1996: 8–9).

Hand in hand with evolution goes the propensity to mate. Mating is not just sex, but rather it is about the ability to communicate and to have something to communicate about. If generations of part-Neanderthals are born to human mothers, or indeed to Neanderthal mothers, which are physically superior? Which are intellectually superior? There can be no assumption that either is physical superior here, or necessarily even always intellectually superior. So what language will they speak?

Theoretical origins: back to the mind

Chomsky (2012: 11), among others, has argued that in humans language is instinctive. It also occurs mainly in the mind, as I-language: 'Now let's take language. What is its characteristic use? Well, probably 99.9 percent of its use is internal to the mind. You can't go for a minute without talking to yourself. It takes an incredible act of will not to talk to yourself.' Furthermore, it is trivial to suggest that, beyond that, language exists for communication. According to Chomsky,

It is perfectly true that language is used for communication. But everything you do is used for communication – your hairstyle, your mannerisms, your walk, and so on and so forth. So sure, language is also used for communication ... As functions are usually informally defined, then, it doesn't make much sense to say that the function of lan-guage is communication. (Chomsky 2012: 12)

Of course, communities will share a language. Yet what is important to Chomsky is that at some point between 100,000 years ago and 60,000 years ago, in one African individual, a mutation took place that gave rise to the abil-ity of that individual to think what another individual was thinking. This ability had tremendous evolutionary advantages, and in a small breeding population it transformed forever the ability of humans to understand, to express things with symbols and to communicate to others what they were thinking. This is not at all implausible, but it still leaves wide open the real question: what on earth is this individual person going to do with her, or his, ability to communicate with children and grandchildren? Or, for that matter, with the earlier generation? In short, what is language really for?

Steven Pinker, notably in his popular text *The language instinct* (1994), is in agreement with Chomsky, although he sees the process of acquiring this instinct as part of the evolutionary adaptation of human hunter-gatherers to converse. I partly agree, yet 'conversation' is only part of the reason we need language. We need it also for playing with symbols, including sexual ones, and for metaphor, poetry and all the rest of things humans have evolved to use language for. Pinker rejects the Whorfian notion that some languages are better for conversing than others. Indeed, the rejection of strong Whorfianism is commonplace among both linguists and anthropologists today. Probably it is even wrong to attribute the idea to Whorf himself. Rather, what we can say is that some languages better lend themselves to certain forms of expression than others. That seems to be all Whorf (1956a: 85) meant in his defence of Hopi as better than English for explaining nuclear physics: *not* that it is impossible to explain physics in English.

Yet, when it comes to incipient forms of linguistic expression, we are not talking about the ability to discuss nuclear physics. We are talking about the evolution of persuasion, accompanied by love and lust. For this can go back earlier than what Chomsky assumes, perhaps to *Homo heidelbergensis* if not *H. erectus*. That is more or less the assumption of Coolidge and Wynn (2009: 174–6). Among the circumstantial evidence they cite is the considerable size of the *H. heidelbergensis* cranium: 1,200 cc, which is well within the modern range. Broca's area is enlarged. The basicranium of the Kabwe or Broken Hill specimen is more angled than in *H. erectus*, and the diameter of the hypoglossal canal is more modern too. These features imply a longer pharynx and greater ability to control the tongue than that of *H. erectus*. Admittedly, such features do not in themselves point to an ability to speak, but they do suggest a modern speech anatomy beyond that, even, of the European specimens of *H. heidelbergensis*.

Putting this evidence together with that from the archaeological record, Coolidge and Wynn propose these cognitive developments that separate *H. heidelbergensis* from *H. erectus*. To quote:

- Spatial cognition with allocentric perception and coordination of spatial quantity and shape recognition.
- Technical cognition with longer, more hierarchically organized procedural routines.
- Shared attention, required for technical learning.
- Ability to maintain two goals simultaneously (suggests a possible increase in working memory capacity).
- Attentive use of indexical signalling. (Coolidge and Wynn 2009: 177).

Thus to see the world through the eyes of one's lover, in the case of several of these points, enabled a kind of cognition not previously known. Cognition, sexual allure and response, metaphor, poetry and grammar all evolve together. This also makes Darwinian evolutionary sense, as Dessalles (2007: 315–35) argues. Animals do not habitually share food, as this would go against the necessity of competition among them. However, humans talk to each other pretty much incessantly. Feelings, love, altruism and cooperation all come to the same thing, and they all require language in order to facilitate them. He argues further or a three-stage theory of language evolution: from pre-language to proto-language to language. In pre-language, communication is through gestures and vocal signals. This leads to immediate verification that one is telling the truth. In proto-language, words are combined but perhaps without clear rules, and the result is deferred verification. He attributes this stage possibly to *Homo erectus*. Finally, language, with clear syntax, with the ability to convey conflicts in cognition, gives us an ability to argue a case. I would add that, with this, myth is possible: language gains purpose as it gains meaning.

Kalahari origins

Henn and her colleagues (Henn *et al.* 2011) found genetic evidence for a southern African origin of modern humans. A year later, Pickrell and his colleagues (Pickrell *et al.* 2012) pointed to similar evidence for a divergence within southern Africa between two population groups. These are loosely identified with north-western and south-eastern Kalahari peoples, who separated within the last 30,000 years. This time period is, of course, beyond the 7,000 or 8,000 years usually supposed as the maximum at which a language family can be identified. Yet it is not unreasonable for us to suppose that languages ancestral to present-day Khoisan ones were being spoken in southern Africa 30,000 years ago. Non-specialists sometimes erroneously describe Khoisan as a language family. Yet in fact it is not a language family at all, but, as I have pointed out, a *Sprachbund*: their common features (insofar as there are common features) are the result of the merging of languages within a geographical area rather than separating after a common origin. Of course there are many common features. The click consonants, found in all Khoisan languages but very rare elsewhere in the world, are one obvious feature. Curiously, clicks are otherwise found only in Bantu languages spoken near the Khoisan (such as Ngoni, Ndebele, Swazi or SiSwati, Zulu, Baca and Xhosa), and in Damin, a ceremonial Australian Aboriginal language used until recently on islands of the Gulf of Carpentaria (Hale and Nash 1997).

Perhaps because of my own ethnographic background, I have great sympathy for the idea of a southern African origin of humankind. This implies, too, a southern African origin for language in general (though excluding Neanderthal and any earlier forms of language). Or perhaps I should say, for languages still in existence today. This not to say that there could not have been evolutionary advances in eastern Africa, either before or after the development of full language, or that evolutionary influences were not at play throughout the continent. The evidence for a southern African origin is, in a sense, stronger because of the large number of languages that survive, and because of their diversity. There is nothing like this in eastern Africa today.

To take three southern African examples, Ju/'hoan, G/ui and !Xóõ are not only separate 'Bushman' languages; they are separate 'Bushman' languages of different language families. Some of these languages are very precise and even lack general terms for things (Ju/'hoan is like this: there is, to my knowledge, no general word for 'tree', just for different kinds of tree). Others have complex grammars, with agglutinating tendencies (like G/ui). Many possess complicated grammars. All have phonological systems that put any other language to shame. I mentioned earlier that !Xũ has 141 phonemes. Ju/'hoan and !Xóõ each have a similar number, and the linguists who specialized in the languages (respectively, Jan Snyman and Anthony Traill) used to argue with each other as to which had more. Of course, which language has more depends on what counts as a phoneme. For example, do we count each click release as a phoneme, or do we count the entire click consonant cluster? (The latter would yield the greater number.) The actual number of phonemes matters very little. The point of the debate is merely that the number is very large, and indeed also that it is far greater in these languages than in any others in the world. This is not only because these are click languages, but because, clicks or no clicks, the languages can be spoken and understood to a degree that is astonishingly difficult for almost anyone else to fathom. For me the problem has never been in pronouncing clicks accurately but rather in being able to hear in *other people's* pronunciation the precise phonological distinctions being made.

Let us look once again at South Africa's motto in the /Xam language. It was invented by rock art expert David Lewis-Williams, at (then) President Thabo Mbeki's instigation. The idea was to represent both South Africa's ancient heritage and ongoing contribution to humanity. In fact, the sentence containing the noun phrase of the motto reads as follows:

Hé	tíkẹn	ē	/kḁammaṅ-a	há
Then	thing	which	/Kuamman-a	this
/ne	kúi:	'Ṅ kaṅ	ka	
(imperative)	say:	'I (stress)	say	
a	≠kákka	kóïṅ,	tssá	ra χá
(to) thee	say/ask	grandfather	why	(interrogative)
ā,	!kóïṅ			
it is	grandfather			
ta		/kŭ		/ḗ
(habitual action)		(continuous action)		among
//ĕ		!k'é		ē
go		people		who
/χárra?'				
(be) different?'				

(Bleek and Lloyd 1911: 32–3; my line-by-line translation)

The character /Kuamman-a is probably a meerkat, although there is some ambiguity here. In any case, the sentence occurs in a folktale told to Lucy Lloyd in 1878. The narrator had learned it from his mother. My point here is that narrative can be much more complicated than it needs to be in order to describe an event. It has to be, in order to tell a story. Like Scheherazade, /Han≠ass'ō (the narrator here) has a complicated story to tell, with quotations within quotations, with deception, and so on, and with something like five levels of recursion all within this one sentence. /Han≠ass'ō was not trying to entice or to seduce anyone, but the implication is clear. Narrative itself is an emotionally powerful and linguistically complex device that goes well beyond what is required just for imparting basic information. Of course, the /Xam were a modern people and until early in the twentieth century, when their language disappeared, spoke a modern language. Yet how old the sentiments expressed might be is anyone's guess. William Labov (2013: 14–43) reflects on the richness of narrative. Narrative has power because a narrator can portray himself or herself in the best possible light or simply use narrative for linguistic effect. /Han≠ass'ō was able to do that because he knew exactly how to tell the story, with truth and falsehood and even with deliberate errors (see Barnard 2013).

Prehistoric technologies

Crudely, prehistory consists of the Palaeolithic, the Mesolithic and the Neolithic. Theoretically, these three ages, eras or periods are defined by the stone technologies that mark them. More commonly, they are associated not only with stone and bone technology but with features of social organization. This has been known since Lubbock (1865) first used the phrase 'pre-historic times' in the mid-nineteenth century, although the emphasis on social organization as a defining feature is more recent.

The Palaeolithic includes the vast majority of prehistory, from early tool-users such as *Homo habilis*, 2,300,000 BP to the much more sophisticated peoples of the Upper Palaeolithic and Mesolithic. The term 'Mesolithic' is more recent than the others, and its meaning has changed through time. Mesolithic groups, appearing first in the Levant about 20,000 BCE, certainly possessed both symbolic thought and language. The Neolithic is the era of pottery, towns, the domestication of goats, sheep and cattle and agriculture. It began (before the invention of pottery) about 10,200 BCE in the Middle East, around 7500 BCE in South Asia and around 6000 BCE in North Africa.

The dates, of course, are not precise nor coincident across the continents but reflect regional differences in evolution and in the diffusion of technology and lifestyles. Bushmen living recently in southern Africa may be thought of as pre-Neolithic, if only since, like earlier hunter-gatherers, they live in bands and are often nomadic or transhumant. Their continued existence highlights the fact that language has nothing to do with advanced technology but was developed in the African Middle Stone Age. That began some 300,000 years ago. In short, to understand the origins of language and its place in modern thought, it is not to the evolution of stone tools in Eurasia we should look but obviously to the beginnings of the Middle Stone Age in southern, central and eastern Africa. Or perhaps to European inhabitants at the same time and since. They, including Neanderthals, also possessed the relevant mutation in the FOXP2 gene that many associate with the faculty of language.

But what does this really mean? When could language have begun? The earliest exponents of Middle Stone Age cultural attributes were, apparently, pre-*Homo sapiens*. Certainly, Neanderthals were, too. If menstrual synchrony lies at the origin of language, as suggested by Ian Watts (2009), among others, then language would seem to have originated rather earlier too. In his scenario, it is related to the incidence of worked ochre, once used as female decoration to simulate menstruation. One thing is clear, though, from this line of reasoning. Although the family has changed a great deal through history, what it was in prehistory was significantly different. Watts and his colleagues (see Knight, Power and Watts 1995) envisage female domination through control over sex, and therefore reproduction, and these linked to the symbolic domains through kinship, gender, ritual, body decoration and even intergenerational roles. I would not go quite that far, but I would look to such forms of family organization rather than to historical ones, in other words, more recent ones, such as those described by Jack Goody (1983, 2000) in *The development of the family and marriage in Europe* and *The European family*.

A glance at Maynes and Waltner's *The family* (2012) illustrates my point. The authors, both historians, explain in splendid fashion the comparative history of families through the ages. In their preface (Maynes and Waltner 2012: ix), and particularly in the abbreviated version on the back cover, it is explained that the family is not natural but is a historical institution, with its history 'stretching 10,000 years into the past'. That is no doubt true, and their wonderful comparative material makes clear the diversity, and generally, though not universally, male dominance in families. However, what is not made clear is that this timespan represents only a tiny fraction of human prehistory and history. A survey of living hunter-gatherer populations shows us a good deal more variety and sheds greater light on the period during which humanity was speaking or signing. I hesitate to put a figure on it, but a duration of at least 130,000 years would seem reasonable. During that time, hunter-gatherers, living in families, possessed symbolic culture. Speech, signs and cognition co-evolved and did so along with grammar, mythology and a greater level of communication than had been possible before that. It is still worth keeping in mind that technological advances were precisely advances in technology; they were not really 'labour-saving' as we normally think of it. If anything, the goal of technological sophistication was saving time so that it could be used for leisure rather than enabling more work to be done. Hunter-gatherers tend to spend as little time as possible in work activities (see Sahlins 1974: 1–39). Their preference is the maximization of free time, not the accumulation of surplus.

Their tools may have been simple, but, as I mentioned earlier, they enable today the utilization of more than a hundred plant species among Ju/'hoansi of the northern Kalahari (Lee 1979: 464–73). There is mainly gender equality, women do most of the food-gathering and men the hunting, there is bride-service and the freedom of marriage and divorce, there are elaborate customs of gift-giving and work effort is very low. That is because the accumulation of free time is valued over the accumulation of wealth. It is to this kind of group I think we should be looking for comparisons, and not merely to examples from history.

8   Conclusions and thoughts for the future

When I was a boy I invented a language. I do not know why, but for some reason I called it Vieth. I knew that the vowel (or vowels) might prove difficult to pronounce and that the *v* and the *th* might cause similar problems for non-English-speakers. I guess I was about eight years old at the time, and certainly knew no click languages or I might have tried to work clicks in as well. Nor did I know any other languages at all then; and really, I still cannot speak anything else fluently, apart from my native English. A smattering of foreign words and phrases were in the back of my head in those days, and a few bilingual dictionaries were in the house. I loved grammar, it seems, so I set about trying to concoct the most difficult grammar I could, with bits and pieces from all the languages that came to mind. Apparently, such an effort is not unknown to science, though it is more common in science fiction. It has probably been around since Babel, as indeed writers like Arika Okrent (2000) and Michael Adams (2011: 1–16) imply.

The point of this story is that I may not have been at all unique. Nor is this common only in science (or science fiction). In many, many other societies through the millennia, languages are invented, diverge from existing languages, build new and complicated grammars, then mix with other languages through conquest or intermarriage. The process is repeated time and time again. Languages are simplified through the development of pidgins, and then as creoles appear they grow complex again. I had grown up in an essentially monolingual environment while nevertheless being exposed to a surrounding world where other languages were indeed being spoken. Children everywhere invent and reinvent. They do this to show cleverness, to fool each other and to fool adults. And when more languages are all around, it must be much easier. Language for me as a child was a game, and I would assume it is a game at least for some other children as well. For those who do not quite believe that languages grow in complexity, then become simplified, James Hurford (2014: 148) gives the example of Faroese, a relatively isolated language which retains a complexity of cases and genders, whereas closely related Norwegian, much more in contact with the outside world, has lost this complexity. For the latter instance, a similar case can be made for another Germanic language, modern English, which is formed by a mixture of Old English, through Middle English, and which is basically English mixed with Norman French, with little of the morphological complexity of its ancestral language remaining.

The late Anthony Traill, the world's academic authority on the !Xóõ language, once told me that his knowledge of !Xóõ was perhaps 10 per cent of that of a native speaker. His own !Xóõ–English, English–!Xóõ dictionary (Traill 1994) numbers 292 pages, so one compiled by a !Xóõ would presumably take up many more pages. For this reason, as I have said, languages are much more complicated than they need to be. I am hesitant to accept any theory of language origins based mainly on the idea that language is merely about communication. If children can play games with language, so too can adults, and I assume this to be much more the case in non-literate societies than among the literate. As Lévi-Strauss (1968: 351) pointed out some 50 years ago, prehistoric thinkers as clever as Plato or Einstein must have been around more than 100,000 years ago. In his scenario, they were playing games with kinship. Yet, as I have suggested, I think it at least as likely they started with words, grammar, metaphor, rhymes and puns. From things such as these, one can build a kinship system, and ultimately a symbolic system, in other words, one can construct 'culture'. That is also, in a sense, about playing games with language, as Mathias Guenther (2006) once speculated.

Social anthropology and the beginnings of language

Anthropology (and social anthropology, in particular) is blessed with many historians of the discipline: in the United States, George Stocking (see e.g., 1968) and Henrika Kuklick, who wrote mainly on the British tradition (see e.g., Kuklick 1991), as well as their many brilliant students, and in the United Kingdom, there are historian-practitioners like Jack Goody (e.g., 1977) and Adam Kuper (e.g., 1973). The difference between these individuals and similar figures in other disciplines is the continual impact they have within the discipline. Anthropologists tend to be much more conscious of the history of their subject than people in other fields. We revisit the work of Malinowski or Evans-Pritchard not simply as a matter of historical awareness but because the debates that engaged them remain an essential part of contemporary discourse. It is not merely that anthropologists today continue old debates, but that the debates of the past return in different forms. An awareness of the earlier versions is an essential part of the training to be a true anthropologist. These debates are, in a sense, the discipline itself – in a way that similar debates in archaeology or genetics are not.

How did language begin? In birdsong, in chimp communication, through the first words of *Homo neanderthalensis* or *H. sapiens*, in their first recognition of grammar, in gesture, from the transition from signing to speech, in mythology, in simile and metaphor or perhaps in verbal deception? Language could *not* have *begun* in birdsong, since there is no evolutionary connection between birds as precursors and humans as descendants. Rather, any relation between birds and humans must be on the level of analogy. Birds may have some 20 different types of call, each with a different function (see Slater 2012). There are differences between the sexes, geographical differences among birds of the same species, as well as differences between species. Some songs are slow, others fast. Songs are used in different kinds of interaction, and certainly in communication within and between species. Some can even use different versions of the same call, apparently so individuals can distinguish each other. Each of these properties, and indeed others, may have analogues in human communication, even though humans are not descended from birds any more than birds are descended from humans. For birds, think merely analogy, not origin.

My view is that the propensity for language appears in virtually all the other precursors mentioned earlier but that none is itself language. Only the later ones are really language at all. Clearly, birdsong is not, although it can still give us *clues* about the nature of communication in humans. So when did language begin? That is a matter of debate, of course, but it is possibly earlier than commonly recognized.

My method throughout this book has been to employ two strategies common in social anthropology: *comparison* and *deduction*. Comparison is part of the very nature of our discipline. Deduction is more specific to theoretical perspectives defined as structuralist. Non-anthropologists, quite legitimately, use other methods: *experiment*, for example. But experiment still requires thinking through the full meaning of what shows up, and that implies deductive reasoning. Experiment is really no better than anthropology's methods for pointing us in the right direction. How and when language began are questions of debate partly because of the diversity of our very means for getting at an answer. There can be no doubt, though, of the usefulness of language, and its evolutionary advantages. For this reason, we must look to its propensity to encourage social transformation more than simply to a Darwinian reason for its existence. For the former, the presence of the FOXP2 mutation is a start (see White 2013), although there may yet be further revelations from genetics. Figure 8.1 shows the difference between a simple evolutionary model and a model drawn from social transformations, dependent on a biologically derived impetus.

Dessalles (2007: 77) poses another curious question when he asks: 'If language is really so advantageous, then why do apes not speak?' Certainly *Homo sapiens* had the capability to speak, and of course to sign, long before agreed notions of the earliest language. But so too did all other species of *Homo*, as well as, to an extent, *Pan paniscus* and *Gorilla gorilla*. In fact, the fictional apes of Edgar Rice Burroughs's Tarzan novels *do* possess a

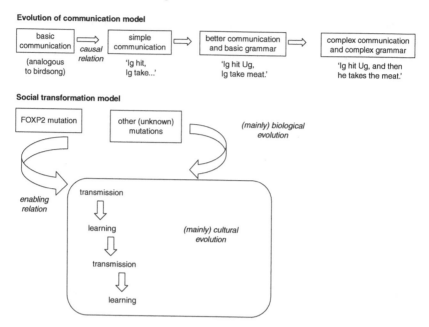

Figure 8.1 Evolution versus social transformation

sort of true *language* (as well as religious ideas and ritual practices). In 1939, Burroughs compiled a 'dictionary' of 'ape' (Griffin 2012: 194–5). It contained a vocabulary of 276 items, each in both 'ape' and English: nouns, verbs and adjectives. Then there is, of course, also the all-purpose interjection *ungawa!*, frequently used by Johnny Weissmuller in his Tarzan films (though that was actually invented by another member of the film crew). This is not to mention the recently discovered capabilities of chimpanzees, bonobos and other higher primates to use and even make tools, which presumably imply the capability to transmit such incredibly difficult and necessarily learned abilities to subsequent generations. Why on earth, then, should apes not speak? If the reason is purely biological, fine: psychologist Peter MacNeilage (2008: 4) notes that human speech requires some 225 different muscle actions in every second of speech. But could apes not at least sign or gesture?

The urge for me to say, 'Well maybe they do speak, or gesture', is very considerable. However, I do not believe that they do. I did spend a short time with chimps in Uganda once (Barnard 1998), and that venture did not disabuse me of the notion. Chimps cannot speak; nor can they sign. But maybe the suggestion of some sort of language among chimps or gorillas implies the use of linguistic skills rather earlier than they were required. Too early for the *necessity* of hominids to develop language! If we assume that the origin of linguistic humanity lies in our adaptation to consuming shellfish (see e.g., Marean 2010), and therefore the requirement no longer to subsist by mainly large, land-based mammals alone, then coastal settlement naturally follows. From early coastal settlement follows coastal migration, and from that the conquest of the world. We did not need language before coastal migration. Perhaps our *Homo erectus* ancestors did not really need anything beyond simple communication either. Rather, language and its richness, that is, its use of simile and metaphor, rhyme and synonymy, alliteration, word-play, complex grammar, etc., all the things that make language more than communication, imply much more. That is why I look to the mythology of the world for clues as to what language *can* be used for. For these clues, we can make sense of the meanings that language enables. Speaking is difficult, and it is unnecessary if one can sign instead. Yet language did evolve into communication through speech, and speech involves the coordination of three distinct systems: the respiratory system, the phonation system and the articulatory system (MacNeilage 2008: 65–87). Only a committed Darwinist could argue, as MacNeilage does, that this degree of coordination could have evolved through the mechanisms of natural selection to produce the extraordinary results it has. Humans needed language, but it evolved well beyond the requirements of communication. That is why only humans can possess it.

Anthropology and contradiction

Anthropology itself, and especially cultural anthropology, is a contradiction. It is a contradiction because its own vocabulary contradicts itself. This comes through, for example, both in Adam Kuper's (1999) rejection of the concept of culture and in his similar rejection of the concept of indigenousness or indigeneity. Culture is problematic on a number of grounds. First of all, it is one of the most abstract of all concepts. Yet it is frequently found in the plural. In modern usage, people do not possess culture itself, but a specific culture: English culture, Scottish culture, Australian culture or whatever. But what is 'Australian' culture? Is it what Aborigines possess? Or what English or Irish immigrants brought to New South Wales in the eighteenth century? Or what has evolved on the continent since then? What about non-European immigrants? Chinese immigrants, for example? Culture is complex partly because its definition is ambiguous, either in the abstract or in usages that suggest specific 'cultures'. For this reason, it is best to avoid the plural if at all possible.

In 'Culture: the indigenous account' (Barnard 2010: 74–5), I noted that even in anthropology, there are many meanings of 'culture': culture in position to (human) nature, culture as what all humans (but not animals) share, culture as symbolic culture, in other words, the thing that distinguishes modern from pre-modern humans, culture as in the concept of culture area, culture as a smaller unit, such as the nation or the ethnic group, culture as subculture or culture as a thing possessed simply by an individual. Some of these are more abstract, some less so, some truly ethereal, others countable things. Culture has to do with nurturing and helping someone to reach maturity, and yet it is what determines one 'cultural' identity. It is a thing of the past, acquired ultimately from one's ancestors, and yet it explains one's own actions within an ongoing, albeit changing, cultural tradition. Indeed, Radcliffe-Brown (1952: 3–5) rejected the idea of culture as a concrete reality or unchanging essence, and substituted the phrase 'cultural tradition' as a way of expressing both the continuity and the transformative aspects of this thing he recognized as nevertheless present. However, this did not really solve the problem. Nor did it convince his opponents within the North American anthropological tradition.

Kuper (2003) also rejects the idea of 'indigenous peoples' and more particularly of special rights for such self-defining groups. For one thing, the definition of indigenous is at least as problematic as that of culture. For another, why should anyone be able to claim rights solely on the basis of their ancestry? And what percentage of ancestry counts? Fifty per cent? Twenty-five per cent? Twelve and a half per cent? For Kuper, such claims are reminiscent of racial classifications in apartheid South Africa, and it may indeed be because of his own South African background that he finds such notions especially repugnant. His critics (including the commentators on his 2003 article in *Current Anthropology*) almost invariably point out that those who claim indigenous status do so from a position of weakness, whereas white South Africans under apartheid did so from a position of privilege. Yet to Kuper, their position is the same. Both white South Africans of the past and 'indigenous' Bushmen are making claims based on spurious grounds, and, in fact, grounds that are difficult to define.

This book is dedicated to the Naro and their language. But would it really matter if the Naro language were to disappear completely? Or indeed to change out of all recognition: linguists tell us that the ancestors of the Naro once spoke a Kx'a language, that is, one related to Ju/'hoan. They switched to Naro (or perhaps rather, to what became Naro) rather late in the day. Or to put it another way, what we now call Naro evolved from a Khoe language in the mouths of some Khoe-speakers, to become 'Naro'. Yes, it would matter to Khoisan linguists if Naro were to disappear. Yes, to UNESCO. Yes, to the Naro themselves, certainly – although virtually all Naro, adults and children alike, are already multilingual. Yes, to me, if only for sentimental reasons: I no longer speak Naro fluently (if ever I did), and certainly I can no longer *think* in Naro. But perhaps that is the point. The ability to *recognize* contradiction is anthropology itself. Virtually all of our disciplinary debates are to do with words and phrases, the way we understand them and the way in which we say we ought to employ them. Our collective ability to engage in such debates is what gives anthropology its very meaning. Indeed, does speaking the language make someone a Naro? If some day the descendants of Naro no longer speak Naro, then do they cease to be Naro at all? This is, of course, a philosophical question, but it is worth some reflection on the part of anthropologists too, and indeed also on the part of linguists.

In truth, when I decided on the dedication, I thought little of the very problem it brought to mind. The Naro are a culturally defined group, but who exactly are they? Like Australian Aborigines, they include people who consider themselves members of the group and who are regarded as such by others. Yet there are Naro, like the famous Morris family who are today prominent in local politics, who are 'mixed'. And what exactly might that mean? If the Naro emerged as an ethnic group out of a mixture of Kx'a-speakers and Khoe-speakers, as almost certainly it did, then what is the 'Naro language'? Was it, at one time, a pidgin, and indeed is this the norm for almost any language spoken in the past? Bushmen are, of course, a collectivity of ethnic groups, and there is no distinct term in any Bushman language that includes them all. Some Bushmen prefer to call themselves San, which is a grammatically incorrect version of what many anthropologists use. Others prefer Kua, some use Ju or Ju/'hoan as a collective term (also the name of one such group), while others prefer Kx'amkakhoe or Kx'amkhoe (which refers to their language) or simply Khoe (with a grammatically appropriate suffix). The geneticist Luigi Cavalli-Sforza (2001: 153) reminds us of what we are dealing with here when he suggests that a gene flow of just 5 per cent over 1,000 years means a possible replacement of 87 per cent of a population's genes during that time. There is, as any anthropologist should know, no such thing as a pure ethnic group, and in a sense, there is no such thing as a pure language either.

In philosophy, the 'later Wittgenstein', that is Wittgenstein (1953) in his posthumous *Philosophical investigations*, is often held up as a key to the perplexities of meaning. I cannot claim to understand it, but the gist seems to be that words do not have meaning except in context. There is no one-to-one correspondence between a word and its meaning, and the latter is derived through shared understandings which seem to depend on both perception and use. The intrinsic argument may be more subtle and certainly deeper than that of, for example, Saussure (1974), although there is a basic similarity: a degree of social interaction and communally recognized cognition, and shared substance of meaning, are implied. Yet building such things into the origin of language, in prehistoric times, entails rather more mutual awareness of purpose than almost any anthropologist might wish to concede to our ancestors. And so, anthropology is not merely a contradiction; it is also an enigma. It is a very big word whose meaning is really quite incomprehensible. Everything depends on what we mean by language, by a particular language at a point in time and on meaning.

Especially in the United States and Canada, the wide subject of 'anthropology' traditionally comprises the four fields: cultural anthropology, physical anthropology, archaeology and linguistics. The four-field subject has been dated to a paper delivered by Franz Boas in St Louis in 1904 (Boas 1904; see also Hicks 2013). Cultural anthropology in many other countries (including the United Kingdom) is known as social anthropology, often with subtle differences in emphasis as well as diverse understandings of 'culture'. That field, along with each of the others, has changed enormously since 1904. Then the field was often known as ethnology and was understood mainly diachronically, with a focus on historical relationships among peoples. The traditional idea of physical anthropology is nowadays commonly replaced by a notion of biological anthropology, whose meaning is much broader: modern biological anthropology includes genetics and often primatology, as well as anatomy through fossil finds. Archaeology is taken here as prehistoric archaeology, since there are also branches of that field that look at historical periods too. Linguistics, of course, means basically anthropological linguistics. This field was not fully recognized in Boas's early work and has since been influenced by great changes in emphasis through time, not least through the work of Edward Sapir. Sapir's writings on 'American Indian' languages and cultures (reprinted in Mandelbaum 1985 [1949]: 167–250, 387–487) anticipate Benjamin Lee Whorf's later supposed romanticization of Native North American or First Nations' linguistic and cultural ways. The paperback edition of Sapir's 'selected writings' (Mandelbaum 1985) remains important, at least in the United States and Canada. In these countries, linguistic anthropology is often still rooted in the Boasian (or Sapirian) notion of linguistic diversity rather than the Chomskyan (for example, Chomsky 1965) notion that languages everywhere are in essence very similar: all containing sentences, noun phrases, verb phrases and so on. Although it is more complicated than that, this is basically what Chomsky's (2012: 59–64) notion of Universal Grammar is all about. And everywhere, linguistics has moved from the philology of the nineteenth century to the synchronic emphasis given to us by Saussure (1974).

Although there have been attacks on the idea of a four-field approach, and generally a tendency for graduate students to concentrate on just one field, the ideal has survived. It has also resisted attempts in some prominent universities, notably at Harvard and at Stanford, to divide into humanist and scientific branches as separate departments. This is perhaps why the relativism of North American anthropology has retained its strength and its exotic appeal, in spite of the influence of Chomsky in mainstream linguistics and philosophy.

In *Social anthropology and human origins* (Barnard 2011: 149–51), I argued against a full incorporation of social anthropology into a new, unified Boasian science of humanity. Yet now, I am not so sure. For one thing, a unification of the arts or sciences of anthropology would make less problematic the difficulty of incorporating social anthropological field research into traditional teaching programmes. One would not have to choose *either* biological *or* social research, *either* linguistic *or* archaeological research, but could combine these as appropriate for a given topic. The feelings of divisiveness and mutual distrust that seem to plague some large North American anthropology departments might cease to exist. These are no doubt caused to a large extent by an excess of postmodernist thinking, and therefore they imply the rejection of much work in biological and archaeological sciences in any case.

Kuper and Marks (2011) date the division to the 1980s, and argue that biological and social anthropologists should now make an effort for greater engagement, for example, by attending each other's conferences. This is hardly difficult: I attended a 'biological' session of the American Anthropological Association meetings myself in late 2012, and learned probably as much about social anthropology there as in any social anthropological session, and of course picked up much more, and much more useful, material from the biological and archaeological areas of the wider discipline than would ever be possible in designated 'sub-discipline'-specific (of any kind) sessions. Sadly, linguistic anthropology is poorly represented in that association, probably for reasons of greater specialization within the wider linguistic sciences as well as because of the separation of them from the other 'anthropologies'. Certainly, the linguistics conferences I attend (mainly on 'origin of language' themes) often have significant attendance and participation by archaeologists and others interested in the big picture, if not by social anthropologists. This makes me wonder if we in our specialization are, in fact, really any longer interested in the interdisciplinary science created by Franz Boas (see Jakobson 1944), and whose implications were taken on by Sapir (Mandelbaum 1985), Whorf (Carroll 1956) and others since.

Towards a reunification of the anthropological sciences?

In the year 2000 the Max Planck Society (*Max-Planck-Gesellschaft* or MPG), overseer of the Max Planck Institutes (MPI) (including the Institute for Evolutionary Anthropology in Leipzig), put together a team. This consisted of three social anthropologists from abroad, plus the five Directors of the MPI in Leipzig and two Directors of other MPIs. The three social anthropologists were Philippe Descola, Adam Kuper and me, and we met privately in a Leipzig café to make up a list of potential candidates for a new Directorship in Social Anthropology. I do not know how the three of us came to be chosen, although it is probably coincidental that we are loosely of structuralist persuasion, as well as interested in evolution.

We drew up our list, and all of our nominees were invited to a small conference, which we attended too. This was held a few months later. While the three of us were in agreement about the kind of person needed for the proposed new Directorship, most of the other members of the committee favoured the appointment of someone of more sociobiological or ethological interests. We argued that in order to represent our discipline properly, the appointment needed a person with proper social anthropological credentials. The appointment was of paramount importance, since the Directorship carried with it the potential to hire dozens of other social anthropologists and support staff, all working together with our evolutionist colleagues. Their disciplines included primatology, linguistics, human evolution, evolutionary genetics and developmental and comparative psychology. In the words of one MPG website (www. mpg.de/eva-en?section=all), 'Scientists from various disciplines work closely together at the Institute: for example, linguists and psychologists aim to discover how languages develop and how people learn languages.' No doubt, all Directors and other senior staff would be eligible for research funding as well, and able to supervise PhD students on a wide variety of topics, including topics combining social and biological interests within the wider frame of the anthropological sciences. The MPI for Evolutionary Anthropology presently has a staff of over 450.

But it was not to be. In the end, Max Planck Society decided that funds were too short to support a sixth Directorship, and funds went instead to the existing Max Planck Institute for Social Anthropology, in nearby Halle. It is impossible to say what might have happened if social anthropology had been added to the MPI for Evolutionary Anthropology's list of subjects. Of course, social anthropology need not be dependent on German government funding. Of course, most departments of anthropology in the United States, for example, include both social and cultural anthropology, and usually anthropological linguistics and archaeology too. Any number of these could have come to the rescue with funding either for a unified science, or perhaps preferably, with funds for specific projects to enable cross-fertilization among the anthropological disciplines. The same is true for several departments in the United Kingdom as well, except that linguistics is usually a department in its own right.

So, what have we learned?

Throughout this book I have argued a number of points on language origins. Some are based on my field experience, some on my training in anthropology, particularly social anthropology, and some on my reading in many relevant disciplines. Let me put it all together in the form of some questions and answers.

Do we know exactly how and when language began? No, not really. However, we can say with some certainty that we were heading towards it, with genetic mutations among our ancestors and the ancestors of the Neanderthals. The FOXP2 mutation was one of these, but it almost certainly was not the only one. Other mutations are yet to be discovered. The scenario I envisage is one of dominant mutations proving extremely advantageous for following generations, a degree of sexual selection for these and their eventual domination in the genome of *Homo sapiens* and possibly in *H. neanderthalensis* too. The earliest mutations may lie even farther back in time, but they became significant when human ancestors were able to use them in communication and in what followed: what I have referred to as the flowering of language (Barnard 2012: 83–103). The invention of grammar was probably rapid, as indeed was the repeated reinvention of grammatical categories as languages evolved and mixed with each other through contact and interbreeding. We do not know when this was, but my own guess is that it occurred at first together with early symbolism, and developed along with the creation of ritual, music and art. And it culminated in complex symbolic thought, mythology and other forms of narrative. This was not necessarily recent: I presume at the very least, 130,000 years ago for early language, with fully developed language in existence before human migrations across the globe around 74,000 years ago. This is rather earlier than supposed by Chomsky (2012: 13–14), who suggests something like 60,000 or possibly 100,000 years ago. It is equally possible that some form of language was in place as far back as 350,000 years ago, before the migration of *Homo heidelbergensis* out of Africa. In other words, Denisovans and Neanderthals had language too, although possibly not a language that was much like the ones spoken by modern humans.

What was the first language? We do not know. Yet in a way, this is the wrong question. It is better to be thinking in terms of a mixing of languages almost from the very beginning. Pidgins are invented, rapidly become creoles as children use them as first languages, spread and evolve and mix again. As they do, they acquire the characteristics of any full language. The rate at which languages pick up and lose grammatical complexity varies, but it is constantly occurring. If there was a first language, then pretty soon there was a second, and a third and so on. And we are talking here about languages in very, very small groups: bands of hunter-gatherers numbering just a few dozen, and speech communities of no more than a few hundred. Comparatively, we know from studies of savannah hunter-gatherers that group size was probably in the order of tens, twenties or thirties, no doubt with a maximum group size of around 'Dunbar's number' (Dunbar 1993), that is, about 150. We also know from recent work in analogous communities that many languages will almost undoubtedly have been spoken, again from the dawn of human interaction. Multilingualism was the norm. Neanderthals had bigger brains than *H. sapiens*, and they could have been multilingual too.

What form did society take? Hunter-gatherers are not nomadic, although they are transhumant. Of course, there are hunter-gatherers on every continent, but it is likely that language began in the human heartland of southern or central Africa. Humans lived then by eating meat as well as vegetable resources. Their diet was varied and included hundreds of species. These had among them large as well as small animals, and fast as well as slow animals, just as among hunter-gatherers in the Kalahari now. The earliest signers and speakers were effective tool-makers. They had hafted spears, and later bows and arrows, though possibly not flighted (modern hunter-gatherers of southern Africa do not use flights on their arrows). They may have used poison to bring down large game (as Kalahari hunter-gatherers do today). They were skilled and inventive, though not innovative, in this the 'original affluent society' (Sahlins 1974: 1–39) which valued free time over the accumulation of resources.

That society also no doubt neither accumulated wealth nor required it, and it probably had means to encourage the redistribution of property, whether through exchange, through gift-giving, through lending and borrowing of material goods, through socially understood sharing mechanisms or indeed through gambling. All of these are prevalent among living hunter-gatherers in southern and eastern Africa. All of these also imply communication about material goods and food resources. Hunter-gatherers have no need to spend their spare moments literally in hunting and gathering. These take far less time than the average Westerner spends in making a living. In Africa, and indeed on all other continents, they spend their time telling myths, legends and stories. To them, the creation and the retelling of these is what is most important, not the truth or falsehood of the stories. That is not to say that they do not conceive of facts in the same way as others, but rather that their significance is not necessarily understood in the same way. It takes a great deal of linguistic ability to tell or even to understand a myth. It does not take that to express a fact, particularly not if it is an obvious truth.

What form did language first take: I-language or E-language? Actually, it has always been both. Humans acquire E-language as soon as they start communicating with their mothers. Humans acquire thinking almost from that time too, and forever find themselves lost in thought. And they form their thoughts with a language (or two). If, as has often been asserted, bilingual people are better at resisting dementia than monolingual ones, it follows that thinking in two languages, or more, is better than thinking in one. Chomsky was right about the constant presence of I-language, but he was wrong that this does not begin through communication.

And finally, are we asking the right questions? The field of language-origin studies has never agreed on what the basic question is. Almost every researcher has their own theory about how language began, and when. That is why we have so many, and contradictory, theories. Yet language did not *begin* just once. It began with proto-language, with the first words, with the process of word-into-thought and with all of these. It was after these beginnings that language evolved, and greater grammatical complexity followed. Then languages dissolved as they became pidgins, which evolved again and again into full languages, and that process began many times over. The process has continued and still continues to this day. We are really looking for a single point of origin that does not easily exist. Everything, in fact, depends on what we mean by 'the origin of language'. We know that the origins were in prehistory, but the question of when exactly will have different answers depending on what we see the point of origin to have been. Language, in short, has many points of beginning. It is about as easy to define as the length of a piece of string.

To sum up

Derek Bickerton (2014: 258) sums up what he found in writing his most recent book in this way: 'Perhaps the most reassuring thing I found out in the course of writing this book was that in trying to explain how humans evolved, almost everybody was right about something. Few of the factors that were mentioned in the literature didn't fit into the story somewhere.' Much the same is true about how language evolved.

We do know quite a bit about the origins of language:

1. There are linguistic universals and therefore that language had to have begun before modern humans populated the earth. In other words, it preceded the migrations of our species across the globe. When humans first arrived in Australia, they arrived with language, having used it on their migration and after their fortuitous settlement of the continent.
2. That being the case, and since modern *Homo sapiens sapien*s spread from eastern Africa, we can assume it began there, or possibly in southern Africa, before human expansion and dispersal.
3. There were once many more languages in the world than there are today. We have plenty of evidence as to how languages come to be complex, and, through the study of pidgins and creoles, how they become simplified and quickly grow, in the hands of native speakers, to become complex once more.
4. We have similar evidence as to how many languages an individual might speak. We also know that our ancestors were not people like us, living in large groups, in essentially monolingual and literate environments. They were pure hunter-gatherers. They lived in small bands, and they came from many places, and their languages and dialects had diversity too.

Multilingualism was the norm, and multilingual peoples were made up of individuals from different linguistic backgrounds, whose groups intermarried and passed on both their genes and their linguistic diversity.

5. We can assume that linguistic sophistication was valued at least as much in the past as today. With the growth of material culture and with its transmission through the generations, humankind became more technologically sophisticated. Symbolic culture replicated this. The poets of the past spread their words and also their learning, just as they spread their material artefacts. The Middle Stone Age succeeded the Old Stone Age, and, just as surely, the Later Stone Age succeeded that. If language had not been formed by the early part of the Middle Stone Age, then by the end of that period, it certainly was.

6. Mythology occurs on every inhabited continent, and often even the same myths occur. Myth is as much part of being human as is the oblique and obscure truths it tells. Arguably at least, humanity thinks through its myths, and we have been doing this since symbolic thought began in the Middle Stone Age. That age is fundamental to human existence as we know it, and we must date language, along with myth, symbolism, art and religion, and no doubt much else too, to around this time. Some say we might even date it earlier, with the use of symbols evolving before their verbal expression. In other words, we might be able to look back to the Late Palaeolithic for the first symbols and the first words.

Mythology may not mark the very beginnings of everything, but it is certainly a good place to start in our quest for the origins of language. It is also a useful place to expect contributions from social anthropology, which still remains absent from discussion of this fundamental question. However, it is an open question as to whether the beginnings of mythology, or indeed some precursor, like simply telling the events of a hunt or other revelations, preceded mythology as we know it. Some hunter-gatherer groups, such as the Naro, simply do not distinguish between 'myths' and any other 'stories'. In spite of an extremely rich and complex language, all stories are described by the same term. They are all *huane* (singular, *hua*).

To put it all together, we might think of the key points of language evolution as the four Ms: *mutation, multilingualism, myth* and *migration*. Included in *myth*, in a sense, is sexual selection. One recent set of authors (Martin *et al.* 2014) might also throw in a fifth M, namely *mindfulness*: the thing that is lost when immediate-return hunter-gatherers (and all others) make the transition to delayed-return economic structures. Immediate-return hunter-gatherers live hand to mouth, whereas delayed-return ones, just like cultivators, must plan ahead and therefore think differently. It could not be simpler: immediate-return hunter-gatherers represent virtually no branch of humankind today but they were the norm through the vast majority of human evolution, and before that, in the time of animals. Therefore, we should not assume that language began with people like us. Rather, it began with people who *became* like us. The dawn of language is like Ingold's (2000: 374–6) bicycle, it is something which humans came into being *ready* to ride: neither quite an instinct nor quite an invention, but a bit of both.

Glossary

Aboriginal	Relating to the original population of Australia. First settlement is commonly dated between 60,000 and 40,000 BP, earlier than *Homo sapiens* in the Middle East or Europe.
accumulation mode of thought	My term for an ideology emphasizing the acquisition of property. This ideology is Neolithic and post-Neolithic. The opposite is the **foraging mode of thought**.
African Eve	A hypothetical mitochondrial ancestor of all humans, purported to have lived in Africa some 130,000 years ago. See also **Y-chromosomal Adam**.
agamy	A rule permitting marriage either inside or outside. Marriage within a group is called **endogamy**, and marriage outside of a group is known as **exogamy**.
agent	In grammatical theory, the person or thing that is the cause of an action. Compare **patient** and **thematic relation**.
allele	In genetics, an alternative form of a gene located at a specific position on a chromosome. It is analogous to an **allophone** in a sound system.
allocentric	Perceiving from a perspective other than one's own.
allophone	A sound that occurs as an alternative within a sound system, either as different dialect choices or according to phonetic rules. For example, in English [p]and [pʰ] are two allophones of /p/. They differ in that the aspirated form occurs initially, and the unaspirated form if preceded by an [s]. Thus, the /p/ in [pʰɪt] and [spɪt] differ in that the former is aspirated and the latter (preceded by an [s]) is not. See **phonetics, phonology**.
articulatory system	That of speech production. This involves a significant number of elements: voice, muscle coordination, and so on.

australopithecines (*Australopithecus*)	The genus which includes 'gracile' forms such as *A. africanus* and 'robust' forms such as *A. robustus* (*Paranthropus robustus*). Australopithecines lived in eastern and southern Africa from about five million to about one million years ago.
avoidance relationship	A kin relationship with required deference and respect, for example commonly between in-laws or among opposite-sex siblings. The opposite is a joking relationship.
balanced reciprocity	Marshall Sahlins's term for exchanges of resources or goods on an equal basis. Cf. **generalized reciprocity, negative reciprocity**.
behavioural modernity	The set of cultural and behavioural traits common to modern humans but not to earlier ancestors. These traits include, among others, language, mythology, religion and art.
Blombos Cave	South African Indian Ocean coastal site excavated by Chris Henshilwood, Francesco d'Errico and others. Important for etched pieces of red ochre (dating from 77,000 BP) and for very early beadwork.
bottleneck	A rapid and significant reduction in the size of a population, due to an event such as a volcanic eruption or an earthquake. It can result in a **founder effect** and resulting genetic drift.
BP	The abbreviation for 'Before Present'. When used as a precise dating measure, it is taken to mean the year 1950 (when radiocarbon dating became practicable).
bride-service	The custom whereby a man performs services, such as hunting, for his parents-in-law. It is common among hunter-gatherers and often lasts for a few years after marriage.
Broca's area	The part of the brain associated with the production of speech and also related to speech comprehension. It lies in the frontal lobe of the dominant (left) hemisphere. Cf. **Wernicke's area, 'Mead's Loop'**.

Brodmann area	A complex area of the left hemisphere of the brain. It is associated with phonological and semantic fluency.
Broken Hill	The site of 'Rhodesian Man', the *Homo heidelbergensis* fossil discovered in a mine in then Northern Rhodesia in 1921. The name is derived from a similar mine in Australia, and the Zambian town is now called Kabwe.
Campi Flegrei	An underwater volcano near Naples. It has been argued that its eruption in about 39,000 BP led to the extinction of the Neanderthals.
capacity for language	The natural ability for humans to develop language both in terms of speaking and in terms of understanding. This capacity, many claim, lies at the biological root of language.
carbon-14	A dating method used by archaeologists to estimate the age of carbon-containing material such as bones, artefacts or charcoal. It is based on the rate of decay of the radioactive isotope of carbon of that name, found in minute quantities along with non-radioactive carbon isotopes.
chromosome	A cellular structure of DNA.
click languages	Languages of southern and central Africa that, famously, contain 'clicks'. These are ingressive consonants (produced by sucking air in rather than blowing out). The consonants are represented by these symbols, from front to back of the mouth: ⊙, /, ≠, // and !, respectively bilabial, dental, alveolar, lateral and retroflex.
click release	The sound immediately following or pronounced simultaneously with a click. For example, the click ! may be released onto a glottal fricative /x/ or nasalized, written either /n!/ or /!n/.
cognates	Two or more words derived from the same original word. They often retain the same meaning, although since meanings can change this is not always the case, for example, English *dish* and German *Tisch* (table). They often sound the same, although through sound shifts these can change too, for example English *heart* and Latin *cardia* (heart).

collective consciousness (collective representation)	Any of the collective understandings which people in a given community or society share. The term is derived from Durkheimian sociology.
collective unconscious	An idea attributable to Adolf Bastian, Lucien Lévy-Bruhl, C. G. Jung and Claude Lévi-Strauss alike. It emphasizes the unconscious, as in dreams, and is sometimes seen in opposition to Emile Durkheim's notion of the **collective consciousness**.
competence	Noam Chomsky's earlier term for the idealized aspect of language: the ability to speak a language and to determine the grammaticality of an utterance. Cf. **performance**.
complex structure	Lévi-Strauss's term for a kinship structure which has negative marriage rules. For example, one must marry someone not classified as a brother or sister. See also **elementary structure**.
core	In archaeology, a stone from which flakes are removed to produce a tool.
creole	A fully formed language that results from a pidgin being spoken as a first language. See also **pidgin**.
Cro-Magnon	Early modern humans of Europe, from a site in southern France excavated in 1868.
cross-cousin	Father's sister's child or mother's brother's child. Cf. **parallel cousin**.
cross-relative	A collateral relative related through an opposite-sex sibling link.
Crow-Omaha structure	Lévi-Strauss's term for a kinship structure which has either a 'Crow' or an 'Omaha' terminology (i.e., one in which given kin terms are applied to entire lineages, matrilineal for 'Crow' or patrilineal for 'Omaha'), and in which the marriage prohibitions extended through such lineages are so extensive that the 'complex' structure comes to resemble an 'elementary' one.
culture area	A geographical region comprising peoples of similar culture.

culture circle	A cluster of related culture traits, or the geographical area where they are found. The idea is fundamental to German-Austrian diffusionists, who saw these circles as spreading progressively over earlier culture circles. From the German *Kulturkreis*.
culture-historical archaeology	Traditional archaeological theory that defines ethnic groups through their material culture. Largely superseded by processual archaeology in the 1960s.
Darwinian	Referring to the ideas of Charles Darwin (1809–82). Specifically, the notion that evolution is through **natural selection**. Cf. **Lamarckian**.
deaf community sign language	A group of deaf people who share the same sign language. The community is not a natural group but made up of people brought together, for example at an educational institution. Cf. **village sign language**.
delayed-return	James Woodburn's term for the economic and social system of 'advanced' hunter-gatherers and non-hunter-gatherers, where time is invested in planning ahead in subsistence activity. The opposite of **immediate-return**.
demonstrative	Specifying the person or thing being referred to.
Denisova Cave	A cave in the Altai Mountains of southern Siberia, home to the **Denisovans**. It was occupied from about 50,000 to 30,000 BP. It is presently being excavated.
Denisovans	A recently discovered hominin species, as yet unnamed, that are descended from *Homo heidelbergensis*. There is evidence of interbreeding with Neanderthals and *H. sapiens* about 40,000 years ago.
descriptive and structural linguistics	Older approaches in linguistics, based on language diversity and emphasis on the structures of particular languages. These are based respectively on the ideas of Leonard Bloomfield and Ferdinand de Saussure.

diffusionism	The diachronic theoretical perspective that stresses migration and diffusion of cultural ideas, rather than evolution.
diglossia	The ability to speak two languages, but with the interesting twist that each is used for a different purpose. For example, one is employed for everyday use and the other for technical use.
discourse	In the social sciences, the term often refers to a body of knowledge or the use of that knowledge, such as in structures of power. In linguistics, a unit of speech longer than a sentence.
DNA	Deoxyribonucleic acid, the substance which contains genetic information. See also **mtDNA, Y-chromosome DNA**.
Early Stone Age (ESA)	Southern African designation of the Palaeolithic, usually assumed to be prior to the invention of art, ritual, language, etc. (the Middle Stone Age). Also called the Earlier Stone Age.
eidos	The form or structure of a cultural tradition. See also **ethos**, which in a sense is its opposite.
Eland Bull Dance	A dance performed by several groups of Kalahari Bushmen, in which a man representing a male eland 'chases' women around the dance fire. It is performed at the time of the female initiate's first menstrual period, and from then on the girl is free to marry.
E-language	Noam Chomsky's term for the external or spoken aspect of language. Cf. **I-language** and **P-language**.
elementary structure	Lévi-Strauss's term for a kinship structure which has positive marriage rules. For example, one is obliged to marry into the category that includes the cross-cousin. The opposite is a **complex structure**. See also **Crow-Omaha structure**.
endogamy	Marriage within a group. (Marriage outside of a group is known as **exogamy**, and a rule permitting marriage either inside or outside a group is called **agamy**.)
Eolithic	A former name for the presumed 'Dawn Stone Age'. It has been replaced by the term **Palaeolithic**.

episodic memory	The memory of events. The relation between episodic memory and autobiographical memory is complex, but broadly the collection of one's episodic memories makes up one's autobiographical memory. This differs from **semantic memory**. See also **mimetic**.
ethos	The distinctive character of an event or a cultural tradition. The opposite is the **eidos**, which represents its form or structure.
evolutionism	In biology, the theory that 'higher' organisms evolve from 'lower' forms. In social anthropology, the diachronic perspective that stresses change for the better or advancement from simple to complex. In contrast to a 'revolutionist' perspective, the term can also refer to slow as opposed to rapid change of this kind. Cf. **diffusionism**.
exaption	A change in the function of a trait. For example, the feathers of birds may have evolved for temperature regulation but later took on the function of enabling flight.
exogamy	Marriage outside of a group. (Marriage within a group is known as **endogamy**, and a rule permitting marriage either inside or outside a group is called **agamy**.)
expensive tissue hypothesis	The hypothesis, formulated by Leslie Aiello and Peter Wheeler, that the ability to digest meat led to an expansion of the brain.
faculty of language	See **language faculty**.
fitness	In Darwinian theory, a measure of the reproductive success of an individual in passing on their genes to successive generations.
five modes	Sir Grahame Clark's set five forms of lithic technology from simple choppers to complex (combining stone with wood and leather or grass) artefacts. Because it is more precise, some archaeologists use this classification in preference to traditional periods or geographical names such as Lower Palaeolithic or Oldowan. See **Modes 1, 2, 3, 4, 5**.
flaked tool	A tool made by striking it from a prepared core.
foraging mode of thought	My term for an ideology emphasizing *not* the acquisition of property, but foraging and sharing. Sometimes known as the **hunter-gatherer mode of thought**. This ideology is common among hunter-gatherers. The opposite is the **accumulation mode of thought**.

Foucauldian	Referring to the ideas of Michel Foucault, especially **discourse**.
founder effect	A loss of genetic variation which occurs as a result of migration and the establishment, by a small number of individuals, of a new population. See also (population) **bottleneck**.
FOXP2	A gene that controls brain and lung development. In humans it also controls speech and the ability of the brain to formulate complex rules of grammar. A FOXP2 mutation during the evolution of *Homo* is believed to be partly responsible for the development of humankind's linguistic abilities.
full language	In contrast to **proto-language**, language with complete grammar and highly developed for communication.
generalized reciprocity	Marshall Sahlins's term for freely giving resources or goods without the expectation of return. Cf. **balanced reciprocity**, **negative reciprocity**.
generative grammar	The set of rules that generates all and only the sentences that are grammatical in a particular language.
genetic distance	In biology, the distance in time between two related species or two population groups. In linguistics, a similar distance between two related languages.
genetic drift	Random fluctuation in the frequency of alleles from generation to generation.
genome	The sum of the genetic information encoded in the genes, chromosomes, etc. of an individual, using genetic mapping and DNA sequencing.
gesture	Non-verbal forms of communication, i.e., communication through finger, hand, arm or body movement.
giving environment	Nurit Bird-David's term for the environments of hunter-gatherers, where the forest or desert gives rather than takes resources.
glottochronology	A lexicostatistical method based on the assumption that words are lost at a common rate, and therefore that the time between the divergence of two related languages, or linguistically genetic distance, can be measured.

Gondwana	According to Michael Witzel, the common source of the mythologies of most of Africa and of Australia and the Andaman Islands.
grammaticalization theory	This is the idea that language evolves as humans become more creative with grammar. The process is not driven by conscious thought but by an evolutionary mechanism within the **capacity for language** itself.
hafting	The attachment of stone to wood artefacts, for example by tying a spear point to a spear handle with leather straps or by inserting it in a slit in the handle.
historical particularism	In archaeology, the school of thought based on the search for evolutionary and diffusionist relations among social groups.
Holocene	The present geological epoch. It followed the Pleistocene, about 10,000 years ago.
hominids (Hominidae)	In present usage, the Linnaean family that includes great apes and humans. In earlier usage, it was employed for *Homo* and immediate ancestors.
hominins (Hominini)	The Linnaean tribe that includes humans and human ancestors. In present usage, it includes australopithecines, but used to be defined more narrowly.
Homo	The genus to which humans belong. All *Homo* are considered, in the broadest sense, 'human'.
Howiesons Poort	An advanced Middle Stone Age cultural tradition that includes hafted microlithic artefacts and the use of ochre, roughly 66,000 to 59,000 BP.
historical linguistics	The study of the historical relations between or among languages.
human revolution	The term employed in 1964 by Charles Hockett and Robert Ascher for the revolutionary set of biological and technological advances that gave rise to humanity, as distinct from the apes. The term is sometimes used today for more recent advances, such as the 'symbolic revolution'.

hunter-gatherer mode of thought	My term for an ideology emphasizing *not* the acquisition of property, but foraging and sharing. Sometimes known as the **foraging mode of thought**. This ideology is common among hunter-gatherers. The opposite is the **accumulation mode of thought**.
Hxaro or *xaro*	An exchange system found among the Ju/'hoansi and some other groups in southern Africa. Individuals give non-consumable possessions upon request, and reciprocity follows at some interval later. This system of delayed **balanced reciprocity** overlies a system of **generalized reciprocity** of rights to hunt or gather in one's *xaro* partner's land. The average number of *xaro* partners among the Ju/'hoansi is 16. (*Xaro* is the correct spelling, but the usage *hxaro* is well established in the literature.)
hyoid	A horseshoe-shaped bone under the chin, which, arguably, is similar in *Homo sapiens sapiens* and Neanderthals.
I-language	Noam Chomsky's term for the internal or cognitive aspect of language. Cf. **E-language** and **P-language**.
immediate-return	James Woodburn's term for the economic and social system of small-scale hunter-gatherers, where time is *not* invested in planning ahead in subsistence activity. The opposite of **delayed-return**.
incest	In social anthropology, sex with a member of a prohibited category of relative (not necessarily with close kin).
indexical	In contrast to symbolic (arbitrary), acquiring meaning through natural, associational or metonymic relations. For example, a crown represents sovereignty not in a totally arbitrary way, but as a physical manifestation of the status and power it implies.
interpretivism	Anti-structuralist, anti-scientistic perspective that uses the analogy that cultures are like languages in that they can be 'translated', one to another.
inverse *mafisa*	Thomas Widlok's term for the Hai//om custom which operates in the reverse manner of the Tswana practice of *mafisa*. A purported hunter-gatherer secretly leaves his goats with an Owambo patron to look after, and the latter gets to keep any offspring produced. Thus the rich get richer at the expense of the poor.

Iron Age	In most of Africa, the age associated with the coming of agriculture and with the Bantu-speaking populations and their migrations. Elsewhere, the age of iron-using populations, following the Bronze Age, from about 1300 BCE.
joking relationship	A kin relationship with permitted licence and informality, for example among same-sex siblings. The opposite is an **avoidance relationship**.
Kabwe	A town in central Zambia formerly known as Broken Hill. The location of the discovery of 'Rhodesian Man'.
Kanzi	A male bonobo (born 1980) who was trained to use a customized keyboard containing lexigrams. He also acquired American Sign Language from watching videos.
Kapthurin	A site of early ochre use in Kenya, dating to the Acheulean to Middle Stone Age transition period.
Kebara	Site of a Neanderthal burial in Israel, dating to about 60,000 BP.
kin selection	The idea, according to W. D. Hamilton, that people (and animals) favour their biological kin above others. This leads to notions of sacrifice for the good of one's relatives, though at the expense of one's own interests.
Koko	A female gorilla (born 1971) who was trained to use American Sign Language and acquired at least 375 signs.
Lake Mungo	A site, in New South Wales, of early habitation in Australia. The site includes evidence of both burial and cremation. Its dating is in dispute, but the date is by around 40,000 BP.
Lake Toba	See **Toba**.
Lamarckian	Referring to the ideas of Jean-Baptiste Lamarck (1744–1829). Specifically, the notion that acquired characteristics may be inherited. Cf. **Darwinian**.
language faculty	The ability to use language. Related to **I-language**, especially in Noam Chomsky's notion of Universal Grammar. This is the internal, biological aspect of language which enables linguistic thought.
language family	A group of languages that share descent from the same ancestral language. See also **proto-language**.

langue	Ferdinand de Saussure's term for language in the sense of linguistic structure or grammar. By analogy, this can be the 'grammar' of culture as well as of language proper. Cf. **parole**.
Later Stone Age (LSA)	The term employed in southern Africa for the most recent stone tool traditions and associated social organization. It comprises modern hunter-gatherers and herders of southern Africa whose lifestyles pre-date the arrival of Iron Age Bantu-speaking populations.
Laurasian	According to Michael Witzel, the common source of South American, Eastern, Indic and European mythologies.
level of intentionality	In psychology, one of the five or six levels of theory of mind. Second-level intentionality, for example, is believing (first level) that someone else believes (second level) something. See also **theory of mind**.
lexical	Pertaining to words (lexemes).
lexicostatistics	A quantitative method employed in comparing the retention of words in languages derived from a common source. Cf. **glottochronology**.
lexigram	A symbol that represents a word.
linguistic anthropology	A synonym for anthropological linguistics. Dell Hymes (1927–2009) championed the phrase 'linguistic anthropology', since it highlighted the place of linguistics within a wider discipline of anthropology.
Lower Palaeolithic	Early period of the Palaeolithic, roughly from 2,600,000 to 100,000 BP. The period of the *Homo erectus* Out of Africa migrations. See also **Oldowan**.
mafisa	The traditional Tswana practice in which a pastoralist leaves his cattle or goats with a client to look after. In return for looking after the animals, the client is allowed to take milk and to eat the remains of animals that die under his care. Sometimes, the patron, upon his return, would give his client a calf or two in payment for his service. Cf. *inverse* **mafisa**.

material culture	The artefacts created by people according to presumed cultural traditions, for example, stone tools uncovered by archaeologists, or the material aspects of cultural life recorded by ethnographers.
matriarchal	Under authority of the mother. Compare **patriarchal**.
matrilateral cross-cousin marriage	Marriage of a man to his mother's brother's daughter. Unlike **patrilateral cross-cousin marriage**, this common form of marriage aligns kin groups and, when repeated, creates a hierarchical relation among them: either the givers of wives are superior to the takers of wives, or vice versa.
matrilineal descent	Descent through females (mother to children). Also known as **uterine descent**.
matriliny	Descent through females. (See also **matrilineal descent**.)
'Mead's Loop'	The ability of humans (and possibly human ancestors) to see things from another person's point of view. Neurologically, it is effected in Broca's area of the brain. It is named after sociologist G. H. Mead, who recognized the social nature of inter-subjective communication.
meme	Richard Dawkins's term for a unit of culture: an idea or behaviour transmitted between individuals within culture. It is analogous to **gene** (within genetics).
memetic	Relating to the theoretical study of memes. Based on ideas in Richard Dawkins's (1976) book *The selfish gene*. (Not to be confused with **mimetic**.)
Mesolithic	The European and Asian stone tool tradition between the Palaeolithic and the Neolithic. The term means 'middle stone age', but is not to be confused with the southern African Middle Stone Age, which is roughly the equivalent of the European Upper Palaeolithic.
metaphor	An analogy or relation of similarity across different levels of meaning. A metaphor is literally untrue (for example, 'The man is a pig').

microlith	A tiny stone tool such as a small projectile point. Significant because these are often assumed to be part of a more complex tool, such as an atlatl or spear-thrower.
Middle Palaeolithic	Middle period of the Palaeolithic, roughly from 300,000 to 30,000 BP. The period associated with Neanderthals in Europe and with the emergence of modern *Homo sapiens* in Africa.
Middle Stone Age (MSA)	The southern African stone tool tradition, around 300,000 to 50,000 BP. Associated with early modern and modern humans, and the symbolic revolution. Abbreviated MSA.
mimetic	Pre-linguistic, symbolic activities such as ritual activities and dance. Attributed by Merlin Donald to **Homo erectus**. (Not to be confused with **memetic**.)
mimesis	The noun form of **mimetic**.
minimalist program(me)	The idea of linguistics as a search for explaining why language possesses the properties it has.
mirror neuron system	The system that regulates the ability to perceive both the actions of another and the actions of oneself in mirror image. It is regulated by Broca's area of the brain.
MIS	Marine isotope stage. Marine isotope stages are calculated by variations in the oxygen isotope ratios. They give estimates that indicate the alternation between warm and cold periods in geological time, and consequently, for example, changes in sea level.
Modes 1, 2, 3, 4, 5	A classification system for stone tools, designed in the 1960s by Grahame Clark in order to unify African and European classifications. See also **five modes**.
moiety	Literally, 'half' (French *moitié*): entailing a division of society into two halves, and a rule that one marries into the half to which one does not belong. The division is through either patrilineal or matrilineal descent. Common in Australia and South America.

molecular clock	A time measure for genetic divergence: it assumes a constant mutation rate between genomes.
molecular biology	The study of biology at the molecular level.
morpheme	A unit of meaning. See **morphology**.
morphology	In linguistics, the study of units of meaning, often shorter than a word. For example, the word *dogs* is made up of the morphemes *dog* (canine animal) and *s* (plural).
Mousterian	Middle Palaeolithic, including Neanderthal, stone tool tradition dating from 100,000 to 35,000 BP. Named after the rock shelter Le Moustier in the Dordogne and characterized by reshaped flakes.
'Movius Line'	In archaeology, the division between supposedly more 'backward' areas of stone tool technology to the west of Southeast Asia and the more evolved areas that lie to the east.
mtDNA	Mitochondrial DNA: a form of DNA that performs specific functions within the cell. Its significance in genetic studies is that, in humans and many other species, it is inherited only through females and thus indicates matrilineal descent. See also **Y-chromosomal DNA**.
Multiregional Continuity Model (MCM)	Another name for the **multiregional hypothesis** (see below). More specifically, the model that suggests that, for example, Asians have evolved from Asian *Homo erectus* and Europeans from European *H. erectus* or from Neanderthals.
multiregional hypothesis	A theory that modern humankind is the product of evolution from several different earlier forms. Cf. **Out of Africa**, **Recent African Origin**.
mutation	In genetics, the change in a DNA sequence that will affect the fitness of an individual and their progeny.
mystical thought	Lévy-Bruhl's term for thought processes present in every human mind but commonly associated with 'primitive' thinking: communication with nature or with the spirit world.

natural language	A language formed and evolving through natural processes, and not purposefully invented.
natural selection	The mechanism of Darwinian evolution, through which heritable traits are passed from generation to generation. This can involve either sexual selection (i.e., competition for mates) or ecological selection. Either way, those who live to breed will propagate future generations.
Neanderthal, Neandertal	The English name for *Homo neanderthalensis* or *H. sapiens neanderthalensis.*
'Neanderthal flute'	A purported, prehistoric musical instrument, the prototype of which is the femur of a cave bear in which four holes (as in a modern recorder) have been made.
negative reciprocity	Marshall Sahlins's term for 'exchange' involving theft or gambling. Cf. **balanced reciprocity**, **generalized reciprocity**.
neocortex	The main part of the brain, excluding the brain stem and limbic system.
Neolithic	Stone tool industry characterized by polished tools and by ceramics. The term is also employed very commonly for the types of social organization and subsistence lifestyles which characterize this industry. These include permanent settlement, village life, and animal husbandry and agriculture. The term means 'new stone age'. See also **Mesolithic**.
Neolithization	The transition from food-gathering to food production, along with accompanying changes in economic and social organization.
New Archaeology	The approach developed by Lewis Binford and others, based on the search for scientific understandings in the field. Also known as **processualism.**
noun class	A grammatically defined class of nouns, indicating characteristics such as male, female, human, non-human, animate, etc.
Oldowan	Referring to the part of the Lower Palaeolithic, the time of the first stone tools in eastern Africa roughly between 2,600,000 and 1,700,000 years ago.
ontogenic behaviour	Behaviour of an individual organism. See also **phylogenic behaviour**.

optimal foraging theory	A perspective within ecology that suggests that organisms maximize energy intake over a given period of time. The term is often used in anthropology with reference to the evolution of human behaviour.
original affluent society	Marshall Sahlins's term for hunter-gatherer social life, in which 'affluence' is measured by free time rather than by accumulated wealth. Hunter-gatherers spend *less* time in subsistence-related activities than non-hunter-gatherers.
Out of Africa	The theory, developed especially since the 1980s, that all modern humankind is descended from a small and relatively recent (less than 200,000 years ago) group of Africans. (The allusion is to the title of an unrelated 1937 book, made into a film in 1985.) Also called the **Recent African Origin** model. Cf. **Multiregional Continuity Model**, **multiregional hypothesis**.
own-kill rule	Chris Knight's term for a rule that forbids a person from eating meat he (normally a male) kills himself. This taboo is often likened to incest, and the meat is given to or exchanged with others.
Palaeolithic	The term means 'old stone age'. Divided into Early or Lower (including Oldowan and Acheulean, from 3,600,000 or 3,500,000 to 100,000 BP), Middle (including Mousterian, from 300,000 to 30,000 BP), and Late or Upper (including several traditions from about 45,000 to 10,000 BP).
Pan-Gaean	According to Michael Witzel, the common mythology of the world, stemming from a source in Africa before the global migrations of *Homo sapiens*.
Paranthropus	The genus name for a robust form of australopithecine. See **australopithecines**.
parole	Ferdinand de Saussure's term for speech in the sense of actual utterances. By analogy, it also refers to social action as opposed to social structure (*langue*). Cf. **langue**.

particle	A short function word or linguistic unit that has no clear definition apart from its grammatical function. For example, a plural indicator such as *s* at the end of a noun.
patient	In grammatical theory, the person or thing that is the object of an action. Compare **agent** and **thematic relation**.
patrilateral cross-cousin marriage	Marriage of a man to his father's sister's daughter. Whereas repeated **matrilateral cross-cousin marriage** aligns kin groups in relation to each other (a man marries the same group his father did), patrilateral cross-cousin marriage has the opposite effect. Therefore, as an institution it is unstable.
performance	Noam Chomsky's earlier term for the practical aspect of language, i.e., speaking. Cf. **competence**.
person-gender-number marker (PGN)	A noun or pronoun that identifies person (first, second or third), gender (for example, masculine, feminine, neuter or common) and number (for example, singular, dual or plural). Sometimes known as **person-number-gender marker**.
phatic communion	Bronislaw Malinowski's term for small talk, such as greetings, talking about the weather and other forms of ritual communication.
phonatory system	That related to speaking, or literally, voicing.
phoneme	The smallest *meaningful* unit of sound in a given language. Symbolized with a slash: /p/. For example, the phoneme /p/ in English includes the allophones [p] and [pʰ]. The latter has aspiration or a 'breath' after the sound. Thus [pit] is not found in English, but is always represented by the aspirated form [pʰɪt]. See **allophone**, **phonetics**.
phonetics	The study of the objective auditory or acoustic nature of sounds, independent of their place in a sound systems (phonemics or phonology). Represented by square brackets, for example, [p].

phonology	The study of sounds as part of the sound system of a particular language. For example, in English the sounds **p**, **t** and **k** form one sequence (unvoiced stops, in order from front to back of the mouth) and **b**, **d** and **g** another (the equivalent voiced stops). Other languages may have fewer or more of these, or lack the distinction between unvoiced and voiced. See also **phoneme, phonetics, morphology, semantics** and **syntax**.
PGN	Person, number, gender: in reference to markers to indicate these attributes in nouns or pronouns.
phylogenic behaviour	Behaviour or evolution of a species. See also **ontogenic behaviour**.
pidgin	A simplified language that develops as a result of contact between two or more speech communities who do not have a language in common. See also **creole**.
Pleistocene	Geological epoch from about 2,600,000 to 10,000 BP (followed by the Holocene). It was characterized by stages of repeated glaciation.
Pliocene	Geological epoch before the Pleistocene. From about 5,400,000 to 2,600,000 BP.
P-language	The idealized notion of language in existence independently of any people. Cf. **E-language** and **I-language**.
polygamous marriage	Marriage to more than one person at a time: either polygyny (more than one wife), polyandry (more than one husband) or 'group marriage'.
population bottleneck	A population decrease that causes a reduction in the genetic variation of a population. Past population bottlenecks (such as one following the Toba volcanic eruption) may be deduced through genetic studies.
post-processual archaeology	A trend in archaeological theory which emphasizes the subjectivity of archaeological interpretation. It originated in the late 1970s and 1980s as a reaction against **processual archaeology**.

postvocalic /r/	In English, phonetic [r] pronounced at the end of a word (as in Ireland, Canada, most of the United States, etc.). In much of the English-speaking world (parts of England, New England, Australia, etc.), this historical phonemic /r/ is not pronounced at all. Cf. **pre-consonantal /r/**.
potassium-argon dating	Dating method employing the measure of the rate of decay of an isotope of potassium into argon. It is used when radiocarbon dating is not possible.
pre-consonantal /r/	In English, phonetic [r] before a consonant. Depending on dialect, English phonemic /r/ before a consonant may be rendered as either a phonetic [r] (for example, in Canada) or as the lengthening of the previous consonant (for example, as in Australia). Cf. **postvocalic /r/**.
processual archaeology	The trend in archaeological theory that advocates a scientific methodology and an emphasis on evolution and cultural ecology. It became prominent in the 1960s, especially in North America. Cf. **post-processual archaeology**.
proto-language	In my theory of language (derived from Derek Bickerton's), words and phrases only, without simple sentences or rules for word order. Cf. **rudimentary language**. In another sense, the ancestral language of a language family.
radiocarbon dating	Dating method employing the measure of the rate of decay of the radioactive isotope carbon-14. Its limit is about 60,000 years. For earlier dates, other methods (such as **potassium-argon dating**) are required.
Recent African Origin model	Another name for the **Out of Africa** theory: that modern *Homo sapiens* have evolved exclusively or mainly from a small African population. Cf. **Multiregional Continuity Model**.
recursion	In linguistics, the property of embedding one unit into another of the same kind, such as sentences within sentences.
relativism	A view of the world that opposes the assumption of cultural universals or universal values. In social anthropology, it usually refers to a form of cultural relativism rather than a theory of values.

retrievability	The ability (suggested by Morrison and Conway) to remember the past through the association between words and events. This suggests a transformation from episodic to autobiographical memory.
'Rhodesian Man'	The *Homo rhodesiensis* or *Homo heidelbergensis* fossil discovered at the Broken Hill mine in then Northern Rhodesia (modern Zambia) in 1921.
rudimentary language	In my theory of language (derived from Derek Bickerton's), language possessing only simple syntax. Cf. **proto-language**.
Sahul	The continental shelf of Australia and New Guinea and the Pleistocene land mass which once occupied much of it. See also **Sunda**.
Saussurian	Referring to the ideas of Ferdinand de Saussure (1857–1913). Specifically the ideas on the synchronic study of language from the posthumous *Course in general linguistics* (French edition, 1916).
Scheherazade	The mythical Persian queen who, in the story *One thousand and one nights*, never completed her narrative. Had she done so, she would, like her predecessors, have been killed.
'Scheherazade effect'	Geoffrey Miller's term for his theory of the origin of language: that it developed in order to attract potential mates.
semantic memory	Memory of the meaning of things, the concepts which form general knowledge. Together with episodic memory, semantic memory forms part of declarative memory, as distinct from procedural (or implicit memory). Procedural memory might include, for example, remembering how to ride a bicycle.
semantics	The level of language or branch of linguistics that concerns meaning. See also **morphology**, **phonology** and **syntax**.
sexual selection	In Darwinian theory, the primary means of natural selection: through competition for mates.
sign	In Saussurian thought, the relation between a word (the signifier) and what it signifies.
signifying	Relating to the relationship between a word (or morpheme) and meaning, or by extension, between any object and its meaning.

signifying revolution	My term for the revolutionary linguistic change to the use of words to signify meaning.
simile	Like **metaphor**, an analogy or relation of similarity across different levels of meaning, but expressed in the form 'as a …' or 'like a …'.
socio-centric category	A category of kin defined in the same way for all members of society (for example a **moiety** or a section).
spandrel	In biology, a structure that acquires function as an accidental by-product of evolution. In linguistics, an analogous concept employed, for example, by Chomsky who explains the **language faculty** as a spandrel. (The term is borrowed from architecture, where it refers to the mortared space between elements of an arch.)
speech	Actual vocalized communication. See also *parole*.
Sprachbund	A group of previously unrelated languages that have come together and acquired characteristics from one another. Also known as **linguistic area**.
Still Bay	Also known as Stillbay or Stillbaai, an advanced Palaeolithic or Middle Stone Age cultural tradition, very roughly 77,000 to 72,000 BP. It was identified in the 1920s, and questioned in the 1970s, but has since taken on renewed interest in view of cave sites such as Sibudu and Blombos.
sui generis	Literally 'of its own kind', referring to that which can only be explained in its own terms. For example, culture can be explained only with reference to culture itself.
Sunda	The land mass which once existed adjacent to **Sahul** and which partly now comprises Southeast Asia.
symbolic revolution	My preferred term for the 'human revolution' of early *Homo sapiens sapiens*, related to full language and to elementary structures of kinship.
syntax	The level of language or branch of linguistics that concerns grammar. See also **morphology**, **phonology**, and **semantics**.
tetradic	A four-part system similar to an Australian section system. Hypothesized by N. J. Allen as the primal human kinship structure, and (controversially) perhaps 100,000 years old. This date would imply that its earliest existence would have been in Africa.

thematic relation	In grammatical theory, the relation between the **agent** and the **patient**.
theory of mind	The ability to understand another person's point of view, in other words to anticipate the thinking of another person or being. This facility is limited in small children, primates, and, presumably also, in early hominins.
Toba	A super-volcano that exploded approximately 74,000 years ago, causing a 'volcanic winter' of perhaps ten years and, arguably, a significant reduction in the world's population and a population bottleneck. The remnants of the Toba volcano today comprise Lake Toba on the island of Sumatra.
totem	In the Ojibwa language, the spirit of a patrilineal clan. By extension, a similar spirit among any people.
transformational grammar	The approach in linguistics based on the idea of a deep structure, within which rules transform that structure into surface structures represented by real sentences.
Twin Rivers	A site in Zambia with the earliest evidence of pigment use. Dated to 400,000 to 260,000 years and attributed at *Homo heidelbergensis*.
universal grammar	The idea that all languages are basically alike, in that they share certain structural attributes presumed to be innate. (Often capitalized: *Universal Grammar*.)
universal kinship, universal kin categorization	Systems in which everyone in a society is classified by a relationship term and treated appropriately. In such systems there is no concept of someone being 'non-kin'.
Upper Palaeolithic	Late period of the Palaeolithic, roughly from 45,000 to (in some regions) 10,000 BP. Comprises a number of diverse stone tool traditions.
village sign language	A sign language invented spontaneously by members of an isolated group of deaf people. Such languages are often used both by hearing and deaf people. Cf. **deaf community sign language**.

vowel harmony	The characteristic whereby the first vowel of a word is maintained throughout that word, in each syllable, contrary to expectation.
Wernicke's area	The part of the brain associated with the comprehension of speech. It lies in the posterior section of the dominant hemisphere. Cf. **Broca's area**.
Whorfian	Relating to the ideas of Benjamin Lee Whorf (1897–1941), specifically the relativistic idea attributed to him that language determines thought. In other words, that people who speak different languages think differently.
xaro	See **hxaro**.
Y-chromosomal Adam	A hypothetical patrilineal ancestor of all humankind purported to have lived in Africa. See also African Eve.
Y-chromosomal DNA	A form of DNA that it is inherited only through males and thus indicates patrilineal descent. See also mtDNA.

References

Adams, Michael. 2011. 'The spectrum of invention', in Michael Adams (ed.), *From Elvish to Klingon: exploring invented languages*. Oxford University Press, pp. 1–16

Aiello, Leslie C. 1998. 'The foundation of human language', in Jablonski and Aiello, pp. 21–34

Aiello, Leslie C., and Robin I. M. Dunbar. 1993. 'Neocortex size, group size, and the evolution of language', *Current Anthropology* 34: 184–93

Aiello, Leslie C., and Peter Wheeler. 1995. 'The expensive tissue hypothesis; the brain and the digestive system in human and primate evolution', *Current Anthropology* 36: 199–221

Aitchison, Jean. 1996. *The seeds of speech: language origin and evolution*. Cambridge University Press

Alexander, Richard D. 1977. 'Review of *The use and abuse of biology* (Marshall Sahlins)', *American Anthropologist* 77: 917–20

Alexiades, Miguel N. 2009. 'Mobility and migration in indigenous Amazonia: contemporary ethnoecological perspectives: an introduction', in Miguel N. Alexiades (ed.), *Mobility and migration in indigenous Amazonia: contemporary ethnoecological perspectives*. Oxford: Berghahn Books, pp. 1–43

Allen, Nicholas J., Hilary Callan, Robin Dunbar, and Wendy James (eds.). 2008. *Early human kinship: from sex to social reproduction*. Oxford: Blackwell Publishing

Ambrose, Stanley. H. 1998. 'Late Pleistocene human population bottlenecks, volcanic winter, and differentiation of modern humans'. *Journal of Human Evolution* 34(6): 633–51

Andresen, Julie Tetel. 2014. *Linguistics and evolution: a developmental approach*. Cambridge University Press

Anon. 2015. 'Jewellery for Neanderthals', *The Week: The Best of British and International Media* 1015 (25 March 2015): 20

Arbib, Michael A. 2012. *How the brain got language: the mirror system hypothesis*. New York: Oxford University Press

Armitage, Simon J., Sabah A. Jasim, Anthony E. Marks, Adrian G. Parker, Vitaly I. Usik and Hans-Peter Uerpmann. 2011. 'The southern route "out of Africa": evidence for an early expansion of modern humans into Arabia', *Science* 331: 453–6

Armstrong, Karen. 2006. *A short history of myth*. Edinburgh: Canongate Books

Atkinson, Quentin D. 2011. 'Phonemic diversity supports a serial founder effect model of language expansion from Africa', *Science* 332: 246–9

Bancel, Pierre J. and Alain Matthey de l'Etang. 2013. 'Brave new words', in Lefebvre, Comrie and Cohen, pp. 333–77

Barham, Lawrence and Peter Mitchell. 2008. *The first Africans: African archaeology from the earliest toolmakers to most recent foragers.* Cambridge University Press

Barnard, Alan. 1976. *Nharo Bushman kinship and the transformation of Khoi kin categories.* Unpublished PhD thesis, University of London

  1978. 'Universal system of kin categorization', *African Studies* 37: 69–81

  1980. 'Sex roles among the Nharo Bushmen of Botswana', *Africa* 50: 115–24

  1988. 'Kinship, language and production: a conjectural history of Khoisan social structure', *Africa* 58: 29–50

  1992. *Hunters and herders of southern Africa: a comparative ethnography of the Khoisan peoples.* Cambridge University Press

  1995. 'Orang Outang and the definition of Man', in Han F. Vermeulen and Arturo Álvarez Roldán (eds.), *Fieldwork and footnotes: studies in the history of European anthropology.* London: Routledge, pp. 95–112

  1998. 'An anthropologist among the primatologists', *Budongo Forest Project* 1(3): 1–3

  1999. 'Modern hunter-gatherers and early symbolic culture', in Dunbar, Knight and Power, pp. 50–68

  2000. *History and theory in anthropology.* Cambridge University Press

  2002. 'The foraging mode of thought', *Senri Ethnological Studies* 60: 5–24

  2003. '!Ke e: /xarra //ke – multiple origins and multiple meanings of the motto', *African Studies* 62: 241–8

  2004a. 'Hunting-and-gathering society: an eighteenth-century Scottish invention', in Barnard 2004b, pp. 31–43

  (ed.). 2004b. *Hunter-gatherers in history, archaeology and anthropology.* Oxford: Berg

  2008a. 'The co-evolution of language and kinship', in Allen *et al.*, pp. 232–43

  2008b. 'Ethnographic analogy and the reconstruction of early Khoekhoe society', in Karim Sadr and Francois-Xavier Fauvelle-Aymar (eds.), *Khoekhoe and the origins of herding in southern Africa* (Southern African Humanities 20). Pietermaritzburg: Natal Museum, pp. 61–75

  2009. 'Social origins: sharing, exchange, kinship', in Botha and Knight, pp. 219–35

  2010. 'Culture: the indigenous account', in Deborah James, Evlie Plaice and Christina Toren (eds.), *Culture wars: context, models and anthropologists' accounts.* New York: Berghahn Books, pp. 73–85

  2011. *Social anthropology and human origins.* Cambridge University Press

  2012. *Genesis of symbolic thought.* Cambridge University Press

  2013. 'Cognitive and social aspects of language origins', in Lefebvre, Comrie and Cohen, pp. 53–71

  2014. 'The Ju/'hoan-Naro contact area', in Alan Barnard and Gertrud Boden (eds.), *Southern African Khoisan kinship systems* (Research in Khoisan Studies 30). Cologne: Rüdiger Köppe Verlag, pp. 209–22

Bar-Yosef, Ofer. 2008. 'Can Paleolithic stone artifacts serve as evidence for prehistoric language?', in Bengtson, pp. 373–9

Beaken, Mike. 2011. *The making of language* (second edition). Edinburgh: Dunedin

162   References

Behar, Doron M., Richard Villems, Himla Soodyall, Jason Blue-Smith, Luisa Pereira, Ene Metspalu, Rosaria Scozzari, Heeran Makkan, Shay Tzur, David Comas, Jaume Bertranpetit, Lluis Quintana-Murci, Chris Tyler-Smith, R. Spencer Wells, Saharon Rosset and the Genographic Consortium. 2008. 'The dawn of human matrilineal diversity', *American Journal of Human Genetics* 82: 1–11

Bengtson, John D. (ed.) 2008. *In hot pursuit of language in prehistory: essays in the four fields of anthropology in honor of Harold Crane Fleming*. Amsterdam: John Benjamins

Bergman, Thore J. 2013. 'Speech-like vocalized lip-smacking in geladas', *Current Biology* 23(7): R268–9

Berent, Iris. 2013. *The phonological mind*. Cambridge University Press

Berlin, Brent and Paul Kay. 1969. *Basic color terms: their universality and evolution*. Cambridge University Press

Berwick, Robert C., Marc D. Hauser and Ian Tattersall. 2013. 'Neanderthal language? Just-so stories take center stage', *Frontiers in Psychology* 4: 671. doi: 10.3389/fpsyg.2013.00671 (2 pages)

Bettinger, Robert L. 1991. *Hunter-gatherers: archaeological and evolutionary theory*. New York: Plenum Press

    2009. *Hunter-gatherer foraging: five simple models*. New York: Eliot Werner Publications

Beyin, Amanuel. 2011. 'Upper Pleistocene human dispersals out of Africa: a review of the current state of the debate', *International Journal of Evolutionary Biology* 2011 (Article ID 615094). doi:10.4061/2011/615094. 17 pages

Bickerton, Derek. 1981. *Roots of language*. Ann Arbor, MI: Karoma

    2009. *Adam's tongue: how humans made language, how language made humans*. New York: Hill and Wang

    2012. 'The origins of syntactic language', in Tallerman and Gibson 2012a, pp. 456–68

    2014. *More than nature needs: language, mind, and evolution*. Cambridge, MA: Harvard University Press

Binford, Lewis R. 1962. 'Archaeology as anthropology', *American Antiquity* 28: 217–25

    1978. *Nunamiut ethnoarchaeology*. New York: Academic Press

    1983. *In pursuit of the past*. London: Thames & Hudson

Bird-David, Nurit. 1990. 'The giving environment: another perspective on the economic system of hunter-gatherers', *Current Anthropology* 31: 183–96

    1992. 'Beyond "The original affluent society": a culturalist reformulation', *Current Anthropology* 33: 25–47

    1999. '"Animism" revisited: personhood, environment, and relational epistemology', *Current Anthropology* 40 (Supplement): S67–S91

Blacking, John. 1973. *How musical is man?* Seattle: University of Washington Press

Blake, Barry J. 2008. *All about language*. Oxford University Press

Bleek, D. F. 1928. *The Naron: a Bushman tribe of the central Kalahari*. Cambridge University Press

    1928/9. 'Bushman grammar: a grammatical sketch of the language of the /xam-ka-!k'e', *Zeitschrift für Eingeborenen-Sprachen* 19: 81–98

    1929/30. 'Bushman grammar: a grammatical sketch of the language of the /xam-ka-!k'e (continuation)', *Zeitschrift für Eingeborenen-Sprachen* 20: 161–74

Bleek, W. H. I. and L. C. Lloyd. 1911. *Specimens of Bushman folklore*. London: George Allen & Co.

Boas, Franz. 1904. 'The history of anthropology', *Science* 20 (512): 513–24
    1940. *Race, language, and culture.* New York: Macmillan
Botha, Rudolf. 2009. 'Theoretical underpinnings of inferences about language evolution: the syntax used at Blombos cave', in Botha and Knight, pp. 93–111
    2012. 'Inferring modern language from ancient objects', in Tallerman and Gibson 2012a, pp. 303–12
Botha, Rudolf and Martin Everaert (eds.). 2013. *The evolutionary emergence of language: evidence and inference.* Oxford University Press
Botha, Rudolf and Chris Knight (eds.). 2009. *The cradle of language.* Oxford University Press
Bowler, James M., Harvey Johnston, Jon M. Olley, John R. Prescott, Richard G. Roberts, Wilfred Shawcross and Nigel A. Spooner. 2003. 'New ages for human occupation and climatic change at Lake Mungo, Australia', *Nature* 421: 837–40
Boyer, Pascal. 1994. *The naturalness of religious ideas: a cognitive theory of religion.* Berkeley: University of California Press
    2001. *Religion explained: the human instincts that fashion gods, spirits and ancestors.* London: Vintage Books
Brody, Hugh. 2000. *The other side of Eden: hunter-gatherers, farmers and the shaping of the world.* Vancouver: Douglas & McIntyre
Brown, Donald E. 1991. *Human universals.* New York: McGraw-Hill
Brown, Kyle S., Curtis W. Marean, Zenobia Jacobs, Benjamin J. Schoville, Simen Oestmo, Erich C. Fisher, Jocelyn Bernatchez, Panagiotis Karkanas and Thalassa Matthews. 2012. 'An early and enduring advanced technology originating 71,000 years ago in South Africa', *Nature* 491: 590–3
Brown, Penelope and Suzanne Gaskins. 2014. 'Language acquisition and language socialization', in Enfield, Kockelman and Sidnell, 2014b, pp. 187–226
Brown, Steven. 2000. 'The "musilanguage" model of music evolution', in Wallin, Merker and Brown, pp. 271–300
Burch, Ernest L., Jr., and Linda J. Ellanna (eds.). 1994. *Key issues in hunter-gatherer research.* Oxford: Berg
Calvin, William H., and Derek Bickerton. 2000. *Lingua ex machina: reconciling Darwin and Chomsky with the human brain.* Cambridge, MA: MIT Press
Cameron, David W. and Colin P. Groves. 2004. *Bones, stones and molecules: 'Out of Africa' and human origins.* Burlington, MA: Elsevier Academic Press
Campbell, Lyle. 1997. *American Indian languages: the historical linguistics of Native America.* Oxford University Press
Cane, Scott. 2013. *First footprints: the epic story of the first Australians.* Crows Nest, NSW: Allen & Unwin
Carroll, John B. (ed.). 1956. *Language, thought, and reality: selected writings of Benjamin Lee Whorf.* Cambridge, MA: MIT Press
Carstairs-McCarthy, Andrew. 1999. *The origins of language: an inquiry into the evolutionary beginnings of sentences, syllables, and truth.* Oxford University Press
Cavalli-Sforza, Luigi. 2001. *Genes, peoples and languages* (translated by Mark Seielstad). London: Penguin Books
Chomsky, Noam. 1965. *Aspects of the theory of syntax.* Cambridge, MA: MIT Press
    1986. *Knowledge of language.* New York: Praeger
    1993. 'A minimalist program for linguistic theory', in Kenneth L. Hale and S. Jay Keyser (eds.), *The view from building 20: essays in linguistics in honor of Sylvain Bromberger.* Cambridge, MA: MIT Press, pp. 1–52

1996. *Powers and prospects: reflections on human nature and the social order.* London: Pluto Press

2002. *On nature and language.* Cambridge University Press

2004. '*Language and mind: current thoughts on ancient problems*', in Lyle Jenkins (ed.), *Variation and universals in biolinguistics.* Amsterdam: Elsevier, pp. 379–405

2005. 'Three factors in language design', *Linguistic Inquiry* 36: 1–22

2011. 'Language and other cognitive systems. What is special about language?', *Language Learning and Development* 7: 263–78

2012. *The science of language: interviews with James McGilvray.* Cambridge University Press

Christiansen, Morten H. and Simon Kirby (eds.). 2003a. *Language evolution.* Oxford University Press

2003b. 'Language evolution: the hardest problem in science?', in Christiansen and Kirby, pp. 1–15

2003c. 'Language evolution: consensus and controversies', *Trends in Cognitive Sciences* 7(7): 300–07

Clark, J. G. D. 1969. *World prehistory: a new outline* (second edition). Cambridge University Press

Clifford, James and George E. Marcus (eds.). 1986. *Writing culture: the poetics and politics of ethnography.* Berkeley: University of California Press

Cohen, Emma. 2012. 'The evolution of tag-based cooperation in humans', *Current Anthropology* 53: 588–616

Comrie, Bernard. 1989. *Language universals and linguistic typology: syntax and morphology.* University of Chicago Press

Conklin, Harold C. 1969 [1962]. 'Lexicographical treatment of folk taxonomies', in Stephen A. Tyler (ed.), *Cognitive anthropology.* New York: Holt, Rinehart & Winston, pp. 41–59

Coolidge, Frederick L. and Thomas Wynn. 2009. *The rise of Homo sapiens: the evolution of modern thinking.* Oxford: Wiley-Blackwell

Corballis, Michael C. 2011. *The recursive mind: the origins of human language, thought, and civilization.* Princeton University Press

Cummings, Vicki. 2013. *The anthropology of hunter-gatherers: key themes for archaeologists.* London: Bloomsbury

Cummings, Vicki, Peter Jordan and Marek Zvelebil (eds.). 2014. *The Oxford handbook of the archaeology and anthropology of hunter-gatherers.* Oxford University Press

Dalrymple, Sir John. 1758. *Essay towards a general history of feudal property in Great Britain* (second edition). London: A. Millar

Damas, David. 1969a. *Contributions to anthropology: band societies.* Ottawa: National Museums of Canada (Bulletin 228)

1969b. 'Characteristics of Central Eskimo band structure', in Damas 1969a, pp. 116–38

D'Anastasio, Rugerro, Stephen Wroe, Cladio Tuniz, Lucia Mancini, Deneb T. Cesana, Diego Dreossi, Mayoorendra Ravichandiran, Marie Attard, William C. H. Parr, Anne Agur and Luigi Capasso. 2013. 'Micro-biomechanics of the Kebara 2 hyoid and its implications for speech in Neanderthals', *PLoS ONE* 8 (12): e82261. doi:10.1371/journal.pone.0082261

D'Andrade, Roy G. 1995. *The development of cognitive anthropology*. Cambridge University Press

Darwin, Charles. 1859. *On the origin of species by means of natural selection*. London: John Murray

   1871. *The descent of man, and selection in relation to sex*. London: John Murray

Davidson, Donald. 1979. 'What metaphors mean', in Sheldon Sacks (ed.), *On metaphor*. University of Chicago Press, pp. 29–45

Davidson, Iain and William Noble. 1992. 'Why the first colonisation of the Australian region is the earliest evidence of modern human behaviour', *Archaeology in Oceania* 27: 135–42

Dawkins, Richard. 1976. *The selfish gene*. Oxford University Press

Deacon, Hilary J. and Janette Deacon. 1999. *Human beginnings in South Africa: uncovering the secrets of the Stone Age*. Cape Town: David Philip

Deacon, Terrence W. 1997. *The symbolic species: the coevolution of language and the brain*. New York: W. W. Norton & Co.

   2003. 'Universal Grammar and semiotic constraints', in Christiansen and Kirby 2003a, pp. 111–39

Debreuil, Benoît and Christopher Stuart Henshilwood. 2013. 'Material culture and language', in Lefebvre, Comrie and Cohen, pp. 147–70

Dediu, Dan and Stephen C. Levinson. 2013. 'On the antiquity of language: the reinterpretation of Neandertal linguistic capabilities and its consequences', *Frontiers in Psychology* 4: 397. doi: 10.3389/fpsyg.2013.00397 (17 pages)

d'Errico, Francesco. 2003. 'The invisible frontier: a multiple species model for the origin of behavioral modernity', *Evolutionary Anthropology* 12: 188–202

   2009. 'The archaeology of early religious practices: a plea for a hypothesis-testing approach', in Renfrew and Morley, pp. 104–22

d'Errico, Francesco, Christopher Henshilwood, Graeme Lawson, Marian Vanhaeren, Anne-Marie Tillier, Marie Soressi, Frédérique Bresson, Bruno Maureille, April Nowell, Joseba Lakarra, Lucinda Backwell and Michele Julien. 2003. 'Archaeological evidence for the emergence of language, symbolism, and music – an alternative multidisciplinary perspective', *Journal of World Prehistory* 17: 1–70

Descola, Philippe and Gísli Pálsson. 1996. 'Introduction', in Philippe Descola, and Gísli Pálsson (eds.), *Nature and society: anthropological perspectives*. London: Routledge, pp. 1–21

Dessalles, Jean-Louis. 2007 [2000]. *Why we talk: the evolutionary origins of language* (translated by James Grieve). Oxford University Press

Diller, Karl C. and Rebecca L. Cann. 2010. 'The innateness of language: a view from genetics', in Smith *et al.*, pp. 107–15

Dixon, R. M. W. 1980. *The languages of Australia*. Cambridge University Press

Donald, Merlin. 1991. *Origins of the modern mind: three stages in the origin of culture and cognition*. Cambridge, MA: Harvard University Press

   2009. 'The roots of art and religion in ancient material culture', in Renfrew and Morley, pp. 95–103

Dor, Daniel and Eva Jablonka. 2010. 'A new theory of language and its implications for the question of evolution', in Smith *et al.*, pp. 116–21

Dunbar, Robin I. M. 1993. 'The coevolution of neocortical size, group size and language in humans', *Behavioral and Brain Sciences* 16: 681–735

1996. *Grooming, gossip and the evolution of language*. London: Faber and Faber

2001. 'Brains on two legs: group size and the evolution of intelligence', in F. B. M. de Waal (ed.), *Tree of origin: what primate behavior can tell us about human social evolution*. Cambridge, MA: Harvard University Press, pp. 173–92

2003. 'The social brain: mind, language and society in evolutionary perspective', *Annual Review of Anthropology* 32: 163–81

2008. 'Kinship in biological perspective', in Allen *et al.*, pp. 131–50

Dunbar, Robin, Chris Knight and Camilla Power (eds.). 1999. *The evolution of culture: an interdisciplinary view*. Edinburgh University Press

Duranti, Alessandro. 2003. 'Language as culture in U.S. anthropology: three paradigms', *Current Anthropology* 44: 323–47

Edwardes, Martin. 2010. *The origins of grammar: an anthropological perspective*. London: Continuum

Eliade, Mircea. 1963. *Myth and reality: religious traditions of the world* (translated by Willard R. Trask). New York: Harper & Row

Ellis, George F. R. 2011. 'Biology and mechanisms related to the dawn of language', in Henshilwood and d'Errico, pp. 163–83

Enfield, N. J., Paul Kockelman and Jack Sidnell. 2014a. 'Introduction: directions in the anthropology of language', in Enfield, Kockelman and Sidnell, 2014b, pp. 1–24

(eds.). 2014b. *The Cambridge handbook of linguistic anthropology*. Cambridge University Press

Englefield, F. R. H. 1977. *Language: its origin and its relation to thought* (edited by G. A. Wells and D. R. Oppenheimer). London: Elek/Pemberton

Evans, Vyvyan. 2014. *The language myth: why language is not an instinct*. Cambridge University Press

Evans-Pritchard, E. E. 1937. *Witchcraft, oracles, and magic among the Azande*. Oxford: Clarendon Press

1956. *Nuer religion*. Oxford: Clarendon Press

Everett, Daniel. 2005. 'Cultural constraints in grammar and cognition in Pirahã: another look at the design features of human language', *Current Anthropology* 46: 621–46

2012. *Language: the cultural tool*. London: Profile Books

Fitch, W. Tecumseh. 2004. 'Kin selection and "mother tongues": a neglected component in language evolution', in Oller and Griebel, pp. 275–96

2010. *The evolution of language*. Cambridge University Press

Fitch, W. Tecumseh, Michael Arbib and Merlin Donald. 2010. 'A molecular genetic framework for testing hypotheses about language evolution', in Smith *et al.*, pp. 137–44

Féblot-Augustins, Jehanne. 1993. 'Mobility strategies in the late Middle Palaeolithic of Central Europe and Western Europe: elements of stability and variability', *Journal of Anthropological Archaeology* 12: 211–65

Feyerabend, Paul. 1978. *Science in a free society*. London: Verso

Fodor, Jerry A. 1983. *The modularity of mind*. Cambridge, MA: MIT Press

Foster, Mary LeCron. 1999. 'The reconstruction of the evolution of human spoken language', in Andrew Lock and Charles R. Peters (eds.), *Handbook of symbolic evolution*. Oxford: Blackwell, pp. 747–75

Foucault, Michel. 1970 [1966]. *The order of things: an archaeology of the human sciences*. New York: Random House

Freud, Sigmund. 1913 [1900]. *The interpretation of dreams* (third edition, translated by A. A. Brill). New York: Macmillan

Gamble, Clive. 2008. 'Kinship and material culture: archaeological implications of the human global diaspora', in Allen *et al.*, pp. 27–40

Gärdenfors, Peter. 2004. 'Cooperation and the evolution of symbolic communication', in Oller and Griebel, pp. 237–56

2013. 'The evolution of semantic: sharing conceptual domains', in Botha and Everaert, pp. 139–59

Geertz, Clifford. 1973. *The interpretation of cultures*. New York: Basic Books

1983. *Local knowledge: further essays on interpretive anthropology*. New York: Basic Books

Gloag, W. M. and R. Candlish Henderson. 2001. *The law of Scotland* (eleventh edition, edited by Hector L. MacQueen, Parker Hood, Morag Wise and Laura Dunlop). Edinburgh: W. Green & Son

Gomes, Christina and Christoph Boesch. 2009. 'Wild chimpanzees exchange meat for sex on a long-term basis', *PLpS ONE* 4(4): e516 (doi:10.1371/journal.pone.000516)

González-José, Rolando, Antonio González-Martín, Miquel Hernández, Héctor M. Pucciarelli, Marina Sardi, Alfonso Rosales and Silvina Van der Molen. 2003. 'Craniometric evidence for Palaeoamerican survival in Baja California', *Nature* 425: 62–5

Goody, Jack. 1977. *The domestication of the savage mind*. Cambridge University Press

1983. *The development of the family and marriage in Europe*. Cambridge University Press

2000. *The European family*. Oxford: Blackwell

Griffin, Scott Tracy. 2012. *Tarzan: the centennial celebration*. London: Titan Books

Güldemann, Tom. 1998. 'The Kalahari Basin as an object of areal typology – a first approach', in Mathias Schladt (ed.), *Language, identity, and conceptualization among the Khoisan* (Research in Khoisan Studies 15). Cologne: Rüdiger Köppe, pp. 137–69

Guenther, Mathias. 1986. *The Nharo Bushmen of Botswana*. Hamburg: Helmut Buske Verlag

2006. 'N//àe (talking): the oral and rhetorical base of San culture', *Journal of Folklore Research* 43: 241–61

Haeckel, Ernst. 1869. 'Editor's preface', in W. H. I. Bleek, *On the origin of language* (translated by Thomas Davidson). New York: L. W. Schmidt, pp. iii–viii

Hahn, Theophilus. 1881. *Tsuni-//Goam: the supreme being of the Khoi-khoi*. London: Trübner & Co.

Hale, Kenneth and David Nash. 1997. 'Lardil and Damin phonotactics', in Darrell Tryon and Michael Walsh (eds.), *Boundary rider: essays in honour of Geoffrey O'Grady*. Research School of Pacific and Asian Studies, Australian National University, pp. 247–59

Hamilton, W. D. 1964. 'The genetical evolution of social behaviour. I, II', *Journal of Theoretical Biology* 7: 1–52

Harari, Yuval Noah. 2014 [2011]. *Sapiens: a brief history of humankind* (translated by Yuval Noah Harari, John Purcell and Haim Wartzman). London: Harvill Secker

Harpaz, Yuval, Yechiel Levkovitz and Michael Lavidor. 2009. 'Lexical ambiguity resolution in Wernicke's area and its right homologue', *Cortex* 45: 1097–103.

Hauser, Marc, Noam Chomsky and W. Tecumseh Fitch. 2002. 'The faculty of language: what is it, who has it, and how did it evolve?', *Science* 298: 1569–79

Hébert, Louis. 2011. 'The functions of language', in Louis Hébert (ed.), *Signo: Theoretical Semiotics on the Web*. Quebec: Rimouski. www.signosemio.com/ jakobson/functions-of-language.asp

Heine, Bernd and Tania Kuteva. 2007. *The genesis of grammar: a reconstruction*. Oxford University Press

Heinz, Hans-Joachim. 1994 [1966]. *Social organization of the !Kõ Bushmen* (edited by Klaus Keuthmann) (Research in Khoisan Studies 10). Cologne: Rüdiger Köppe Verlag

Henn, Brenna M., Christopher R. Gignoux, Matthew Jobin, Julie M. Granka, J. M. Macpherson, Jeffrey M. Kidd, Laura Rodríguez-Botigué, Sohini Ramachandran, Lawrence Hon, Abra Brisbin, Alice A. Lin, Peter A. Underhill, David Comas, Kenneth K. Kidd, Paul J. Norman, Peter Parham, Carlos D. Bustamante, Joanna L. Mountain and Marcus W. Feldman. 2011. 'Hunter-gatherer genomic diversity suggests a southern African origin for modern humans', *Proceedings of the National Academy of Sciences (PNAS)* 108(13): 5154–62

Henshilwood, Christopher. 2009. 'The origins of symbolism, spirituality, and shamans: exploring Middle Stone Age material culture in South Africa', in Renfrew and Morley, pp. 29–49

Henshilwood, Christopher S. and Francesco d'Errico (eds). 2011. *Homo symbolicus: the dawn of language, imagination and spirituality*. Amsterdam: John Benjamins

Henshilwood, Christopher S. and Benoît Dubreuil. 2009. 'Reading the artefacts: gleaning language skills from the Middle Stone Age in southern Africa', in Botha and Knight, pp. 41–61

Henshilwood, Christopher S. and Curtis W. Marean. 2003. 'The origin of modern human behaviour: critique of the models and their test implications', *Current Anthropology* 44: 627–51

Herder, Johann Gottfried. 1986 [1772]. 'Essay on the origin of language' (translated by Alexander Gode), in Rousseau and Herder, pp. 85–166

Hewes, Gordon W. 1973. 'Primate communication and the gestural origins of language', *Current Anthropology* 14: 5–24

Hicks, Dan. 2013. 'Four-field anthropology: charter myths and time warps from St. Louis to Oxford', *Current Anthropology* 54: 753–63

Hobaiter, Catherine and Richard W. Byrne. 2014. 'The meanings of chimpanzee gestures', *Current Biology* 24(14): 1–5. http://dx.doi.org/10.1016/j.cub.2014.05.066

Hobbes, Thomas. 1991 [1651]. *Leviathan* (revised student edition, edited by Richard Tuck). Cambridge University Press

Hodder, Ian. 1985. 'Postprocessual archaeology', *Advances in Archaeological Method and Theory* 8: 1–26

Hoefler, Stefan H. and Andrew D. M. Smith. 2009. 'The pre-linguistic basis of grammaticalisation: a unified approach to metaphor and reanalysis', *Studies in Language* 33: 886–909

Honken, Henry. 2013. 'Genetic relationships: an overview of the evidence', in Rainer Vossen (ed.), *The Khoesan languages*. London: Routledge, pp. 12–24

Hurford, James. 2007. *The origins of meaning: language in the light of evolution*. Oxford University Press

2012. *The origins of grammar: language in the light of evolution.* Oxford University Press

2014. *The origins of language: a slim guide.* Oxford University Press

Hurford, James R., Michael Studdert-Kennedy and Chris Knight (eds.). 1998. *Approaches to the evolution of language: social and cognitive bases.* Cambridge University Press

Hymes, Dell. 1964. 'General introduction', in Dell Hymes (ed.), *Language in culture and society: a reader in linguistics and anthropology.* New York: Harper and Row, pp. xxi–xxxii

Ichikawa, Mitsuo. 2004. 'The Japanese tradition in central African hunter-gatherer studies, with comparative observations on the French and American traditions', in Barnard 2004b, pp. 103–28

Ingold, Tim. 2000. *The perception of the environment: essays in livelihood, dwelling and skill.* London: Routledge

Jablonski, Nina G. (ed.). 2002. *The first Americans: the Pleistocene colonization of the New World.* San Francisco: California Academy of Sciences

Jablonski, Nina G. and Leslie C. Aiello (eds.). 1998. *The origin and diversification of language.* San Francisco: California Academy of Sciences, Memoirs 24

Jakobson, Roman. 1944. 'Franz Boas' approach to language', *International Journal of American Linguistics* 10(4): 188–95

1999 [1960]. 'Linguistics and poetics', in Adam Jaworski and Nikolas Coupland (eds.), *The discourse reader.* London: Routledge, pp. 54–62

James, Wendy. 2003. *The ceremonial animal: a new portrait of anthropology.* Oxford University Press

Jesperson, Otto. 1922. *Language, its nature, development and origin.* London: Allen & Unwin

Johnson, Matthew. 2011. *Archaeological theory: an introduction* (second edition). London: John Wiley & Sons

Jung, Carl G. 1959 [1948–54]. *Four archetypes: mother, rebirth, spirit, trickster* (translated by R. F. C. Hull). Princeton University Press (Bollingen Series)

1964. 'Approaching the unconscious', in Carl G. Jung (ed.), *Man and his symbols.* New York: Dell, pp. 1–94

1971 [1933]. 'The structure of the psyche', in Joseph Campbell (ed.), *The portable Jung.* New York: Penguin Books, pp. 23–46

Kegl, Judy. 2002. 'Language emergence in a language-ready brain: acquisition', in Gary Morgan and Bernice Woll (eds.), *Directions in sign language acquisition.* Amsterdam: John Benjamins, pp. 207–54

Kelly, Robert L. 2013 [1995]. *The lifeways of hunter-gatherers: the foraging spectrum* (second edition). Cambridge University Press

Kenneally, Christine. 2007. *The first word: the search for the origins of language.* New York: Viking Penguin

Kirk, G. S. 1970. *Myth: its meaning and functions in ancient and other cultures.* Cambridge University Press

Klein, Richard G. 2009. *The human career: human biological and cultural origins* (third edition). University of Chicago Press

Klein, Richard G. with Blake Edgar. 2002. *The dawn of human culture.* New York: John Wiley & Sons

Kluckhohn, Clyde. 1953. 'Universal categories of culture', in A. L. Kroeber (ed.), *Anthropology today: an encyclopedic inventory*. University of Chicago Press, pp. 507–23

  1959. 'Common humanity and diverse cultures', in David Lerner (ed.), *The human meaning of the social sciences*. New York: Meridian Publishing, pp. 245–84

Kluckhohn, Clyde and Dorothea Leighton 1974 [1946]. *The Navaho* (revised edition), Cambridge, MA: Harvard University Press

Knight, Chris. 1998. 'Ritual/speech coevolution: a solution to the problem of deception', in Hurford, Studdert-Kennedy and Knight, pp. 68–91

  2010. 'The origins of symbolic culture', in Ulrich J. Frey, Charlotte Störmer and Kai Willführ (eds.), *Homo novus – a human without illusions*. Berlin: Springer-Verlag, pp. 193–211

Knight, Chris and Camilla Power. 2012. 'Social conditions for the emergence of language', in Tallerman and Gibson 2012a, pp. 346–9

Knight, Chris, Camilla Power and Ian Watts. 1995. 'The symbolic revolution: a Darwinian account', *Cambridge Archaeological Journal* 5(1): 75–114

Knight, John. 2012. 'The anonymity of the hunt: a critique of hunting as sharing', *Current Anthropology* 53: 334–55

Krause, Johannes, Qiaomei Fu, Jeffrey M. Good, Bence Viola, Michael V. Shunkov, Anatoli P. Derevianko, and Svante Pääbo. 2010. 'The complete mitochondrial DNA genome of an unknown hominin from southern Siberia', *Nature* 464: 894–7

Krause, Johannes, Carles Lalueza-Fox, Ludovic Orlando, Wolfgang Enard, Richard E. Green, Hernán A. Burbano, Jean-Jacques Hublin, Catherine Hänni, Javier Fortea, Marco de la Rasilla, Jaume Bertranpetit, Antonio Rosas, Svante Pääbo. 2007. 'The derived FOXP2 variant of modern humans was shared with Neandertals', *Current Biology* 17(21): 1908–12

Kuklick, Henrika. 1991. *The savage within: the social history of British anthropology, 1885–1945*. New York: Cambridge University Press

Kuper, Adam. 1973. *Anthropologists and anthropology: the British school, 1922–1972*. London: Allen Lane

  1982. *Wives for cattle: bridewealth and marriage in southern Africa*. London: Routledge & Kegan Paul

  1999. *Culture: the anthropologists' account*. Cambridge, MA: Harvard University Press

  2003. 'The return of the native', *Current Anthropology* 44: 389–402

Kuper, Adam and Jonathan Marks. 2011. 'Anthropologist unite!', *Nature* 470: 166–8

Labov, William. 2013. *The language of life and death: the transformation of experience in oral narrative*. Cambridge University Press

Lane, P. J. and R. T. Schadla-Hall. 2004. 'The many ages of Star Carr: do "cites" make the "site"', in Barnard 2004b, pp. 145–61

Layton, Robert. 1986. 'Politics and territorial structures among hunter-gatherers', *Man* (n.s.) 21: 18–33

Layton, Robert and Sean O'Hara. 2010. 'Human social evolution: a comparison of hunter-gatherer and chimpanzee social organization', in Robin Dunbar, Clive Gamble and John Gowlett (eds.), *Social brain, distributed mind*. Oxford University Press, pp. 83–113

Leacock, Eleanor. 1969. 'The Montagnai-Naskapi band', in Damas 1969a, pp. 18–50

Lee, Richard B. 1979. *The !Kung San: men, women and work in a foraging society.* Cambridge University Press

Lee, Richard B. and Irven DeVore (eds.). 1968a. *Man the hunter.* Chicago: Aldine

1968b. 'Problems in the study of hunters and gatherers', in Lee and DeVore 1968a, pp. 3–12

Leech, Geoffrey. 1974. *Semantics.* Harmondsworth: Penguin Books

Lefebvre, Claire, Bernard Comrie and Henri Cohen (eds.). 2013. *New perspectives on the origins of language.* Amsterdam: John Benjamins

Levinson, Stephen C. 2003. *Space in language and cognition: explorations in cognitive diversity.* Cambridge University Press

2014. 'Language evolution', in Enfield, Kockelman and Sidnell, 2014b, pp. 312–24

Lévi-Strauss, Claude. 1963 [1945–58]. *Structural anthropology* (translated by Clare Jacobson and Brook Grundfest Schoepf). New York: Basic Books

1966 [1962]. *The savage mind.* University of Chicago Press

1968. 'The concept of primitiveness', in Richard B. Lee and Irven DeVore (eds.), *Man the hunter.* Chicago: Aldine, pp. 349–52

1969a [1962]. *Totemism.* Harmondsworth: Penguin Books

1969b [1949]. *The elementary structures of kinship* (revised edition, translated by James Harle Bell, John Richard von Sturmer and Rodney Needham). Boston, MA: Beacon Press

1978. *Myth and meaning.* University of Toronto Press

1981 [1971]. *The naked man: introduction to a science of mythology* (translated by J. Weightman and D. Weightman, volume 4). London: Jonathan Cape

1985 [1983]. *The view from afar* (translated by Joachim Neugroschel and Phoebe Hoss). Oxford: Basil Blackwell

Lévy-Bruhl, Lucien. 1975 [1949]. *The notebooks on primitive mentality* (translated by Peter Rivière). Oxford: Basil Blackwell & Mott

Lewis, Jerome. 2009. 'As well as words: Congo Pygmy hunting, mimicry, and play', in Botha and Knight, pp. 236–56

Lewis-Williams, David. 2010. *Conceiving God: the cognitive origin and evolution of religion.* London: Thames & Hudson

Lieberman, Philip. 1984. *The biology and evolution of language.* Cambridge, MA: Harvard University Press

2006. *Toward an evolutionary biology of language.* Cambridge, MA: Harvard University Press

2008. 'A wild 50,000-year ride', in Bengtson, pp. 359–71

Lourandos, Harry. 1997. *Continent of hunter-gatherers: new perspectives in Australian prehistory.* Cambridge University of Press

Lubbock, John. 1865. *Pre-historic times, as illustrated by ancient remains, and the manners and customs of savages.* London: Williams and Northgate

1874 [1870]. *The origin of civilisation and the primitive condition of man.* New York: D. Appleton and Company

Lucy, John A. 1992. *Language and cultural diversity: a reformulation of the linguistic relativity hypothesis.* Cambridge University Press

Lupyan, Gary and Rick Dale. 2010. 'Language structure is partly determined by social structure', *PLoS ONE* 5(1): e8559. doi:10.1371/journal.pone.0008559

McBrearty, Sally. 2007. 'Down with the revolution', in Paul Mellars, Katie Boyle, Ofer Bar-Yosef and Christopher Stringer (eds.), *Rethinking the Human Revolution: new behavioural and biological perspectives on the origin and dispersal of modern humans.* Cambridge: McDonald Institute for Archaeological Research, pp. 133–51

McBrearty, Sally and Alison S. Brooks. 2000. 'The revolution that wasn't: a new interpretation of the origin of modern human behavior', *Journal of Human Evolution* 39: 453–63

MacDonald, Katharine and Wil Roebroeks. 2013. 'Neanderthal linguistic abilities: an alternative view', in Botha and Everaert, pp. 97–117

McMahon, April and Robert McMahon. 2013. *Evolutionary linguistics.* Cambridge University Press

MacNeilage, Peter F. 2008. *The origin of speech.* Oxford University Press

McNeill, David. 2012. *How language began: gesture and speech in human evolution.* Cambridge University Press

McWhorter, John H. 2003. *The power of Babel: a natural history of language.* New York: Perennial

   2005. *Defining creole.* Oxford University Press

   2011. *Linguistic simplicity and complexity: why do languages undress?* Boston: De Gruyter Mouton

   2014. *The language hoax: why the world looks the same in any language.* Oxford University Press

Maggs, Tim. 1967. 'A quantitative analysis of the rock art from a sample area in the western Cape', *South African Journal of Science* 63: 100–4

Maine, Henry Sumner. 1913 [1861]. *Ancient law: its connection with the early history of society and its relation to modern ideas.* London: George Routledge & Sons

Malinowski, Bronislaw. 1944 [1939–42]. *A scientific theory of culture and other essays.* Chapel Hill: University of North Carolina Press

   1953 [1923]. 'The problem of meaning in primitive languages', in Charles K. Ogden and I. A. Richards (eds.), *The meaning of meaning: a study of the influence of language upon thought and of the science of symbolism* (ninth edition). London: Routledge & Kegan Paul, pp. 451–510

Mandelbaum, David G. (ed.). 1985 [1949]. *Selected writings of Edward Sapir in language, culture and personality.* Berkeley: University of California Press

Marean, Curtis W. 2010. 'When the sea saved humanity', *Scientific American* 303: 55–61

Marett, R. R. 1909. *The threshold of religion.* London: Methuen

Marshall, Lorna. 1961. 'Sharing, talking, and giving: relief of social tensions among !Kung Bushmen', *Africa* 31: 231–49

Martin, Leonard L., Matthew A. Sanders, Amey Kulkarni, Wyatt C. Anderson and Whitney L. Heppner. 2014. 'I-D compensation: exploring the relations among mindfulness, a close brush with death, and our hunter-gatherer heritage', in Amanda Ie, Christelle T. Ngnoumen, and Ellen J. Langer (eds.), *The Wiley-Blackwell handbook of mindfulness* (two volumes). Chichester: Wiley-Blackwell, pp. 290–311

Marwick, Ben. 2003. 'Pleistocene exchange networks as Evidence for the evolution of language', *Cambridge Archaeological Journal* 13(1): 67–81

Maturana, Humberto R., and Francisco J. Varela. 1992 [1987]. *The tree of knowledge: the biological roots of human understanding.* Boston, MA: Shambhala Publications

Maynes, Mary Jo and Ann Waltner. 2012. *The family: a world history.* Oxford University Press

Mead, Margaret. 2005. *The world ahead: an anthropologist anticipates the future.* New York: Berghahn Books

Mead, Margaret and Rhoda Métraux. 2005 [1966]. 'One world—but which language?', in Mead 2005, pp. 111–18

Meir, Irit, Wendy Sandler, Carol Padden and Mark Aronoff. 2010. 'Emerging sign languages', in Marc Marschark and Patricia Elizabeth Spencer (eds.), *Oxford handbook of deaf studies, language, and education* (volume 2). Oxford University Press

Mellars, Paul and Chris Stringer (eds.). 1989. *The human revolution: behavioural and biological perspectives in the origins of modern humans.* Edinburgh University Press

Meyer, Matthias, Martin Kircher, Marie-Theres Gansauge, Heng Li, Fernando Racimo, Swapan Mallick, Joshua G. Schraiber, Flora Jay, Kay Prüfer, Cesare de Filippo, Peter H. Sudmant, Can Alkan, Qiaomei Fu, Ron Do, Nadin Rohland, Arti Tandon, Michael Siebauer, Richard E. Green, Katarzyna Bryc, Adrian W. Briggs, Udo Stenzel, Jesse Dabney, Jay Shendure, Jacob Kitzman, Michael F. Hammer, Michael V. Shunkov, Anatoli P. Derevianko, Nick Patterson, Aida M. Andrés, Evan E. Eichler, Montgomery Slatkin, David Reich, Janet Kelso and Svante Pääbo. 2012. 'A high-coverage genome sequence from an archaic Denisovan individual', *Science* 338: 222–6

Miller, Geoffrey F. 1999. 'Sexual selection for cultural displays', in Dunbar, Knight and Power, pp. 71–91

2000a. 'Evolution of human music through sexual selection', in Wallin, Merker and Brown, pp. 329–60

2000b. *The mating mind: how sexual choice shaped the evolution of human nature.* New York: Anchor Books

Mithen, Steven. 1996. *The prehistory of the mind: a search for the origins of art, religion and science.* London: Thames & Hudson

2005. *The singing Neanderthals: the origins of music, language, mind, and body.* London: Weidenfeld & Nicholson

2009. 'Out of the mind: material culture and the supernatural', in Renfrew and Morley, pp. 123–34

Monboddo, Lord. 1774 [1773]. *Of the origin and progress of language* (second edition, volume 1). London: T. Cadell

Montesquieu, Baron de. 1989 [1748]. *The spirit of the laws* (translated and edited by Anne M. Cohler, Basia Carolyn Miller and Harold Samuel Stone). Cambridge University Press

Morgan, Lewis H. 1871. *Systems of consanguinity and affinity of the human family.* Washington, DC: Smithsonian Institution

Morrison, Catriona M. and Martin A. Conway. 2010. 'First words and first memories', *Cognition* 116: 23–32

Movius, Hallam L. 1948. 'The Lower Palaeolithic cultures of southern and eastern Asia', *Transactions of the American Philosophical Society* (n.s.) 38: 329–420

Mufwene, Salikoko S. 2001. *The ecology of language evolution.* Cambridge University Press

Müller, F. Max. 1861. *Lectures on the science of language delivered at the Royal Institution of Great Britain in April, May, and June, 1861.* London: Longman, Green, Longman, and Roberts

1881a. *Selected essays on language, mythology and religion* (volume 1). London: Longmans

1881b [1856]. 'Comparative mythology', in *Selected essays*, pp. 299–424

1881c [1871]. 'On the philosophy of mythology', in *Selected essays*, pp. 577–623

Murdock, George Peter. 1945. 'The common denominator of cultures', in Ralph Linton (ed.), *The science of man in the world crisis*. New York: Columbia University Press, pp. 123–42

Nelson, Katherine and Robyn Fivush. 2004. 'The emergence of autobiographical memory: a social cultural developmental theory', *Psychological Review* 111: 486–511

Nettle, Daniel. 1999. *Linguistic diversity*. Oxford University Press

Nettle, Daniel and Suzanne Romaine. 2000. *Vanishing voices: the extinction of the world's languages*. Oxford University Press

Newmeyer, Frederick J. 2003. 'What can the field of linguistics tell us about the origins of language?', in Christiansen and Kirby 2003a, pp. 58–76

Nichols, Joanna. 1997. 'Sprung from two common sources: Sahul as a linguistic area', in Patrick McConvell and Nicholas Evans (eds.), *Archaeology and linguistics: Aboriginal Australia in global perspective*. Melbourne: Oxford University Press, pp. 135–68

1998. 'The origin and dispersal of languages: linguistic evidence', in Jablonski and Aiello, pp. 127–70

2002. *Linguistic diversity in space and time*. University of Chicago Press

2012. 'Monogenesis or polygenesis: a single ancestral language for all humanity?', in Tallerman and Gibson 2012a, pp. 558–72

Nicolaï, Robert. 2006. 'Origine du langage et origine des langues: réflexions sur la permanence et le renouvellement d'un questionnement des Lumières', *Marges linguistiques* 11: 93–129

Noble, William and Iain Davidson. 1996. *Human evolution, language and mind: a psychological and archaeological enquiry*. Cambridge University Press

Okrent, Arika. 2000. *In the land of invented languages*. New York: Spiegel & Grau

Oller, D. Kimbrough and Ulrike Griebel (eds.). 2004. *Evolution of communication systems: a comparative approach*. Cambridge, MA: MIT Press.

Oppenheimer, Stephen. 2004. *The real Eve: modern man's journey out of Africa*. New York: Carroll & Graf

2009. 'The great arc of dispersal of modern humans: Africa to Australia', *Quaternary International* 202: 2–13

Osmond-Smith, David. 1981. 'From myth to music. Lévi-Strauss's *Mythologiques* and Berio's *Sinfonia*', *The Musical Quarterly* 67: 230–60

Perry, William James. 1923. *Children of the sun: a study in the early history of civilization*. London: Methuen

Pickrell, Joseph K., Nick Patterson, Chiara Barbieri, Falko Berthold, Linda Gerlach, Tom Güldemann, Blesswell Kure, Sununguko Wata Mpoloka, Hirosi Nakagawa, Christfried Naumann, Mark Lipson, Po-Ru Loh, Joseph Lachance, Joanna Mountain, Carlos D. Bustamante, Bonnie Berger, Sarah A. Tishkoff, Brenna M. Henn, Mark Stoneking, David Reich and Brigitte Pakendorf. 2012. 'The genetic prehistory of southern Africa', *Nature Communications* 3, Article number: 1143 doi:10.1038/ncomms2140

Pilley, John W. and Alliston K. Reid. 2011. 'Border collie comprehends object names as verbal referents', *Behavioural Processes* 86: 184–95

Pinker, Steven. 1994. *The language instinct: how the mind creates language*. New York: William Morrow & Co.

1997. *How the mind works*. London: Penguin Books

2011. *The better angels of our nature: a history of violence and humanity*. London: Allen Lane

Pinker, Steven and Ray Jackendoff. 2005. 'The faculty of language: what's special about it?', *Cognition* 95: 201–36

Pluciennik, Mark. 2014. 'Historical frames of reference for "hunter-gatherers"', in Cummings, Jordan and Zvelebil, pp. 55–68

Ponelis, Fritz. 1993. *The development of Afrikaans*. Bern: Peter Lang

Porter, James N., Paul F. Collins, Ryan L. Muetzel, Kelvin O. Lim and Monica Luciana. 2011. 'Associations between cortical thickness and verbal fluency in childhood adolescence and young adulthood', *Neuroimage* 55: 1865–77

Postal, Paul M. 2005. 'Foreword', in Geoffrey Sampson, *The 'language instinct' debate* (second edition). London: Continuum, pp. vii–xi

Powell, Adam, Stephen Shennan and Mark G. Thomas. 2009. 'Late Pleistocene demography and the appearance of modern human behaviour', *Science* 324: 1298–1301

Power, Camilla. 1998. 'Old wives' tales: the gossip hypothesis and the reliability of cheap signals', in Hurford, Studdert-Kennedy and Knight, pp. 111–29

2015. 'Review of Melvin Konner, *Women after all: sex, evolution, and the end of male supremacy*,' *Times Higher Education* 2,196 (26 March–1 April 2015): 52–3

Preston, Stephanie D. and Frans de Waal. 2003. 'Empathy: its ultimate and proximal bases', *Behavioral and Brain Sciences* 25: 1–72

Proctor, Robert N. 2003. 'Three roots of human recency: molecular anthropology, the refigured Acheulean, and the UNESCO response to Auschwitz', *Current Anthropology* 44: 213–39

Pullum, Geoffrey K. 1991. *The great Eskimo vocabulary hoax and other irreverent essays on the study of language*. University of Chicago Press

Rabinow, Paul. 1984. 'Introduction', in Paul Rabinow (ed.), *The Foucault reader: an introduction to Foucault's thought*. London: Penguin Books, pp. 3–30

Radcliffe-Brown, A. R. 1951. 'The comparative method in social anthropology', *Journal of the Royal Anthropological Institute* 81: 15–22

1952. *Structure and function in primitive society: essays and addresses*. London: Cohen and West

Rappaport, Roy. 1999. *Ritual and religion in the making of humanity*. Cambridge University Press

Renfrew, Colin. 2008. *Prehistory: the making of the human mind*. London: Phoenix

Renfrew, Colin and Iain Morley (eds.). 2013. *Becoming human: innovation in prehistoric material and spiritual culture*. Cambridge University Press

Renfrew, Jane M. 2009. 'Neanderthal symbolic behaviour?', in Renfrew and Morley 2013, pp. 50–6

Robinson, Jennie. 2014. 'The first hunter-gatherers', in Cummings, Jordan and Zvelebil, pp. 177–90

Rousseau, Jean-Jacques. 1973 [1750–62]. *The social contract and discourses* (translated by G. D. H. Cole). London: J. M. Dent & Sons

1986 [1781]. 'Essay on the origin of languages' (translated by John H. Moran), in Rousseau and Herder, pp. 1–74

Rousseau, Jean-Jacques and Johann Gottfried Herder. 1986. *On the origin of language: two essays.* University of Chicago Press

Rowley-Conwy, Peter. 2006. 'The concept of prehistory and the invention of the terms "prehistoric" and "Prehistorian": the Scandinavian origin, 1833–1850', *European Journal of Archaeology* 9: 103–30

Ruhlen, Merritt. 1994a. *The origin of language: tracing the evolution of the mother tongue.* New York: John Wiley & Sons

   1994b. *On the origin of languages: studies in linguistic taxonomy.* Stanford University Press

Sahlins, Marshall. 1974. *Stone age economics.* London: Tavistock Publications

   1976. *The use and abuse of biology: an anthropological critique of sociobiology.* Ann Arbor, MI: University of Michigan Press

Sampson, Geoffrey. 2005 [1997]. *The 'language instinct' debate* (second edition). London: Continuum

Samuels, Andrew. 1985. *Jung and the post-Jungians.* London: Routledge & Kegan Paul

Sapir, Edward. 1933. 'Language', in *Encyclopaedia of the social sciences*, volume 9. New York: Macmillan, pp. 155–96

Saussure, Ferdinand de. 1974 [1916]. *Course in general linguistics* (edited by Charles Bally and Albert Sechehaye, translated by Wade Baskin). Glasgow: Fontana/Collins

Savage-Rumbaugh, E. Sue and Duane M. Rumbaugh. 1993. 'The emergence of language', in Kathleen R. Gibson and Tim Ingold (eds.), *Tools, language and cognition in human evolution.* Cambridge University Press, pp. 86–108

Schepartz, L. A. 1993. 'Language and modern human origins', *American Journal of Physical Anthropology* 36 (Issue Supplement 17): 91–126

Schmidt, Wilhelm. 1939 [1937]. *The culture historical method of ethnology:} the scientific approach to the racial question* (translated by S. A. Sieber). New York: Fortuny's

Schurr, Theodore G. 2004. 'The peopling of the New World: perspectives from molecular anthropology', *Annual Review of Anthropology* 33: 551–83

Senghas, Richard J., Ann Senghas and Jennie E. Pyers. 2005. 'The emergence of Nicaraguan Sign Language: questions of development, acquisition, and evolution', in Sue Taylor Parker, Jonas Langer and Constance Milbrath (eds.), *Biology and knowledge revisited: from neurogenesis to psychogenesis.* London: Lawrence Erlbaum Associates, pp. 287–306

Shennan, Stephen. 2001. 'Demography and cultural innovation: a model and its implications for the emergence of modern human culture', *Cambridge Archaeological Journal* 11: 5–16

Silberbauer, George B. 1963. 'Marriage and the girl's puberty ceremony of the G/wi Bushmen', *Africa* 33: 12–24

Slater, Peter. 2012. 'Bird song and language', in Tallerman and Gibson 2012a, pp. 96–101

Smith, Adam. 1767. *The theory of moral sentiments, to which is added a dissertation on the origins of languages* (third edition). London: A. Millar, A. Kincaid and J. Bell.

   1978. *Lectures on jurisprudence* [Lectures delivered 1762–63], edited by R. L. Meek, D. D. Raphael and P. G. Stein. Oxford: The Clarendon Press

Smith, Andrew D. M. and Stefan Höfler. 2014. 'The pivotal role of metaphor in the evolution of human language', in Javier E. Díaz-Vera (ed.), *Metaphor and metonomy across time and cultures: perspectives on the sociohistorical linguistics of figurative language.* Amsterdam: De Grouter Mouton, pp. 123–40

Smith, Andrew D. M., Marieke Schouwstra, Bart de Boer and Kenny Smith (eds.). 2010. *The evolution of language: Proceedings of the 8th International Conference (EVOLANG8).* Singapore: World Scientific

Soodyall, Himla (ed.). 2006. *The prehistory of Africa: tracing the lineage of modern man.* Johannesburg: Jonathan Ball

Spikins, Penny A., Holly E. Rutherford and Andrew P. Needham. 2010. 'From homininity to humanity: compassion from the earliest archaics to modern humans', *Time and Mind* 3(3): 303–26

Stam, James H. 1976. *Inquiries into the origin of language: the fate of a question.* New York: Harper & Row

Stewart, Pamela J. and Andrew Strathern. 2002. *Violence: theory and ethnography.* New York: Continuum

Stix, Gary. 2008. 'The migration history of humans: DNA study traces human origins across the continents', *Scientific American* 299 (1): 56–63

Stocking, George W., Jr. 1968. *Race, culture, and evolution: essays in the history of anthropology.* New York: The Free Press

Stringer, Chris. 2011. *The origin of our species.* London: Allen Lane

Swadesh, Morris (edited by Joel F. Sherzer). 2006 [c.1967]. *The origin and diversification of language.* New Brunswick: AldineTransaction

Swann, Joan. 2009 [2000]. 'Language in interaction', in Rajend Mesthrie, Joan Swann, Ana Deumert and William L. Leap, *Introducing sociolinguistics* (second edition). Edinburgh University Press, pp. 183–212

Taçon, Paul S. C. 2009. 'Identifying ancient religious thought and iconography: problems of definition, preservation, and interpretation', in Renfrew and Morley 2013, pp. 61–73

Tallerman, Maggie and Kathleen R. Gibson (eds.). 2012a. *The Oxford handbook of language evolution.* Oxford University Press

2012b. 'Introduction: the evolution of language', in Tallerman and Gibson 2012a, pp. 1–45

Tattersall, Ian. 1998. *Becoming human: evolution and human uniqueness.* Oxford University Press

2008. *The world from beginnings to 4000 BCE.* Oxford University Press

Tilly, Christopher. 1990. 'Claude Lévi-Strauss: structuralism and beyond', in Christopher Tilly (ed.), *Reading material culture: structuralism, hermeneutics and post-structuralism.* Oxford: Basil Blackwell, pp. 3–81

Tomasello, Michael. 1999. *The cultural origins of human cognition.* Cambridge, MA: Harvard University Press

2008. *Origins of human communication.* Cambridge, MA: MIT Press

Tomasello, Michael and Josep Call. 2007. 'Ape gestures and the origins of language', in Josep Call and Michael Tomasello (eds.), *The gestural communication of apes and monkeys.* London: Lawrence Erlbaum Associates, pp. 221–39

Traill, Anthony. 1994. *A !Xóõ dictionary* (Research in Khoisan Studies 9). Cologne: Rüdiger Köppe Verlag

Traugott, Elizabeth Closs. 2003. 'Constructions in grammaticalization', in Brian D. Joseph and Richard D. Janda (eds.), *The handbook of historical linguistics.* Oxford: Blackwell, pp. 624–47

Trigger, Bruce. 2006 [1989]. *A history of archaeological thought* (second edition). Cambridge University Press

Trivers, Robert L. 1971. 'The evolution of reciprocal altruism', *Quarterly Review of Biology* 46: 35–57

Tyler, Stephen A. (ed.). 1969. *Cognitive anthropology*. New York: Holt, Rinehart & Winston

Tylor, Edward B. 1871. *Primitive culture: researches into the development of mythology, philosophy, religion, art, and custom* (volume 2). London: John Murray

Ulbaek, Ib. 1998. 'The origin of language and cognition', in Hurford, Studdert-Kennedy and Knight, pp. 30–43

Vico, Giambattista. 2002 [1725]. *The first new science* (Leon Pompa). Cambridge University Press

Visser, Hessel. 2001. *Naro dictionary: Naro-English, English-Naro* (fourth edition). Gantsi: Naro Language Project / SIL International Swann

Wade, Nicholas. 2006. *Before the dawn: recovering the lost history of our ancestors*. New York: Penguin Books

Wallin, Nils L., Björn Merker and Steven Brown (eds.). 2000. *The origins of music*. Cambridge, MA: MIT Press

Watts, Ian. 2009. 'Red ochre, body painting, and language: interpreting the Blombos ochre', in Botha and Knight, pp. 62–92

Wells, Spencer. 2007. *Deep ancestry: inside the genographic project*. Washington, DC: National Geographic

2010. *Pandora's seed: why the hunter-gatherer holds the key to our survival*. London: Penguin Books

Whallon, Robert, William A. Lovis and Robert K. Hitchcock (eds.). 2011. *Information and its role in hunter-gatherer bands: ideas, debates and perspectives*. Los Angeles: Cotsen Institute of Archaeology at UCLA

White, Stephanie A. 2013. 'FoxP2 and vocalization', in Lefebvre, Comrie and Cohen, pp. 211–35

Whitehouse, Paul. 2008. 'Some speculations on the evolution of language, and the language of evolution', in Bengtson, pp. 401–16

Whorf, Benjamin Lee. 1956a. 'A linguistic consideration of thinking in primitive communities', in Carroll, pp. 65–86

1956b. 'The relation of habitual thought and behavior to language', in Carroll, pp. 134–59

Widlok, Thomas. 1999. *Living on mangetti: 'Bushman' autonomy and Namibian independence*. Oxford University Press

Wiessner, Pauline Wilson (Polly). 1977. *Hxaro: a regional system of reciprocity for reducing risk among the !Kung San* (two volumes). Ann Arbor, MI: University of Michigan (University Microfilms International)

1982. 'Risk, reciprocity and social influence on !Kung San economics', in Eleanor Leacock and Richard Lee (eds.), *Politics and history in band societies*. Cambridge University Press, pp. 61–84

2014. 'Embers of society: firelight talk among the Ju/'hoansi Bushmen', *Proceedings of the National Academy of Sciences (PNAS)* 111(39): 14027–35

Willis, Roy. 1974. *Man and beast*. London: Hart-Davis, MacGibbon

Wilson, Daniel. 1851. *The archaeology and prehistoric annals of Scotland*. Edinburgh: Sutherland and Knox

Wilson, David Sloan. 2011. 'The human major transition is relation to symbolic behavior, including language, imagination, and spirituality', in Henshilwood and d'Errico, pp. 133–39

Wilson, Edward O. 1975. *Sociobiology: the new synthesis*. Cambridge, MA: Belknap Press of Harvard University Press

Winterhalder, Bruce and Eric Alden Smith (eds.). 1981. *Hunter-gatherer foraging strategies: ethnographic and archaeological analyses*. University of Chicago Press

Wittgenstein, Ludwig. 1953. *Philosophical investigations*. Oxford: B. Blackwell

Witzel, E. J. Michael. 2012. *The origins of the world's mythologies*. Oxford University Press

Woodburn, James. 1980. 'Hunter-gatherers today and reconstruction of the past', in Ernest Gellner (ed.), *Soviet and Western anthropology*. London: Duckworth, pp. 95–117

  1982. 'Egalitarian societies', *Man* (n.s.) 17: 431–51

Wrangham, Richard. 2009. *Catching fire: how cooking made us human*. London: Profile Books

Wray, Alison. 1998. 'Protolanguage as a holistic system for social interaction', *Language and Communication* 18: 47–67

  2000. 'Holistic utterances in protolanguage: the link from primates to humans', in Chris Knight, Michael Studdert-Kennedy and James Hurford (eds.), *The evolutionary emergence of language: social function and the origins of linguistic form*. Cambridge University Press, pp. 285–302

Wynn, Thomas and Frederick L. Coolidge. 2012. *How to think like a Neandertal*. Oxford University Press

Zegura, Stephen L. 2008. 'Current topics in human evolutionary genetics', in Bengtson, pp. 343–57

Zilhão, João. 2014. 'The Neanderthals: evolution, palaeontology, and extinction', in Cummings, Jordan and Zvelebil, pp. 191–213

Zuberbühler, Klaus. 2013. 'Primate communication', in Lefebvre, Comrie and Cohen, pp. 187–210

Index